GA**OKS

Also by Peggy Kaye

GAMES FOR WRITING

GAMES FOR LEARNING

GAMES FOR MATH

GAMES FOR READING

GAMES WITH BOOKS

28 OF THE BEST CHILDREN'S BOOKS AND HOW TO

USE THEM TO HELP YOUR CHILD LEARN—FROM

PRESCHOOL TO THIRD GRADE

WRITTEN BY **Peggy Kaye**

WITH ILLUSTRATIONS
BY THE AUTHOR

FARRAR, STRAUS AND GIROUX

NEW YORK

FOR PAUL

Farrar, Straus and Giroux
19 Union Square West, New York 10003

Copyright © 2002 by Peggy Kaye
All rights reserved
Distributed in Canada by Douglas & McIntyre Ltd.
Printed in the United States of America
First edition, 2002

Grateful acknowledgment is made to the following for permission to
reprint previously published material:
Excerpt from *Many Moons* by James Thurber. Copyright © 1943 by
James Thurber. Copyright © renewed 1971 by Helen Thurber and
Rosemary A. Thurber. Reprinted by arrangement with Rosemary A.
Thurber and The Barbara Hogenson Agency. All rights reserved.
Excerpt from *Blueberries for Sal* by Robert McCloskey, copyright 1948,
renewed © 1976 by Robert McCloskey. Used by permission of Viking
Penguin, an imprint of Penguin Putnam Books for Young Readers, a
division of Penguin Putnam Inc.
Excerpt from *Chrysanthemum* by Kevin Henkes. Copyright © 1991 by
Kevin Henkes. Used by permission of HarperCollins Publishers.
Excerpt from *The Carrot Seed* by Ruth Krauss. Text copyright © 1945 by
Ruth Krauss. Used by permission of HarperCollins Publishers.
Excerpt from *Ten Black Dots* by Donald Crews. Used by permission of
HarperCollins Publishers.

Library of Congress Cataloging-in-Publication Data
Kaye, Peggy, 1948–
    Games with books : 28 of the best children's books and how to use them to help your
child learn—from preschool to third grade / written by Peggy Kaye ; with illustrations by
the author.— 1st ed.
        p. cm.
    ISBN 0-374-23455-8 (alk. paper) — ISBN 0-374-52815-2 (pbk. : alk. paper)
    1. Children—Books and reading.   2. Educational games.   3. Education, Preschool—
Activity programs.   4. Education, Primary—Activity programs.   5. Best books.
6. Children's literature—Bibliography.   I. Title.

Z1037.A1 K38 2002
028.5'34—dc21
                                                                                2001033342

www.fsgbooks.com

10 9 8 7 6 5 4 3 2 1

CONTENTS

INTRODUCTION

HOW TO PLAY WITH BOOKS

One of the best things you can do in life is to sit with a child and read a good story aloud. You will enjoy yourself, and so will the child. By reading aloud and turning the pages and admiring the pictures and the print, you will teach the child to treasure books—to see books as beautiful objects, offering many delights. But you can also linger over the book a little longer by playing a few carefully chosen games, and in that way you can teach many other lessons, too. You can help the child learn to read and write and calculate—the same skills that are needed for success in school. My purpose in *Games with Books* is to show you how to do that—how to have a good time reading aloud to your child, and how to extend the experience by playing a few simple and amusing games that will help the child learn.

If you glance at the children's shelves of a bookstore or in the children's room of a public library, you will see at once that thousands of books have been written for children. I have picked twenty-eight of those books, the ones I think are the very best for reading aloud—though you could certainly choose others. Some of the twenty-eight books on my list are classics of children's literature, well known to generations of readers. I remember quite a few from my own childhood. I loved those books then, and I still love them. But I have also picked a number of books written more recently. I love those books, too, and I believe that, eventually, they will be considered classics.

In the following pages, I have described each of these twenty-eight books, so that you can select a few that you would like to read aloud to your child. And for each book that I have described, I propose a number of games that you and your child can play, based on that particular story. Playing the games will give the child a more vivid appreciation of whichever book you choose to read—a deeper understanding of the story and of the characters. The child will find playing the games entertaining, too, and take a very special pleasure in the fact that they are based on the book.

But I have also designed these games to help children sharpen some very specific and crucial academic skills. There are counting games, measurement games, geometry games, alphabet games, reading games, writing games, poetry games, spelling games, and several other kinds as well. Playing these games will give a child valuable practice grappling with some of the most important aspects of elementary education.

The first half of *Games with Books* describes fourteen picture books—that is, books in which the pictures as much as the words tell the story. Some of the picture books are suited for preschoolers and kindergartners, and I have labeled them as such. Others are suited for first and second graders. Those books, too, are clearly labeled. How can you pick out one of these books for reading aloud? You will need to drop by the library or a bookstore and see which are available. All of these books are excellent, and any one of them that strikes your fancy will make a good choice. You might discover that you already know several of them. You may even have read one or another of them aloud to your child. Did the child enjoy it? If so, you might want to read the same book again. Children love hearing a good story over and over.

In any case, once you have chosen a book and have it in hand, turn back to *Games with Books* and examine the activities that I propose. You might need to gather a few household items and do a little planning to play some of these games—

though with other games you won't need any supplies, and you won't need to plan, either. Sometimes it's a good idea to play a few games immediately after reading the book, but sometimes it's perfectly okay to wait a day or two, so long as your child remembers the book. Most of the games take between five and ten minutes to play. Other games require a bit more time. Your child might enjoy playing a certain game day after day. Repetition can be a very good thing. Skills get hammered home that way, and the fact that the child wants to keep playing proves that the game is still stimulating.

The second half of *Games with Books* describes chapter books—books with so many words that, in order to be readable, they must be divided into chapters. The chapter books I have picked are suited to children from kindergarten to third grade, and my descriptions of them are duly labeled. A wordy chapter book takes much more time to read aloud than a picture book. You and your child may end up spending a week or even longer poring over the book from start to finish. You want to be sure, therefore, that you pick the right volume for your child.

Sometimes you will pick a book and begin reading it aloud, only to discover, after a few pages or a chapter, that your child is groaning with boredom. That does happen, even with the best of books and the best of children. If that is the case, try to convince your child to give the book another chance and let you read another chapter. But if, after listening to a new chapter, the child remains unmoved, give up and find a different book. There's no purpose in reading aloud if the child isn't having fun. And, with very little extra effort, you will find the right book and the child will be content.

When should you start playing the games I've matched with the book you selected? You might want to slip a game or two in between chapters. Or you might wait until you have finished reading the entire book. Sometimes a game bears on a specific twist in the plot, and, in that case, you wouldn't want to play until you have read the appropriate part of the story.

For each chapter book, I have suggested at least one game that requires very little preparation and very little time to play. But other games are fairly elaborate and will require several days' effort by you and your child. A short and simple game is sometimes just the thing, and other times a long and complicated project is what you'll want.

Most young children love listening to an adult reading aloud, but some must be encouraged to sit still and pay attention. If your child shies away when you pull out a book, you might try alternative approaches. It can be a good idea if, instead of reading the story verbatim, you recount the events in your own words, pointing to the illustrations as you do so. "Here's Sal picking blueberries. Look how she's gobbling them up. They must taste yummy."

Sometimes children have the power of concentration sufficient for listening to only one or two pages of a book at a time. That's all right, you don't have to read more than that. A child who enjoys three pages today might happily listen to four or even five pages tomorrow. Soon enough, the child will cheerfully listen to a whole book—if it is a short one.

What should you do if your child already reads fluently? Should you still read aloud? Yes, you should. Often, a child understands a book more thoroughly when an adult reads it aloud, especially if a book happens to be difficult. Sometimes children who are good readers simply insist on reading for themselves. If that is the case with your child, perhaps each of you can read the story on your own and then talk about it. If you are in an extravagant mood, you could even get two copies of the same book, and you and your child could sit side by side, each of you with your own copy. In any event, after reading for a while, you should turn back to *Games with Books* and pick a couple of games to play.

It is never a bad idea to take books or games labeled for a younger child and share them with an older child. To cite an example, *Frederick* is an excellent book for kindergartners and first graders, but second and even third graders enjoy it, too, and they will enthusiastically play games based on the story. Older children are not wasting their time when they play games designed for younger children. The older children are getting valuable practice at simple skills, which is always useful. Even the greatest baseball players benefit from a game of catch.

On the other hand, it is not a good idea to read an older child's book to a younger child. *Mr. Popper's Penguins* is a splendid book for first, second, and third graders, but there is no point in reading it to a kindergartner. The kindergartner might enjoy the story or might not, but in either case will certainly appreciate the book much more if you wait a year or two before reading it. It's also a mistake to ask a younger child to play a game intended for someone older. When you push a child to do something that is too difficult, the child is likely to get frustrated and upset, and no good can come of that.

Sometimes you might begin playing a game that is correctly labeled with your child's grade level, only to discover that the child flounders. Don't be alarmed. The game may be too difficult at the moment but in a month or two it might be easier. What should you do if the game does not become any easier? What if your child consistently struggles with one or another type of game—with counting games, for instance, or with alphabet games? If these struggles seem worrisome, talk to the child's teacher. In the meantime, though, keep leafing through *Games with Books*, looking for good books to read and amusing activities to play. Pleasure is the guiding principle here. The child who is having a good time will discover that books are wonderful things, and that books are important to your family. The child will find that playing with words and numbers is entertaining, and that working hard to finish a project is satisfying. These are some of the most valuable lessons a parent can provide.

All twenty-eight of the books that I discuss in *Games with*

Books, and all the games (there are eighty-nine of them), are equally appropriate for boys and girls. In the course of the book, I recount playing games with children; sometimes I describe playing with a girl, and sometimes with a boy. These are composite stories, putting together experiences I've had with several different children. In every case, therefore, I could have told a similar story about the opposite sex. After all, boys and girls both enjoy playing games. And both boys and girls do some of their best learning when they are having fun.

That is the goal of *Games with Books*—to help you create a setting in which your child can have fun, and can enjoy gazing at the pages of a marvelous children's book, and can learn important skills, all at the same time.

PART ONE
HOW TO PLAY WITH PICTURE BOOKS

THE CARROT SEED

WRITTEN BY RUTH KRAUSS
ILLUSTRATED BY CROCKETT JOHNSON
1945
GOOD READING FOR PRESCHOOL AND KINDERGARTEN

*S*hould children always listen to their parents? Most adults will say yes, but many thoughtful children will argue otherwise. *The Carrot Seed* tells the story of a little boy who refuses to mind his parents' sensible advice. In so doing, he sets an elegant example of childhood independence. Should grownups introduce children to such a seditious tale? Yes, absolutely.

The little boy plants a carrot seed, and he is sure his carrot will grow. His mother doubts, his father doubts, his big brother doubts, but the little boy has faith. Despite the naysayers, the boy patiently cares for his plant. "And then, one day, a carrot came up just as the little boy had known it would." How often does a young child manage to prove that he is right and that the grownups are grandly and gloriously wrong? In real life, not often. But it happens every single time you read *The Carrot Seed*.

Ruth Krauss, the author, creates her carrot fable with just one hundred one words. After a few readings, therefore, your child may memorize some of the pages and start reciting words with you. Such pretend reading is extremely valuable for young children. A child who pretends to read, even if his eyes never land on words, begins to think of himself as a reader. He gets lost in books—the way all avid readers do. He will love his books. A child who already loves books will work hard, when the time is right, to learn to read in the non-pretend version.

In between readings of *The Carrot Seed*, you might consider turning your attention to one or another of the following three activities. All three relate directly to the book. All three will set your child to thinking in valuable ways. Take a few minutes to read through the activities and pick one you believe will intrigue your child and that you, too, might find amusing. If more than one game appeals, better yet. So long as you and your child enjoy yourselves, you are doing the right thing.

HOW MANY CARROTS?

GRADES

preschool and kindergarten

MATERIALS

three bunches of carrots, masking tape

SKILLS

learning about measurement

What a carrot the boy grows! It is huge. It is as big as the boy himself. How does the height of a normal, everyday carrot compare to the height of a normal, everyday preschooler or kindergartner? Why not find out with your child? Before you begin, make sure you have three bunches of carrots—leafy tops removed—in your kitchen.

When you are ready to measure, have your child lie down on a wood or linoleum floor, then run a long strip of masking tape from his feet to the top of his head.

Once the masking tape is in place, your child can stand up. Spend a minute or two studying the tape. If your child has never seen his horizontal length before, he may be surprised at how far the tape stretches across the floor. Next, take the carrots and help your child line them up, tip to stem, until you have a row that matches the tape. If your child is between four and five carrots tall, snap off the top of the fifth carrot so that you get a match. Count and you will know your child's carrot height. It might be four carrots, or it might be four and a little bit more.

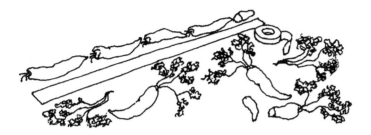

If your child enjoyed discovering his carrot height, he might like to find out yours. Go ahead, measure yourself. In fact, measure anyone who happens to be at home.

Why should you measure with carrots instead of in inches or centimeters? First, it is a fine way to expand the fun of *The Carrot Seed*. Second, it is good to have a child measure with a variety of materials—carrots, or pencils, or paper clips, or all kinds of things—before introducing him to the standard measures. Measuring with various household objects helps a child see the value in comparing different lengths. Eventually the child may notice that not all carrots are alike, and a uniform, universally accepted length, such as an inch or a centimeter, might be more useful. But that realization is for later. It is a bad idea to use carrot-measuring to teach about inches and centimeters. Trying to teach too much will ruin the fun of this game. So stick with carrots for the time being.

Why do you need a row of carrots? Why not grab a single one and push it along the masking tape? When you create a row of carrots, it is very simple to count how many stretch from top to bottom. It is harder, much harder, for a young child to appreciate what a single carrot moving along the masking tape represents. True, your child may attentively watch as you maneuver the carrot along its path, but he will not really understand what you are doing or the reason you are doing it. So it is better to give the child lots of experience in measuring rows of objects he can see and touch—a row of carrots, for instance.

PAINTING WITH CARROTS

GRADES

preschool and kindergarten

MATERIALS

newspaper, old T-shirts, colored construction paper or plain white paper, several lids from plastic containers, a large plastic container full of water, paper towels, tempera or poster paint, a knife, carrots

SKILLS

learning about color combinations, developing artistic expression

*W*hat should the little boy in *The Carrot Seed* do with his colossal carrot? It is a logical question to ask after finishing the book, and that is exactly what I did with Joe, a creative kindergarten student. Joe suggested several interesting ideas. The little boy could cook his carrot, or wave it like a sword, or maybe lay it down and use it as a table. Then, being a polite child, Joe asked me for my opinion.

"He should use it to make a painting," I said.

Assuming I was kidding, Joe laughed. "He couldn't do that!"

"Sure he could, and we can, too, if you want," I said.

"How?"

"I'm glad you asked. I just happen to have a few carrots handy, and I can show you."

Joe smiled.

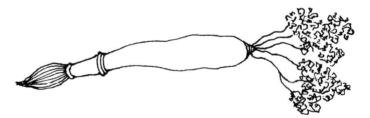

"First, we need to clear a painting space on the tabletop and cover it with newspaper," I said.

After establishing our work area, I found old T-shirts for us to wear in order to protect our clothes. Then I placed a few sheets of construction paper, a few sheets of plain white paper, some plastic lids, a container of water, a roll of paper towels, a set of tempera paints, a knife, and four carrots on the table.

This work done, I said, "Go ahead, Joe, and pick your first color for carrot painting."

Joe pointed to green. I took that jar and poured some of its paint into one of the plastic lids.

"Now, what color paper do you want?" I asked.

Joe picked a sheet of yellow construction paper. I took a plain white sheet for myself.

"We're just about ready to paint," I said.

"But we don't have paintbrushes," Joe observed.

"We're not painting with brushes today, Joe. Remember, we're creating carrot art."

Quickly I took one of the carrots and cut it into four more or less equal sections.

Then I dipped the end of one section into the paint. Using the coated carrot, I began to dab paint on my paper. After a few dabs, I "refilled" my carrot.

Joe caught on right away, took his own piece of carrot, and began dabbing. Before long, I suggested that we add a second color. Joe wanted red. We dipped our green fingers in the bowl of water, and dried our clean hands with paper towels. I

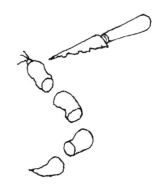

poured some red paint in a clean plastic lid and handed us each a fresh section of carrot. We were ready to go. This time, though, I took my carrot, dipped it lengthwise in the paint, and rolled it until the entire length was paint-covered. Then I rolled the carrot over the paper, creating a thick, weaving red line. Joe liked this method and copied me.

After rolling and dabbing with red for a bit, we decided to mix red and yellow paint together, using the end of a carrot to stir, thus producing orange. We kept adding colors, mixing colors, dabbing and rolling, until our paintings were done. One artistic triumph was not enough for Joe. He wanted to make a second carrot painting and then a third.

If you decide to try this odd way of painting with your child, you can be assured that you are helping him learn a great deal about colors and what happens when you mix them together. When red and blue blend, they make purple. Red and yellow together make orange. These are valuable pieces of basic knowledge—the kind of facts every child should know by first grade. You are also encouraging your child to express himself artistically. Many young children love to draw and paint. These youngsters do not need inspiration to pick up crayons and paintbrushes. Other children, though, lacking confidence in their abilities, shy away from using art materials. Not every child will grow up to be an artist, but every child—especially every young child—should have the chance to freely and confidently express his artistic side.

*A*fter reading *The Carrot Seed*, your child might be eager to grow his own carrot. Despite the little boy's surprising success in the story, it is not always practical to grow carrots at home. Carrots fail to thrive in winter, and although you can grow them inside, it takes a lot of work and a lot of time to get results. You could, however, direct your child's gardening enthusiasm in a less problematic direction.

After reading the book, for the first or the hundredth time, ask your child if he would like to have his very own plant. This would not be any old plant. This would be his own personal PET PLANT. The PET PLANT will belong exclusively to him, and he will be in charge of its well-being.

For his pet, tell your child he can choose any plant he likes—big, small, flowering, or prickly cactus, any plant at all—within set economic limits. Then explore your neighborhood florist or nursery. You might ask the salesperson which plants are most likely to flourish in your house or apartment. After your child selects his PET PLANT, take it home and find a perfect place for it to live. If you can find a spot in your child's room, so much the better.

Once the plant is settled in, think of ways to make it special—different from all other houseplants you own. First off, your child can name his plant. This might seem like an odd thing to do, but sometimes odd is good. Your child might enjoy decorating his plant's container. He can start by making a name tag. Take a piece of paper and cut it down to an appro-

GRADES

preschool and kindergarten

MATERIALS

houseplant, paper, colored marker, glue

OPTIONAL MATERIALS

stickers, colored ribbon, camera, photo album

SKILLS

developing responsibility, learning about plant life

priate size. Have your child write the plant's name, using a colored marker, and then glue the tag to the container. After the tag is in place, he can further glamorize the pot. He might want to cover it with stickers, draw on it with permanent markers, or glue on strips of colored ribbon.

If you have a camera handy, snap a few photos of your child standing proudly by his new "pet." After a few weeks, take the camera out again and shoot more pictures. You might even make a PET PLANT album with dated photographs that record the plant's growth.

Naturally, your child will have to care for his plant. He must water it regularly. Occasionally, he must fertilize the soil. From time to time, he might need to trim leaves. Someday, if the plant gets big enough, he may have to transfer it to a larger pot. This is a lot of responsibility for a young child, and that is exactly the point. Owning a PET PLANT gives your child a clear reason to act responsibly. Don't expect perfection, though. Your child will undoubtedly need help from you. He may need reminders to carry out his chores or require your assistance with the more difficult tasks. Even if your child is very conscientious, his plant might fail to thrive. This will be very sad and your child is likely to feel discouraged and frustrated. Perhaps a new plant will comfort him. But if he wants to mourn his first plant for a while, let him do so. On the other hand, with luck and care, his PET PLANT just might live and grow for years and years.

HAROLD AND THE PURPLE CRAYON

WRITTEN AND ILLUSTRATED BY CROCKETT JOHNSON
1955
GOOD READING FOR PRESCHOOL AND KINDERGARTEN

*H*arold and the Purple Crayon, one of the most imaginative books in children's literature, features a little boy, Harold, who does not live in our everyday world. He lives on blank pages, and on those pages, with the help of his miraculous purple crayon, he creates his own universe. When Harold draws, each and every purple object he renders springs to life.

One evening, Harold decides to take a moonlight walk—but first he must draw the moon. Then he draws a road and starts walking. On the roadside, he draws an apple tree and then a dragon to guard the apples. He falls into a purple ocean, but he quickly sketches a boat and saves himself. He falls off a purple mountain, but manages to create a balloon rigged with a basket so that he can float safely to earth. When he gets tired, he draws his very own purple bed, pulls up his purple covers, and goes to sleep.

As Harold wields his purple crayon, he gives young listeners a fine lesson in imaginative thinking. Adults like to think that all children have active imaginations, but that is only somewhat true. All children have the capacity to imagine creatively, but this ability must be encouraged and nurtured. And Harold, in conjuring up purple mountains, oceans, and dragons, is an expert nurturer.

If your child loves Harold, he might also love the following games. Each one will put a purple crayon in your child's hand.

WITH MY PURPLE CRAYON

GRADES

preschool and kindergarten

MATERIALS

large-size sheets of drawing paper, a stapler, two purple crayons

SKILLS

developing the ability to tell a story

"*R*ead it again," Leslie insisted after I finished *Harold and the Purple Crayon* for the second time. I was not surprised that Leslie loved the book. Having an active fantasy mind herself, it was only natural that she would enjoy meeting a boy who could bring his imagined world to life. I put off her request for a third reading, though. Instead I asked, "Would you like to have a magic crayon like Harold's?"

"Oh, yes," she said.

"Unfortunately, I can't give you a real magic crayon. I do have an ordinary purple crayon and a very large blank book, though. Using them, we can make up our own purple story. It won't come alive, but with your wonderful imagination, I bet you can make our story seem almost real."

Then I showed Leslie an oversized book I had constructed earlier in the day. It had been a simple job, calling on me to do nothing more than staple together four 18″ × 24″ sheets of newsprint. Where did I get such large paper? From a pad that I purchased in an art supply store. You can also find such pads in many stationery stores.

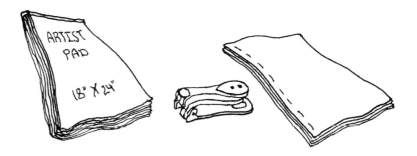

Impressed by the book's size, Leslie was eager to begin. I took a purple crayon from my crayon collection and, on the first sheet, wrote "*A Purple Crayon Story* by Leslie and

Peggy." I read the title aloud and then I turned the page so that we were facing two blank sheets.

"We're ready to go," I said. "Should we take a walk, just like Harold?"

"Yes," she said.

"Shall we walk in the moonlight or the daylight?" I asked.

"Daylight," Leslie said.

"In that case, we need a sun. Would you like to draw one?"

Leslie nodded her head, took the crayon, and got to work. She placed a small purple sun near the top of the right-hand sheet. That done, we were ready for our stroll.

"I want to visit a forest," I said, taking the crayon and starting to draw simple trees on both sheets. Leslie asked if she could draw some, too. I rummaged through the crayon box until I found a purple crayon for her to use.

"Do we meet anyone in the forest? A dog? An army tank? A monster?" I asked.

"A monster," she announced. "A big one."

I nodded my approval and told her to start drawing. She objected, complaining that she was not a good enough artist.

"That's the great thing about drawing a monster: it can look any way you want. Which means anything you draw will be perfect."

Reassured, she began scribbling and wound up with a wide-eyed, toothy beast.

"What should happen next?" I asked.

"Another monster," she answered.

"Oohh, that's a scary idea," I said. "Can I draw it?"

"All right," she said.

I sketched a duplicate of her creature—or as close to it as I could muster. "With two monsters on the loose, we need a way to protect ourselves," I said. "Have you got any ideas?"

"We could draw rocks and throw them," she replied.

I nodded my approval again, and Leslie set to drawing.

"I think those monsters are still after us," I said as soon as she finished.

"So do I!" she shouted.

"We could add a thunderstorm. Maybe lightning will scare them," I said.

Leslie thought this was a fine idea. Working together, we made big dark clouds, lots of raindrops, and then some lightning bolts.

"They don't seem upset," I said. "We need another plan."

"We could run away," she suggested.

"Okay, let's run." With that I drew a wavy purple line across the bottom of the pages—all the way from the left-hand edge until the crayon hit the right-hand edge.

Leslie flipped the page, and we found ourselves once again facing two blank sheets of paper. "I wonder what is going to happen now?" I asked.

"I think we should draw a garden with lots of flowers," she said.

We did. Then we drew a few birds, and then a huge vulture, then we tamed the vulture, and then we turned the page.

We ended our story after one more adventure-filled span of pages. I could have stapled more sheets to the end of the book, but Leslie and I were fully satisfied with our tale. Over the next months, we pulled the book off the shelf now and then and spent a few splendid moments savoring our purple escapades.

"It's my favorite book," Leslie said one day after we turned the last page.

How grand that Leslie's favorite book, at least for the moment, happened to be a volume of her own creation!

PURPLE MAZE

GRADES

preschool and kindergarten

MATERIALS

blank paper, pencil, purple crayon

SKILLS

developing control over finger movements

*I*n Jody's kindergarten class, the children were learning how to handle pencils and then using controlled—or somewhat controlled—pencil strokes to write letters and numbers. But not Jody. Jody tried and tried, but her letters were a mess and her numbers were even worse. "My fingers won't listen to me," Jody explained the first day I met her.

I knew that Jody often felt embarrassed by her work. She was frustrated and beginning to feel angry whenever anyone asked her to write. If I insisted that Jody form letters over and over, she would balk—and I would not blame her. I needed to take a different approach.

I began by reading *Harold and the Purple Crayon*, and Jody thought the book was great.

Her positive response made it easy for me to introduce PURPLE MAZE, a game based on the book.

"Harold was certainly adventurous. He traveled all over the place before climbing into bed," I said.

Jody nodded, and I went on. "I'm going to make a special maze for you starring Harold. It's going to include some of the places he visited on his walk."

I took a blank sheet of paper, and, using a pencil, I drew the following:

"What are those circles?" Jody asked.
"This circle

is Harold. This circle

is the apple tree. This circle

is the ocean. This circle

is the balloon.

And this last circle

is Harold's bed," I said.

As I pointed to each circle, I looked at Jody to make sure she understood. "Here is your part. You have to draw a line from Harold to all the places he visited, in the right order, and then take him to his bed. And, of course, you have to use a purple crayon," I said.

"That's easy. I remember everything," Jody said.

"Except I'm going to make it harder for you. I'm going to draw lots of lines on the page. Each line represents a barrier," I said.

"You have to take Harold for his walk and visit every circle in order, but you cannot touch any of the barriers. That is not easy. That is hard," I said.

"Hard," she repeated.

Undaunted, though, she picked up her purple crayon and

began journeying across the page. In less than a minute she was done.

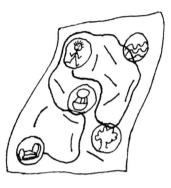

"That was fun," she said. "Can I do another?"

"Sure," I said, "but I think Harold should visit new places this time. Will you help me think of new places?"

"Okay," she said.

I drew a circle for Harold. Then, as Jody suggested, albeit with a little help from me, I added a zoo, a garden, a toy store, a lake, a sailboat, an airplane, a rocket ship, a pizza parlor, and, finally, Harold's bed. Next I put in barriers, many more barriers than in Jody's first PURPLE MAZE.

This time Jody could let Harold travel in any order she wanted, except that she had to start at the Harold circle and finish at his bed.

Once again, Jody managed to complete her mission with no mishaps. She was delighted with herself—understandably so—and wanted to do another maze right away.

Jody did not realize it, but as she maneuvered her purple crayon this way and that to avoid barriers, she was practicing many of the same movements needed to form the letter *c* or write the number *3*. Because the practice took the form of a maze, though, she did not get frustrated or angry or balk. No, she was eager to play. Of course, any very simple maze would have helped Jody with her problem. Unfortunately, most commercial mazes are too hard for young children. Not so with a PURPLE MAZE. Limit the number of circles and barriers and you can make mazes easy enough for children just beginning preschool. Even if I could have found a printed maze appropriate for Jody, I would not have used it. Why? My PURPLE MAZES featured Harold, and Jody completed them with a purple crayon. This gave them a special appeal and accounted, at least in part, for Jody's desire to do maze after maze after maze.

In this game, players make up a story, just as Harold does. And players use a purple crayon, just like Harold. But, in PASS THE PURPLE CRAYON, players work as a team to create a single story, unlike Harold, who invented his tale by himself. And, unlike Harold, who used words and drawings to create adventures, players in this game weave their tale using words alone.

You can play PASS THE PURPLE CRAYON with two people, but the fun increases when you involve more players. Children of several different ages can play, as well as grownups. And, although it is best if everyone is familiar with Harold and his purple crayon, it is not necessary to know the book.

Bring everyone together and give one player a purple crayon. The crayon is like a royal scepter—while a player holds it, he becomes the official storyteller. The first person to hold the crayon, therefore, begins your tale. He can begin in any way he wants. He might announce that when he greeted his favorite teddy bear this morning, the bear answered back, "Good morning to you, too."

Or the storyteller could declare that once upon a time a magical elf came to live with a little boy named Steve.

Or that yesterday when a girl named Joyce left her house, she found a helicopter and a pilot waiting for her in her front yard.

Whatever his beginning, the first player must not contribute more than an idea or two before passing the purple crayon to someone else. The new bearer of the crayon takes over the story, for a short time, and then passes the crayon to yet another storyteller. Players keep passing the crayon until somebody ends the story and, in doing so, ends the game. Sometimes, upon receiving the crayon, a player will not know what to say. It happens, but it does not need to be a problem. PASS THE PURPLE CRAYON is a cooperative game, and so it is perfectly okay for you, or for anyone else, to make suggestions in order to get the story going again.

PASS THE PURPLE CRAYON

GRADES

preschool and kindergarten

MATERIALS

purple crayon

SKILLS

developing the ability
to tell a story

You and your child might have lots of ideas for beginning stories. If you do not, however, here are a few possibilities.

Last night a whale was traveling across the ocean. He was having a fine time splashing, diving, and floating. Suddenly, though, everything changed, and the whale felt sad and terribly lonely.

Mary was walking home from school when without warning it began to rain. Only there was something very strange about this rain. Instead of water, it was raining rose petals.

On the news this morning, the President of the United States announced that friendly visitors from the planet Raggeran are, at this very moment, flying toward Earth.

One Halloween night, all the witches went out to play. The youngest and smallest witch, Witcharella, fell behind all the others. Soon the little witch realized that she was lost.

Julie could not wait until her birthday party. She was positive it would be the best party ever. When the party began, everything was perfect—until something very surprising happened.

And when you and your child and anyone else you included finish a story, you can always turn back to *Harold and the Purple Crayon* and simply enjoy the book.

TEN BLACK DOTS

WRITTEN AND ILLUSTRATED BY DONALD CREWS
1968
GOOD READING FOR PRESCHOOL AND KINDERGARTEN

*T*here are dozens of counting books on the market, and quite a few of them are excellent. In clever or amusing ways, these books help children understand the numbers from one to ten. A favorite of mine is Donald Crews's sleek *Ten Black Dots*.

Crews begins the book with a question: "What can you do with ten black dots?" He spends the next twenty-four pages giving answers. He starts by telling what you can do with one dot. "One dot can make a sun or a moon when day is done." He does not just tell, though; he also shows with pictures that spread across two pages. On the left-hand side, we see a black dot converted into a sun, which, with orange rays, illuminates a yellow sky. On the right-hand side, we see the dot again, only this time Crews places it in a blue nighttime sky surrounded by stars. Turn the page and Crews tells, in a rhyming sentence, and shows, with elegant illustrations, how two dots can be both fox eyes and the eyes of door keys. Page after page, number by number, Crews transforms dots until, at last, ten dots become a collection of pennies and a tree full of balloons.

As with all good picture books, children enjoy hearing *Ten Black Dots* over and over again. And, as with all good counting books, children feel compelled to count along, at least they do after the first several readings.

The following three games offer you and your child even more opportunities to count dots.

DOT BOOK

After reading *Ten Black Dots*, it is fun to imagine other ways you could deploy a dot on the page, or two dots, or three. It can be even more fun to make your own DOT BOOK. You will need a few supplies to get started, namely paper, pencil, crayons or colored markers, and stick-on dots that you can find in any good stationery store.

Stick-on dots come in black, but you can also buy them in other colors—red, green, purple, and blue as well as some fluorescent hues. The dots come in several sizes, too. I like using ½″ dots, but you and your child might prefer slightly smaller or larger ones. You can, if you want, mix things up by using a variety of colors and sizes throughout your book.

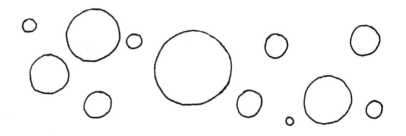

Four sheets of 8½″ × 11″ paper will be the initial pages of your book. You will want more pages before you are done, but these will get you started.

To begin, take a single dot and place it prominently on one of your blank pages.

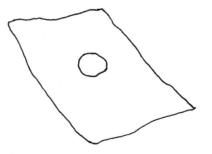

What can you do with this dot? Using crayons or colored markers, you could turn it into

a lollipop,

an ice-cream cone,

an apple,

or an interesting design.

Pick the one-dot suggestion you like, or come up with your own idea. When you finish your picture, write a short description of the illustration. If your child wants to do the writing, or part of it, let him. It does not matter if he misspells every word or misses words altogether. You can always rewrite the caption in a more readable version. Some children, though, will ask to dictate their ideas, which is fine, too.

Now, what can you create with two dots? Put a pair on a second piece of paper and see what springs to mind. Of course, if you prefer, you can make your choice before sticking on the dots.

Two dots can be

a cat,

a pair of eyeglasses,

the eyes on a face,

or another interesting design.

Completing two pages might be enough for the moment, but when you come back to the project in a day or so, here are some other ideas for dotted pages.

Three dots can make a stoplight.   Four can be car wheels.

Five could be a school of fish.   Six might be a bunch of grapes.

Seven—flowers.   Eight—chocolate chip cookies.

 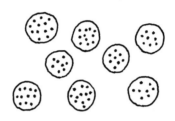

Nine—a caterpillar.   Ten—a beaded necklace.

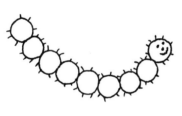 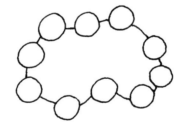

Even if your child only scribbles, make sure that he does as much of the drawing as possible. The school of fish might not look like any fish anyone has ever seen, you might have page after page of interesting designs, but who cares?

It will surely take you many days to complete all your pages. As soon as you have your first page, though, you can start binding the book—if you use the loose-leaf ring method. Just be sure, when you buy those stick-on dots at that well-stocked stationery store, to pick up three loose-leaf binding rings as well.

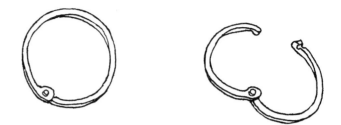

As you complete each page, punch three holes along the left-hand margin and then snap three binding rings into place. After your first day working on the book, you might have two or three pages set to punch. When they are in the rings, add one more sheet, a blank one. Rest the blank sheet on top of the others in order to protect them. Put the partially finished book in a safe place until you want to work on it again.

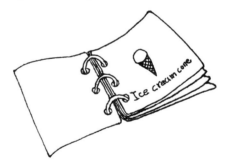

You and your child might discover that you have lots of ideas for a single number—one, for instance. In that case, you might end up with several pages dedicated to the number one. On the other hand, you might fail to think of any good ideas for certain numbers. You can leave those numbers out of the book for the time being. If inspiration strikes in a week or a month, you can add pages then.

When you finish most, if not all, of your pages and they are bound into the rings, you will want an official cover to replace the blank protective sheet. Although you can use regular paper for this job, it is a good idea to pick something sturdier, such as construction paper. First, you must cut this paper down to 8½″ × 11″. Next you must consider a title for your book. *Ten Dots* is a possibility, of course, but you and your child might have other, more original ideas. Once you have written the title, your child can add illustrations. Then punch holes on the left-hand side and snap it inside the rings ahead of the other pages. You might also put a piece of construction paper behind the completed pages to serve as a back cover.

As you add pages to the book, stop now and again and count dots. After your first day's work, find out how many dots you and your child put on paper. How many do you have after your second day? After finishing six pages, count all of the yellow dots in the book, or all of the green ones. Count the dots on your fifth, sixth, and seventh pages—once you have them in rings. Count the dots on every other page, or every third page. On your last day of work, count all the dots from the cover to the final page. Completing all the pages does not mean you have to stop counting. From time to time, pull the book off its shelf, and after you and your child go through the volume enjoying your creative work, go through it again. This time, though, your child will count. He can count all the big dots, or the small ones, or the dots with drawings on them, or all the ones without drawings, or—well, you get the idea.

DOTS GALORE

GRADES

preschool and kindergarten

MATERIALS

3" × 5" index cards, scissors,
black and red colored pencils,
paper, game tokens

SKILLS

counting

*W*hen Beth was in preschool, Alice, her mother and my old friend, gave me a call. Young Beth liked numbers, and Alice, eager to promote her daughter's interest, hoped I could suggest a few math games. Alice's timing was perfect. I had just invented a game, DOTS GALORE, and I was happy to have a child test its virtues. First, I told Alice to read *Ten Black Dots* to Beth. As I hoped, Beth loved the book and thoroughly enjoyed counting the dots. Terrific. The book would prime Beth for the game.

I warned Alice that DOTS GALORE would require about fifteen minutes of her time to prepare. First, she had to make a deck of dotted playing cards—a deck that consisted of fourteen cards made from seven 3" × 5" index cards cut in half.

On ten of the cards, Alice drew black dots:

Two cards with one dot

Two cards with two dots

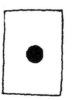 

Two cards with three dots

Two cards with four dots

 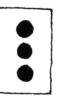 

One card with five dots

One card with six dots

On the four remaining cards, Alice drew red dots:

One card with one dot

One card with two dots

One card with three dots

One card with four dots

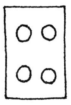

Next, Alice needed to make a simple playing board. On a blank sheet of paper, she drew a winding road divided into twenty-four sections.

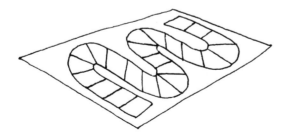

Finally, she selected two game tokens, one for her and one for Beth. Paper clips, pennies, dimes, or anything else that fit into the sections of the playing-board road would have done. Alice picked a penny and a dime.

Now Alice and Beth started playing. Both of them put their game tokens on the first section of the road. Alice shuffled the playing cards and spread them out facedown on the table. Then Beth picked any card she wanted, turned it over, and counted the dots. If the dots were black, she advanced that number of spaces up the road. If the dots were red, she went back that number of spaces. Players cannot go farther back, however, than the first section of the road. That meant, if Beth drew a red card on her initial turn, she would stay put. After Beth made her move, she returned her card, facedown, to the pile and hid it by scrambling all the cards around. Then it was Alice's turn. She picked a card, counted dots, and advanced her token—if she got black dots. Mother and daughter took turns, moving ahead with black dots and retreating with red, until one of them reached the end of the road and won.

For a few days, DOTS GALORE was a big hit. Beth insisted on playing every day, and since a game only took about ten minutes from start to finish, it was easy for Alice to meet this demand. Then Beth lost interest. But Alice did not mind; it had not cost her any money to buy DOTS GALORE and yet it had kept her daughter happily counting for the better part of a week.

*M*aking FINGERPRINT DOTS is usually great fun for children, and for adults, too—at least for those adults who don't mind cleaning up a mess when fingerprinting time is over.

Begin by spreading a newspaper on a table or countertop. Then have your child press his index finger on an ink pad. Have him roll his finger around until it is inked up. Then take a blank sheet of paper and have him use his inky fingertip to create dots. Simple as that.

How many dots should he make? That is up to your child, but here is one idea that calls on you to ink one of your own fingers. Have the child begin by making one dot. Then you draw a circle around it with a brightly colored crayon. Next you make two dots and have your child circle them in a different color. The child makes three dots and you ring them in a colorful circle. Then you make four. Keep taking turns, using as many sheets of paper as necessary, until you have ten dots in a single circle.

FINGERPRINT DOTS

GRADES

preschool and kindergarten

MATERIALS

newspaper, paper, ink pad, crayons

SKILLS

counting

That's a lot of dots. Can your child count them all? Let him try. Help him if he runs into difficulty. Or let him count his own FINGERPRINT DOTS and you count yours. Whichever way you go, in a few inky minutes your child will have counted and counted some more and counted even more. And then it will be time for the two of you to wash your hands.

THE SOMETHING

WRITTEN AND ILLUSTRATED BY NATALIE BABBITT

1970

GOOD READING FOR PRESCHOOL AND KINDERGARTEN

*A*t some point, almost every child develops a fear of the dark. Night falls, and a child finds it easy to imagine monsters lurking and demons smirking. What can a parent do to help a child overcome those nighttime worries? One fine way to reassure an anxious child is to read the right book aloud. The right book should address a child's fears without belittling them. The right book should have a bit of humor to help a child confront the serious and scary subject of night frights. The right book is one your child (and you, too) will want to hear over and over again. To my mind, *The Something* is, in each of these crucial ways, definitely the right book.

The story stars Mylo, a hairy, bucktoothed, warty, and totally appealing, though certainly monstrous, young creature. Mylo has a problem. He is afraid of the dark. He fears that in the night a something will come creeping and crawling through his window. He cannot describe the something. It's just—a something. His hairy, bucktoothed, warty, and totally appealing mother, looking for a way to distract her son, buys him some modeling clay. Mylo rolls, squeezes, and pinches the clay, trying to create a statue of his something. Finally, he succeeds. Now he knows what his something looks like. Late that night, Mylo dreams, and who should stroll into his dream but his something.

To our surprise, relief, and amusement, Mylo's something is a lovely, longhaired, and completely human little girl. Somehow, seeing the object of his fears walk and talk, Mylo over-comes his fright. Then, in a second wonderful twist, the little girl announces that she is not afraid of Mylo either—she just wants him to get out of her dream. *Her* dream? Is it her dream? Or is it Mylo's? Is the girl Mylo's something? Or is Mylo the girl's something? Will we ever know for sure?

No, and we don't really want to. The author of the book, Natalie Babbitt, leaves us in nowhere-land between competing somethings, and that is just fine with young listeners. After all, if scary monsters get scared themselves, how awful can they be?

Reading *The Something* aloud can help your child cope with nighttime fears. Playing the following games can help him develop a few academic skills, which is a useful daytime thing to do.

THE FACE OF A SOMETHING

*"H*ave you ever been afraid of something in the dark?" I asked Timothy after reading *The Something* to him.

"Hmm," he replied—a very noncommittal hmm.

"I have," I said. "But, like Mylo, I can't picture my something."

"Yeah," Timothy responded.

"I sort of think my something's face has lots of colors."

"Yeah," he replied again.

"I also think my something's face has spots and stripes."

A third "yeah," this time with an added giggle.

"Using Play-Doh, I might be able to show you my something's face. Do you think you can make a Play-Doh portrait of your something?" I asked.

"What's a portrait?" he asked in return.

"It's when you make a picture or mold a sculpture of a person. You can create a portrait that shows a person's whole body. That's what Mylo did when he made a statue of his

GRADES

kindergarten

MATERIALS

Play-Doh, waxed paper, pencil, white glue, paintbrushes, glass of water, plastic lid

SKILLS

developing control over finger movements, promoting artistic expression, learning how colors combine

The Something
35

something. Or you can create a portrait that just shows a person's head. I figured we'd work on face portraits. Want to try?"

"I guess," he answered.

"Let's get started, then," I said. I put some waxed paper on top of a table and pulled out a few canisters of colored dough. Timothy hesitated, not sure how to begin, but I started working right away. I hoped that by watching me turn Play-Doh into the face of my something—especially if I commented on my actions—he would feel comfortable starting his own. I took a handful of blue dough and pressed it into a circle.

"That's the face. I know it needs eyes, ears, nose, and—"

"A mouth!" Timothy interrupted.

"Yes, and a mouth. I'm going to start with the eyes. What color should they be? Purple. But there isn't any purple dough. I guess I'll make some. Do you know how I can do it?"

"No," said Timothy.

"I have to mix two colors: red and blue," I said.

I began mixing, and, when I was done, I used the new color to form two small balls. Then I pushed my thumb into the blue face, making an indented spot to place the first of the little purple balls.

I dropped the ball into the dent and, using my fingertips and a pencil point, pinched the blue and purple pieces together so that the ball would stay in place.

"That's an eye," I said.

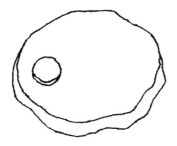

I did the same thing again for the second eye. The embedded purple mounds looked unfinished. So I placed a tiny yellow ball in the middle of each one to give the eyes pupils.

All this time, Timothy watched me work. After I placed the eyes, though, he reached for the dough. With some effort, and a little help from me, he made his own circular shape for a face and started molding features. We talked while we worked. We considered our choices. We discussed colors. Timothy copied many of my face's features, and that was fine with me. Sometimes he had trouble getting his creature's teeth to stay put or keeping its nose in place, so I gave him a few Play-Doh technique tips. After about fifteen minutes, we

were smiling down on a pair of absolutely astonishing somethings.

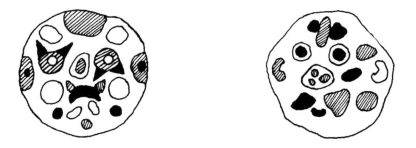

After Timothy left my office, I did a little touch-up work on his creation. I repinched each juncture between bits of dough to secure the connections. Unless the joints are firm, teeth fall out and noses drop away. Then I put our faces on fresh sheets of waxed paper and left them to dry. This took a couple of days and required my very carefully flipping the faces over now and again so they would dry evenly front and back.

The next time Timothy came to my office, I presented him with his sculpture. He was delighted and wanted to take it home that day.

"You can take it today, Timothy, after we do one more thing to finish our faces," I said.

"But mine is how I want it," he complained.

"I know, and it's terrific. But unless we take this last step, your face might crumble. You don't want that to happen."

Timothy shook his head no.

"Here's how we'll strengthen your face: we'll coat it with a thin layer of glue," I said.

Timothy looked skeptical, but watched closely as I covered the table with waxed paper, took out a container of white glue, two inexpensive paintbrushes, a glass of water, and a lid I had removed from a tub of margarine. I squeezed a dollop of glue on the lid and then added an equal quantity of water. I stirred the mixture with a paintbrush. Then I began spreading a thin layer of watery glue over the top of my Play-Doh face. I handed Timothy a brush and told him to do likewise. I also told him to brush on extra glue wherever two pieces of Play-Doh met. Timothy worried that the white glaze would dull his bright colors, but I assured him that the dried glue would be invisible. When the glue on the front of our faces dried, we painted the undersides. Since the glue and water mixture dries quickly, Timothy's face was, as promised, ready to go home when our hour together was done.

SOMETHING SPEAK

Mylo and his something have no problem communicating, and that is surprising. When I think about somethings, I do not imagine them speaking English. In my mind, somethings speak weird tongues seldom heard on Earth. Their exotic languages inspired the game SOMETHING SPEAK.

To introduce SOMETHING SPEAK to your child, tell him that last night you saw a something in your dreams, and the something talked! Only, he didn't use English words. Instead, he said, *"Smish, glam, smish, glam, smish, glam."* And, a second later, he said it again. *"Smish, glam, smish, glam, smish, glam."* He waited a few more seconds and then he said it once more. *"Smish, glam, smish, glam, smish, glam."* You knew he was trying to communicate with you, but you could not figure out what he was saying. It was so frustrating, and you knew the creature was frustrated, too. And then the dream ended, and you woke up.

All morning, you have tried to discover the key to understanding the creature's language. A moment ago, you had an idea. Maybe there is a pattern in your something's words, and, if you can figure it out, maybe you and the creature can communicate. There are only two problems. First, can you figure out the pattern? Second, will your something enter your

GRADES
preschool and kindergarten

SKILLS
identifying, extending, and creating patterns

dreams tonight so that you can test your theory? Then ask for your child's help. Tell him that if he can repeat the something's words, continue the pattern, and then teach you how the pattern works, you will be most grateful. And, if your something does visit you while you sleep tonight, and if knowing the pattern is the key, tomorrow morning you will tell your child exactly what your something said.

It may be that your child is willing to search for the pattern, but is unable to cope with the task. If that is the case, assist him. How? By repeating the nonsense words *"Smish, glam, smish, glam, smish, glam."* Then wait a few seconds and repeat them again. *"Smish, glam, smish, glam, smish, glam."* Before long your child is bound to catch on and start chanting the nonsense words. When he does so, pretend to talk back to him. Have a *smish, glam* conversation.

If your child enjoyed himself, continue the game. Announce that you suddenly remember a second part of the dream. Your something was talking, but he didn't say *smish* or *glam*. Instead he said, *"Tig, snoof, bloop, tig, snoof, bloop."* Explain that tonight, in order to keep communicating with the something, you must figure out this pattern, too.

After your child deciphers the new pattern, stop playing. If you both liked the game, you can return to it in a day or two. By then, your child may report a dream adventure with his own something and have nonsense words for you to hear. Don't be surprised if his idea of a patterned sequence leaves a lot to be desired. Accept his efforts, however unpatterned they may be, with pleasure. It is a huge intellectual challenge to create a true pattern. A child's first attempts, therefore, deserve applause—even if they are less than perfect.

Why spend so much time playing with patterns? Young children who are able to observe, analyze, and create patterns will find these skills of great use. Children who realize that rhyming words are often spelled with the same pattern of letters, for instance, can use this fact to aid them in reading and writing. Children who notice patterns in the number system can use those patterns to help them memorize addition and subtraction facts.

But before a child can make such good use of patterns, he must understand how they work, and that does not happen automatically. It takes time. It takes practice. So, although talking in SOMETHING SPEAK may seem like a very silly thing to do, it actually has a very serious purpose.

Here are a few simple patterns for SOMETHING SPEAK, to get your conversations going.

Zif, zif, zof, zif, zif, zof
Kadoom, kadoom, pluff, kadoom, kadoom, pluff
Drub, drub, moof, lub, drub, drub, moof, lub
Drim, cluz, drim, slin, drim, cluz, drim, slin
Gloff, gloff, gloff, flim, gloff, gloff, gloff, flim
Flump, dop, flump, zar, flump, dop, flump, zar

ALL ABOUT MY SOMETHING

GRADES

preschool and kindergarten

SKILLS

imagining a fictional character, encouraging an active imagination

After reading *The Something* to Lynn, I talked with her about creatures. Lynn said that she had a something and that from time to time, in the dark, it scared her.

"Maybe it scares you," I said, "because you don't know your something very well. Just this morning, I was thinking about what my something likes to eat. It's either pizza topped with liverwurst or poison-ivy pie with a cellophane crust. Which idea do you like best?"

Lynn giggled and then voted for the pizza. Next we talked about her something's culinary preferences. After some discussion, she settled on spaghetti smothered in raspberry jelly.

Two days later, I read *The Something* to her again. Following the reading, we had another talk about our own somethings. This time we considered what makes our somethings cry. My something cries whenever it sees the full moon. Lynn's something cries when you pull its hair.

Lynn enjoyed thinking about her something's likes and dislikes. These talks gave her power over her something, and that felt good. Our occasional discussions had other benefits as well. When deciding on her something's favorite things, Lynn was using her imagination to create a character—a full-bodied character with likes and dislikes, worries and feelings. She was creating a personality the way novelists and short-story writers do. Not bad for a kindergartner.

If you and your child would like to imagine more about your somethings, you might begin by answering the following questions.

What does your something like to eat?
What does your something hate to eat?
What games does your something like to play?
What does your something hate to do?
What animals does your something like?
What scares your something?
What makes your something mad?
What does your something do when it gets angry?
What makes your something happy?
What does your something do when it feels happy?
What makes your something laugh?
What makes your something cry?
What is your something's favorite color?
What is your something's favorite way to spend the day?
What is your something's favorite holiday?
What is your something's favorite ice-cream flavor?

By the time you and your child answer all those questions, your somethings may feel like old friends rather than scary monsters.

CAPS FOR SALE

WRITTEN AND ILLUSTRATED BY ESPHYR SLOBODKINA
1940
GOOD READING FOR PRESCHOOL AND KINDERGARTEN

*T*he most beloved peddler in children's literature makes his living selling caps. He sells gray caps and brown ones, blue caps and red. He does not tote his caps in a box or wheel them in a cart. Instead, he carries them, cap above cap, on top of his head. One day, the peddler, wearing his tower of caps, falls asleep under a tree. When he wakes, he discovers that all of his caps, save one, have vanished. Where can they be? He looks to the left—no caps. He looks to the right—no caps. Then he looks up and sees a band of monkeys sitting in the tree branches above his head. Each monkey is wearing a cap. His caps! How can he retrieve them? He makes threatening gestures. He wags his finger, shakes his hands, and stamps his feet. The monkeys, in true "monkey see, monkey do" fashion, copy each wag, shake, and stamp. But they do not return the caps. Finally, in a fury, the peddler takes his sole remaining cap and hurls it to the ground. The imitating monkeys follow suit, and caps rain down from the tree. The peddler scoops them up, piles them on his head, and walks away.

Why do children so love this story about naughty monkeys and a frustrated peddler? Youngsters know that sometimes they, too, are naughty. They know that, on occasion, they will defy their parents and refuse to do as they are told. And they cannot help but worry about the consequences of such behavior. Their parents will get angry, they know, but how long will the anger last? Forever? It is a troublesome thought, and although children certainly laugh at the monkeys' antics, if you listen carefully you will sometimes hear a trace of apprehension in their giggles. In short order, though, Esphyr Slobodkina, the writer and illustrator of the book, offers children relief. For as soon as the disobedient monkeys return the peddler's caps, his anger disappears. Adults, it seems, can get angry, stamping and shouting angry, but they will not stay furious indefinitely—a soothing thought for a young child.

Of course, children are not always defiant. Request that a child play a game, for instance, and, in general, they are delightfully eager to comply.

GETTING IN ON THE ACT

GRADES

preschool and kindergarten

OPTIONAL MATERIALS

two caps

SKILLS

bringing a story to life

*O*h, those monkeys, how they torment the poor peddler! Generations of children have laughed at his troubles. And, as generations of parents and teachers have discovered, by the second or third reading of the book, a good many of the laughing children cannot resist jumping out of their seats to imitate the monkeys imitating the peddler. Rather than dissuading your child from acting out, consider encouraging him to do a bit of monkeying around. When you reach the scene where the peddler settles down for his nap, close the book and say, "Here's an idea. Since we both know what is going to happen next, let's make a play out of this part of the story. I'll be the peddler and you be a monkey. How does that sound?"

Assuming your child likes this suggestion, the drama can commence. Find two caps and put them on your head—one on top of the other. If you do not have real caps, put on make-believe ones. Then sit under an imaginary tree and pretend to sleep. While you sleep, your child should sneak to your side and snatch the top cap. Then he should climb up on a chair, or tiptoe to a corner of the room, and put the cap on his head. In a moment or two pretend to wake up, and then, with an appropriately shocked expression, notice that one of your caps is missing. Look here. Look there. And then, in alarm, discover your child attired in your cap. Demand its return. Shake your fists. Jump up and down. Stamp your feet. Make praying and pleading gestures. Your child should imitate your every move. In case he doesn't, remind him to do so. If you decide to verbally plead, beg, or cajole for your cap's return, your child can copy you, but he should replace your words with monkeyish squeaks and squeals. When the time seems right, toss down your own cap, and be sure your child follows suit. Make a big production of picking up the two caps and returning them to your head. Then smile contentedly and stroll away.

When you finish reenacting the story, your child might insist on an encore. That will be excellent. Only this time, switch roles. Cast your child as the irate peddler while you become a mimicking monkey.

There is a good reason to dramatize the book. Some young children automatically transform an author's words and illustrator's drawings into a fully imagined world. These children love listening to stories, and once they learn to read they tend to do so with enthusiasm, even if, at first, reading is difficult for them. They know that when they do read a story, they will enter a vividly pictured new experience. And so they throw themselves into reading because they understand that reading produces wonderful rewards. But many children have a hard time exercising their literary imaginations. Listening to stories is not particularly exciting to them—especially when compared to watching TV or playing computer games. All too often, these children find that learning to read is a struggle with few compensations. It is very important, therefore, to help your child breathe life into the stories that you read aloud. And a nearly perfect way to do so is to let the child pretend to be one of the characters, which in this case means letting him shake his fists and stamp his feet.

PATTERNS

GRADES

kindergarten

MATERIALS

3˝× 5˝ index cards, pencil,
crayons, scissors, pen

SKILLS

learning about patterns

*I*n the book *Caps for Sale*, the
the peddler arranges his seventeen caps in a very particular
order. First he puts on his own checked cap. Above that he
places four gray caps, then four brown ones, next four blue
ones, and finally four red. This is a fine way to arrange his
caps, but it is not the only way. He could have arranged them
according to this pattern: gray, brown, blue, red, gray, brown,
blue, red, checked, gray, brown, blue, red, gray, brown, blue,
red. And that is only a single possibility. I thought Dori, one of
my kindergarten students, would enjoy learning about patterns by helping me create a few alternative arrangements for
the peddler's caps.

Before this could happen, though, I needed to make caps. I
did not make cotton or wool caps. Instead I cut seventeen
ovals out of index cards to represent the peddler's wares. To
begin my millinery duties, I took a 3˝ × 5˝ index card and in
pencil drew four ovals on it. Each oval was about 2˝ across
and a little more than 1˝ top to bottom. I colored each oval
gray, and then I cut them out.

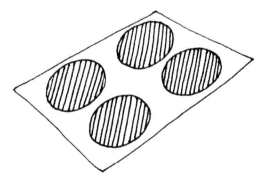

I took a second index card and repeated all the steps, except I colored the ovals red. On a third index card, I colored
the ovals blue, and on a fourth, I colored the ovals brown.
Now I needed to make the peddler's very own checked cap. I

took a fresh index card, drew a single oval on it, with a black pen covered the cap with checks, and cut it out.

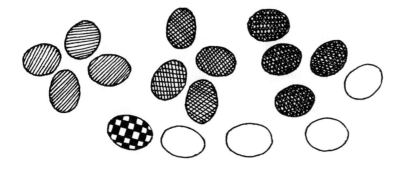

When Dori arrived, the seventeen ovals were scattered about my table.

"What are these?" she asked.

"Caps," I answered, "like the peddler's in *Caps for Sale*, except these are very small and made of paper. See, we have gray, brown, blue, and red ones. I even made a checked one. Do you remember how the peddler arranged his caps?"

She shook her head no.

"He began with his checked cap," I said as I slid the checked oval directly in front of us. "Next he put on all of his gray caps."

I found a gray oval and put it on top of the checked one.

"Would you like to help me, Dori? Can you find the three other gray caps and put them in place?" I asked.

Instead of answering me directly, Dori set about the job, and soon the four gray caps were resting on top of the checked one. Next I asked her to find the brown caps and add them to the column. Then she added the blue caps and finally the red. In less than a minute, Dori had reproduced the peddler's tower of caps.

"Good job, Dori. I was thinking, though, about another arrangement. How about this?" I asked.

I moved the ovals around and positioned them in a pat-

terned column: red, blue, red, blue, red, blue, red, blue, checked, gray, brown, gray, brown, gray, brown, gray, brown.

"That looks nice," Dori said.

"Thank you, I like it, too. I arranged the caps in a pattern. Would you like to make your own cap arrangement?" I asked.

"Okay," she answered. She started moving the ovals, and in a minute she had them in an attractive, although totally random, order.

After praising her work, I started a new tower. Again, I placed ovals following a simple repetitive pattern: red, blue, brown, gray, red, blue, brown, gray, red, blue, brown, gray. After putting down the twelfth oval, I turned to Dori and said, "Here's a tricky job for you. If I want to keep the same pattern, red, blue, brown, gray, red, blue, brown, gray, what should I do with the next four caps?" As I asked the question, I pushed the remaining red, blue, brown, and gray ovals in front of her.

Dori looked puzzled for a moment, and then her eyes lit up. "I get it," she said as she put the ovals in place. "But what about the checked one?"

"That's a good question. I don't want to mess up the pattern. Hmmmm. I guess I'll put it on the very top. How does that look?" I asked.

"Good," she answered.

What would I have done if Dori did not understand how to continue the pattern? I would have put the red cap in place for her while repeating the words, "Red, blue, brown, gray, red, blue, brown, gray." And if this extra assist did not help, I would have finished the tower myself and ended the game. There is no point forcing a child to see patterns before she is ready.

Dori did get the idea, though, and so we kept playing. I told Dori she could make a new arrangement, and she did, but she made no attempt to order the colors. Next it was my turn, and I arranged the ovals according to this pattern: red, red, blue, blue, gray, gray, brown, brown, red, red, blue, blue. Again, I stopped before placing the last four caps and asked Dori to finish my work. After giving the problem some thought, she slid the ovals into their proper locations.

"Fantastic, Dori, you figured out my pattern," I said.

And then, much to Dori's disappointment, I called a halt to the game. She was mollified, though, when I promised that we would play next week. I also promised to change one of the colors, if she wanted. Pinks. Dori wanted pink caps instead of gray ones. No problem.

Over the next weeks, Dori and I played PATTERNS first thing during our work time. I never directly discussed how to make a pattern, but I always created one and I almost always asked Dori to finish my column. When it was Dori's turn, she did not try to make a pattern, but I did not mind. It was enough that she could analyze what I was doing. I knew that over the years Dori would learn more about patterns. She would discover patterns in numbers, patterns in words, patterns in art, patterns in science, patterns in each and every area of intellectual life. Would she remember that her first serious study of patterns began with a peddler and his caps? Probably not, but for her it was a good way to begin, and it might be a good way for your child to begin, too.

*T*he monkeys in *Caps for Sale*, with nearly perfect precision, copy the peddler's every move. This talent—the ability to accurately duplicate the things you see—is of more than passing value. Good penmanship, for instance, relies in part on the facility to make exact copies of letters and numbers. Monkeys do not need penmanship, but people do. And so the art of copying is a good thing to develop in your child.

How can you increase your child's ability to copy? You might try spending a few minutes playing MONKEY SEE, MONKEY DO. To begin the game, you say, "Monkey see,

MONKEY SEE, MONKEY DO

GRADES

preschool and kindergarten

SKILLS

learning to reproduce the things you see

monkey do." When you have captured your child's attention, make a face—a really weird face. Once your features are thoroughly snarled, hold that position. Your child's job is to twist his own face in imitation of yours. It might be hard to stay in your positions without breaking into giggles, but once your child's face looks as much like yours as possible, go ahead and laugh.

Next contort your body in some strange manner and give your child a chance to contort himself in kind. Or move with a hop and a twist and have your child hop and twist, too. Then hold your hands in an odd way and wait for your child to reproduce the positions of your fingers.

After this much seeing and doing, call an end to the game. Your child might protest, but assure him that you will play tomorrow or the next day. Indeed, this is such a quick and easy game, you can almost always find a moment for a couple of rounds. While you are putting away groceries, for instance, turn to your child and say, "Monkey see, monkey do," then make a face. When sorting laundry, shout out, "Monkey see, monkey do," and swivel yourself this way or that. If you are willing to embarrass yourself while waiting in line at the supermarket, you can suddenly announce, "Monkey see, monkey do" there, too. Of course, your child might want to pose in peculiar positions and command you to copy him. Go ahead. It's only fair—after all, MONKEY SEE, MONKEY DO.

CHRYSANTHEMUM

WRITTEN AND ILLUSTRATED BY KEVIN HENKES
1991
GOOD READING FOR PRESCHOOL AND KINDERGARTEN

*U*ntil she starts school, Chrysanthemum, a spunky little mouse, believes that she has an absolutely perfect name. She simply loves how it looks on an envelope, on her birthday cake, or when "she wrote it herself with her fat orange crayon. Chrysanthemum, Chrysanthemum, Chrysanthemum."

On the first day of school, however, the other children ridicule her. Chrysanthemum is such a long name—thirteen letters long. Chrysanthemum is a name for a flower, not a child. As the day wears on, her classmates' taunts take their toll, and Chrysanthemum wilts. The next day, Chrysanthemum suffers anew, and it seems possible that school will be absolute misery always and forever.

Everything changes on the third day of classes, however, when the children meet their music teacher, the very wonderful and very pregnant Mrs. Twinkle. As luck would have it, Mrs. Twinkle's first name is—Delphinium. And, as if that were not excellent enough, Mrs. Delphinium Twinkle announces that if her soon-to-arrive baby turns out to be a girl, she will name the baby Chrysanthemum. Why? Because Chrysanthemum is an absolutely perfect name.

Chrysanthemum succeeds in large part because the book's author and illustrator, Kevin Henkes, creates watercolor drawings that flawlessly display the extreme emotions of childhood. Look at the picture of Chrysanthemum as she leaps to school on that first day. Pure joy. Faster than you can say kindergarten, though, she falls into deepest despond. Chrysanthemum does not go on her emotional roller-coaster ride alone. Readers join her, and, in the end, when Chrysanthemum knows once again that her name is absolutely perfect, readers smile almost as broadly as the little mouse herself.

There are a few amusing touches for adults, too, in the book. On one page, Chrysanthemum's father is reading a large tome which, if you look closely, turns out to be entitled *The Inner Mouse, vol. 2: Childhood Anxiety*. And *Chrysanthemum* is indeed a useful book for dealing with childhood anxiety.

I think it's a useful book for encouraging a few academic skills, too—by playing the following games.

THE NAME GAME

GRADES

preschool and kindergarten

MATERIALS

blank paper, pencil

SKILLS

counting, comparing numbers

*W*hen Victoria, one of Chrysanthemum's classmates, announces to everybody that *Chrysanthemum* has thirteen letters, my student Max interrupted to declare, "My name has three letters."

"You're right about that. Do you know how many letters are in your last name?" I asked.

Max raised his fingers, preparing to count, but I interrupted him. "We'll figure it out after I finish reading the story, okay? In fact, we can do a couple of neat things with our names, if you'd like," I said.

Max nodded his consent.

As soon as I closed the book, and we both agreed that it was a great story, Max asked, "Can we do those name things now?"

"Sure," I answered. "Just let me get the supplies we need and set things up."

I pulled out a sheet of blank paper and a pencil. While Max watched attentively, I turned the page lengthwise and drew lines so that the paper looked like this:

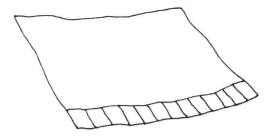

Now I had a row of thirteen boxes. In each box I wrote one of the letters in *Chrysanthemum*.

"That's how long *Chrysanthemum* is. Would you like to see how long your name is compared to hers?" I asked.

"Okay," he answered.

With that, I picked up the pencil again and drew a second row of thirteen boxes above *Chrysanthemum*. In the first three boxes of this new row, I wrote *MAX*—one letter per box.

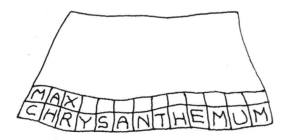

"My name looks so short next to Chrysanthemum's," Max observed.

"Your name only comes up to *C, H, R.* There are a lot more letters than *C, H,* and *R* in *Chrysanthemum,*" I said, running my finger across the string of letters, beginning with *Y.* After observing my finger's movement, Max sent his own finger along the same route, only he took the time to count each letter as he traveled from left to right. When he was done, he announced, "*Chrysanthemum* has ten more." Then he asked, "How about your name?"

"You want to see how my name looks on top of yours and Chrysanthemum's?"

"Yup," he said.

I added another row of boxes and inscribed my name—two letters longer than *Max* but eight shorter than *Chrysanthemum.* After that Max wanted to add his brother's name, his cat's name, his best friend's name, and his middle name to the chart.

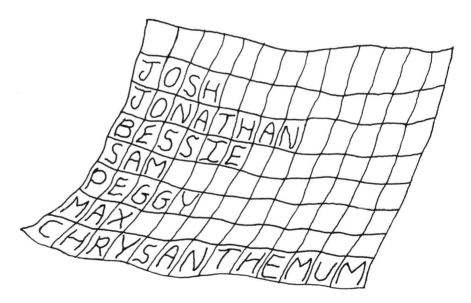

As the chart grew, we counted. We counted how many letters were in each name, and we counted how much longer one name was than another. Most preschoolers and kindergartners can say the numbers from one to thirteen without difficulty. Determining how much larger one number is than another is a far more daunting task. True, children will know that thirteen is greater than three. That's pretty simple stuff. Ask how much greater, though, and things get murky. Typically, and to the surprise of many adults, a young child will answer that thirteen must be thirteen more than three because thirteen is the bigger number.

This is certainly the answer Max would ordinarily give to such a question. Today, then, why was he able to correctly assert that *Chrysanthemum* is ten letters longer than *Max*? Had I asked him to compare the numbers without a picture to guide him, he would have been confused. But by placing *MAX* directly above *CHRYSANTHEMUM* so that each letter in his name matched a letter in hers, he could see the difference. He could even touch the letters—*YSANTHEMUM*—that made up the difference. Seeing the letters, touching the letters, made it possible for Max to successfully compare three and thirteen.

What if, even with the words lined up, Max could not tell how much longer one name was than the other? I would have pointed out the ten extra letters in *Chrysanthemum*, but I would not have goaded him into accepting that thirteen is ten more than three. Insisting that a child grasp a concept he is not prepared to understand is pointless. Much better for Max to enjoy himself and, therefore, be willing to play again another day. Perhaps the second time we played, or the third or the fourth, he would announce, without prompting, that *Greenberg*, his last name, is exactly five letters longer than my last name, *Kaye*, and only four letters shorter than *Chrysanthemum*.

CHRY-SAN-THE-MUM

GRADES

kindergarten

SKILLS

hearing syllables in words

*C*hrysanthemum—not only is it an absolutely perfect name, it is a wonderful mouth-filling word. No wonder the little mouse adores chanting "Chrysanthemum, Chrysanthemum, Chrysanthemum." When I read the story to Jane, she loved hearing all those repeated Chrysanthemums, and soon she was chanting along, "Chrysanthemum, Chrysanthemum, Chrysanthemum."

"Jane," I said when I finished reading, "you say Chrysanthemum's name so beautifully. I wonder, though, can you clap her name?"

"What do you mean?" she asked.

"Like this," I said. Then I carefully pronounced *Chrysanthemum* syllable by syllable: *Chry-san-the-mum*. As I enunciated each syllable, I clapped my hands. Four claps later, Jane was smiling. I said *Chrysanthemum* a second time—syllable by syllable, clap by clap. I repeated myself again and then again. By the third *Chry-san-the-mum*, Jane was clapping with me.

"I like that," she said when we finally stopped.

"Me too. *Chrysanthemum* is a four-clap name, but most names call for fewer claps. Mine, for instance, only needs two. Do you want to hear?" I asked.

Jane did, and so I said, "*Peg-gy*," clapping with each syllable. Almost immediately, Jane was singing and clapping along, "*Peg-gy, Peg-gy, Peg-gy.*"

Suddenly she stopped clapping, turned to me and asked, "How about my name?"

"Yours is a one-clap name. *Jane,*" I said with a single loud explosion of hands.

Jane was disappointed about having a one-clap name. So I suggested we test her last name, Cooperman. *Coo-per-man—* three claps. Now, that was impressive, and we clapped it many times before Jane was willing to stop.

"*Chrysanthemum* is still the clap winner. I wonder if we can think of a word that has just as many claps. It doesn't have to be a name. It could be any word at all."

Jane looked around the room. She mumbled several words before asking aloud, "Computer?"

"Let's check. *Com-pu-ter*, that's a three-clapper," I said. Then we both clapped the word.

"How about lemonade?" she asked after taking a sip of the drink I had given her for snack.

"*Lem-on-ade.* Another three-clapper," I said.

"Radiator?" she asked.

"*Ra-di-a-tor!* Yes, that's four claps. Good for you, Jane!"

Just then the doorbell rang signaling the end of our work time. When Jane's mother entered my office, I explained our hunt for four-clap words, and I suggested that she and Jane continue the quest on their own. I even challenged them to find a word with more than four claps.

The next week, Jane ran up the stairs to my office. As soon as she got to the door, she shouted, "Six!"

"Six?" I asked.

"Six claps. We found a six-clap word," she announced.

"Wow! Tell me," I said.

"*Encyclopedia!*" she bellowed.

"*En-cy-clo-pe-di-a,*" I repeated with claps. "You're right. It is a six-clap word. Amazing. How did you ever think of it?"

Jane explained that during her weekly Saturday trip to the library with her mother, she saw the encyclopedia on the shelf. She said the word, and she said it again. She figured that *encyclopedia* is such a long word it must have lots and lots of claps. She asked her mother to help her count. When they reached six, they both let out such a loud cheer that the librarian had to ask them to be quiet.

The game CHRY-SAN-THE-MUM helped Jane arrive at a major realization: words are composed of smaller bits of sound. For the moment, Jane called these bits "claps," but eventually she would learn their more conventional name—syllables. Claps, syllables, the name did not matter. What mattered was the brand-new way Jane was thinking about words.

SO THAT'S A CHRYSANTHEMUM

GRADES
preschool and kindergarten

SKILLS
learning about flowers

*D*oes your child know what a chrysanthemum looks like? How about a delphinium? After reading the book, consider wandering over to your neighborhood florist. There, if the season is right, you and your child can sniff chrysanthemums or gaze at delphiniums. You might even buy a mixed bunch to take home.

Aside from the fun, why should you take your child to the florist? It is always a good idea to broaden your child's interest in and knowledge of the world. And the book *Chrysanthemum* with its lead characters, Chrysanthemum and Delphinium, offers a perfect opportunity to increase your child's knowledge of flowers.

BLUEBERRIES FOR SAL

WRITTEN AND ILLUSTRATED BY ROBERT McCLOSKEY
1948
CALDECOTT HONOR BOOK
GOOD READING FOR PRESCHOOL, KINDERGARTEN,
AND FIRST GRADE

*O*ver fifty years ago, Robert McCloskey wrote a simple tale of a young woman and her daughter gathering blueberries. Many things have changed in the intervening time, but *Blueberries for Sal* is as charming and delightful as ever.

The story begins one summer morning when a little girl named Sal and her mother climb Blueberry Hill to pick berries. As it happens, on the other side of the hill a she-bear and her frisky cub are engaged in their own berry search. While Sal's mother and the she-bear diligently go about their work, little Sal and the bear cub wander off, as children do. After a time, Sal and the bear cub end up, each of them, trailing the wrong mother—Sal tramps after the she-bear, the bear cub hustles after Sal's mother. What a mix-up! Soon, however, all is set right, and the humans head down one side of the hill and the bears descend the other.

Throughout the story, McCloskey shows how similar the two mothers and the two children happen to be. Both mothers are getting food to store for the winter. Both children drift off and find themselves merrily following the wrong adults. And when the two mothers turn and face the wrong youngsters, their reactions are identical. Sal's mother backs away because she is shy of bears. Mother bear backs away because she is shy of people. Neither of the children is worried, though. The children have not yet learned to be afraid.

As an experiment, try going through the book looking just at the pictures without reading the words. McCloskey's illustrations are drawn in a deep, blueberry blue, and the pleasure they afford makes you turn the pages eagerly, and the story unfolds before you. The vividness of the illustrations makes *Blueberries for Sal* especially appealing for young children who cannot yet read the words. After hearing the story once or twice, a child can grab the book from the shelf and, using the pictures as guides, tell the tale to himself whenever he wants to spend time on Blueberry Hill.

A few years after publishing *Blueberries for Sal*, McCloskey wrote *One Morning in Maine*, starring a somewhat older Sal. It is a pleasure to report that the follow-up story is just as delicious as the original. Before reading about Sal's additional adventures, though, consider playing the following math games.

KUPLINK, KUPLANK, KUPLUNK

GRADES

preschool, kindergarten, and first

MATERIALS

bowl, ten paper clips

SKILL

counting

*K*uplink, kuplank, kuplunk—those are the sounds of blueberries hitting the bottom of Sal's empty pail. When I read *Blueberries for Sal* out loud to Lisa, she smiled every time she heard one of those words. I was pleased about this because I planned to use *kuplink, kuplank, kuplunk* as a starting point for a counting game.

Lisa was finishing kindergarten and could recite the numbers from one to one hundred in order—more or less. When I asked her to count the pencils on a table, though, she had a hard time. She said two numbers when pointing to a single pencil and skipped numbers altogether when pointing to others. As with many young children, Lisa did not understand that a correct count depends on assigning one and only one number to each and every object counted. How could I help her appreciate this idea? I knew that lecturing would not do the trick, but I hoped that playing a game would.

After reading the book to Lisa, I turned to her and said,

"Those *kuplinks, kuplanks,* and *kuplunks* are so much fun. Don't you agree?"

"Yeah," she said.

"Which sound is your favorite?" I asked.

"*Kuplunk*. I like it best," she answered.

"I bet we can use sounds, sounds almost like *kuplunks*, to play a counting game."

"What kind of counting game?" she asked.

"This kind: using sounds, I try to count paper clips with my eyes closed. If I can, I'm doing a good job in the game," I said.

"With your eyes closed?" she repeated.

"Yup, with my eyes closed. Do you want to test me?"

"Sure," she said with real enthusiasm.

"Here's what we'll do. I have an empty bowl and a pile of ten paper clips. I'm going to close my eyes, and while they are closed, you'll drop clips into the bowl the way Sal dropped blueberries in her pail. You might drop five or three or eight. I won't see you drop the clips, but I will hear each clip go *kuplunk* as it lands.

"Using the *kuplunk* sounds, I'll try to figure out how many clips you put in the bowl. There is only one rule you have to follow: you must leave a moment or two between dropping each clip. That way if a clip bounces and *kuplunks* more than once, I won't be confused. Got the idea?"

"I think so. Can I start now?" she asked.

"As soon as I close my eyes you can," I said.

I shut my eyes and Lisa began dropping clips in the bowl. Every time one fell, I mumbled, "*Kuplunk,*" while lifting one of my fingers.

When I had six fingers in the air, she announced, "That's it." And then she asked, "How many?"

"I think there are six clips in the bowl. Am I right?" I asked as I opened my eyes.

Lisa shrugged her shoulders. Although she had dropped the clips, she had not bothered to count while doing so. No problem, we would count now. Slowly and deliberately, I took a clip from the bowl.

"One," I said. Then I took another clip. "Two."

I kept removing clips, and saying numbers—one number for each clip—until the bowl was empty.

Lisa cheered. "Six. There were six. You got it right!"

"Good for me. Now, I wonder if you can count *kuplunks.* Want to try?" I asked.

"Okay."

Lisa covered her eyes, and I dropped clips in the bowl. The whole time, Lisa never said a word. When I finished, I said, "That's it. How many clips do you think are in the bowl?"

"Four?" she asked.

"Open your eyes, and we can count to find out."

We counted and there were five. "You were very close," I said. "How did you keep track of the numbers? Did you count them in your head? I prefer to count them out loud. Test me again, and you'll see what I mean."

I closed my eyes and Lisa began casting clips in the bowl. Every time I heard one fall, I said a new number. When Lisa stopped dropping clips, I declared my results. Then I opened my eyes. We counted the clips, and sure enough, by keeping careful track of *kuplunks*, I had arrived at the right number.

"I think my method works," I said. "You can use it, too, if you want."

"Okay," she said.

This time, with each *kuplunk*, I heard her murmur a number. When the moment came to check her results, she had the correct answer, and she squealed with delight.

Over the next few weeks, we played KUPLINK, KUPLANK, KUPLUNK many times, and our playing brought results. Soon Lisa was counting pencils, paper clips, and anything else presented to her with both ease and accuracy.

*S*al and the bear cub love eating blueberries. Very likely you and your child do, too. Apart from gobbling the delicious little berries by the fistful, you might try throwing a few blueberries into your favorite pancake mix or tossing them into your muffin batter. Or you can try out the recipes below.

Aside from the good time and resulting good food, there are two educational reasons for preparing these BLUEBERRY TREATS with your child. First, to be successful in school, children must learn to follow directions accurately and in sequence. That is exactly what they do when they cook from a recipe. A cook who goes step by step ends up with delicious food. A cook who fails to follow directions may end up with mush. Second, when children cook, they have lots of opportunities to measure. Most recipes are written in customary units: cups, tablespoons, and teaspoons. It is a good idea for children to learn these measurements, but nowadays it's an even

BLUEBERRY TREATS

GRADES

preschool, kindergarten, and first

MATERIALS

cooking equipment, ingredients for recipes

SKILLS

metric measuring, following directions

better idea for children to learn metric units: liters and milliliters. The United States has been slow to convert to the metric system, but in much of the rest of the world and in all scientific circles metrics are standard. Someday we Americans will switch over—more than likely in your child's lifetime. It is important, then, to give your child lots of opportunities to measure in liters and milliliters. And so I've written these recipes using metric units (with the old-fashioned cups, tablespoons, and teaspoons in parentheses). All you need to get started are the right tools—easy to arrange, since you can buy cups and spoons marked with both systems of measurement in almost any housewares store.

Blueberry Honey Sandwich
Makes 6 sandwiches

Pound cake
250 milliliters (1 cup) blueberries (fresh berries are best, but
        you can use frozen if you drain off the juice)
15 milliliters (1 tablespoon) honey

    1. Cut 2 very thin slices of pound cake for each sandwich.

    2. Mash the blueberries in a bowl. You can use a fork or your fingers.

    3. Mix the mashed blueberries with the honey.

    4. Spread the blueberry-honey mix on one slice of pound cake and top it with the second slice.

    5. Eat the sandwich quickly, before it gets soggy.

    6. Refrigerate any remaining blueberry-honey mix for future sandwiches.

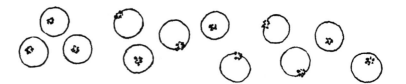

Blueberry Ice Pops

Makes 12 pops

250 milliliters (1 cup) blueberries (fresh berries are best, but
      you can use frozen if you drain off the juice)
250 milliliters (1 cup) lemonade
15 milliliters (1 tablespoon) sugar
Ice cube tray
12 Popsicle sticks (called craft sticks when you buy them in
      stationery or toy stores)

   1. Mash the blueberries in a bowl until they are almost liquid. You can use a fork or your fingers.

   2. Thoroughly mix the blueberries with the lemonade and the sugar.

   3. Pour the blueberry-lemonade mix into the ice cube tray. (You might want to transfer it to the measuring cup first to make it easier to pour.) Make sure some mashed blueberry gets in each ice cube hollow.

   4. Put the tray in the freezer and leave it there until the cubes begin to freeze. This will take about 2 hours.

   5. Stick one Popsicle stick in the middle of each cube.

   6. Leave the tray in the freezer until the ice cubes are frozen solid.

   7. Eat.

You can make the pops without sticks, if you want. When the cubes are frozen, your child can eat them with his fingers. Alternatively, he can drop a couple of cubes into a glass of lemonade. As the cubes melt, they add a delicious blueberry taste and an amusing bluish tone to the drink.

Blueberry Balls

Makes about 10 balls

725 milliliters (2½ cups) cornflakes
125 milliliters (½ cup) powdered sugar for making the balls
90 milliliters (6 tablespoons) cream cheese
125 milliliters (½ cup) fresh (not frozen) blueberries (although you may want to add a few more)
60 milliliters (about ¼ cup) powdered sugar to coat the balls

1. Crush the cornflakes in a bowl with your fingers.
2. Mix in 125 milliliters (½ cup) powdered sugar.
3. Knead the cream cheese into the cornflake and powdered sugar mix until you thoroughly combine the three ingredients.
4. Blend in the blueberries, being careful not to crush them.
5. Sprinkle a plate with some powdered sugar.
6. Put a small amount of the mix in the palm of your hand. Make sure you include a few blueberries. Roll the mix into a ball a little smaller than a Ping-Pong ball.
7. Coat the ball with powdered sugar and roll it in your hands again. Then put the ball on a clean plate.
8. Keep making balls and coating them in powdered sugar. Add more powdered sugar to the plate as needed. You might have to blend a few extra blueberries into the mix before forming the last couple of balls.
9. Refrigerate the balls for at least 1 hour—except for the one you can't resist gobbling right away.

Happy eating!

Some afternoon shortly after introducing *Blueberries for Sal* to your child, why not bring home a container of blueberries to share with him? Don't start eating right away, though. Instead, use the berries to play a mathematical game. Begin by giving your child a tablespoon and asking him to estimate how many berries he thinks he can place in the hollow. After making an estimate, let him either drop berries in the spoon or scoop them up. When the spoon is full, he should empty it and count the berries. How does his estimate compare with the actual number? When you have learned the answer, the two of you can eat the results. Then pull out a butter knife and estimate how many blueberries long it happens to be. Or find out how many berries fit into the lid of a jar of jam. Or how many berries are needed to outline a folded paper napkin. And when you have done enough estimating and eating, you could reread the book just for fun.

BLUEBERRY COUNT

GRADES

kindergarten and first

MATERIALS

blueberries, tablespoon, butter knife, lid from a jar of jam, napkin

SKILLS

counting and estimating

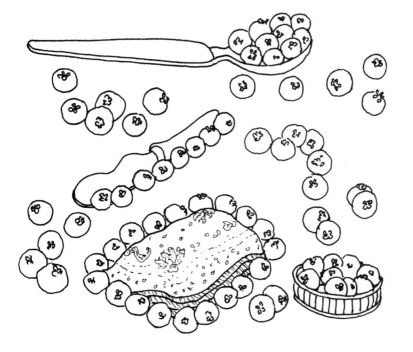

KATY NO-POCKET

WRITTEN BY EMMY PAYNE
ILLUSTRATED BY H. A. REY
1944
GOOD READING FOR PRESCHOOL, KINDERGARTEN,
AND FIRST GRADE

Katy No-Pocket tells the tale of Katy, an indomitable kangaroo, and Freddy, her irrepressible son. It is a wonderful story of mother love and tenacity.

All great heroes of literature confront terrible problems, and so does Katy Kangaroo. By a fluke of nature, she was born without a cozy, comfy, baby-toting pocket. Imagine the troubles this presents for her and her son! With no pocket to slide into, poor little Freddy must hop as best he can alongside his mother. The young kangaroo attempts to keep up, but how can he when Katy's legs are so large and powerful and his own are so small and weak?

Katy tries all sorts of ways to carry Freddy, but nothing works. Finally Owl, the wisest animal in the forest, makes a clever suggestion. Katy must go to the city and buy a pocket.

Katy does not hesitate. Off she hops, with Freddy by her side. Before long the two kangaroos arrive in the city, where they see a workman wearing a carpenter's apron. Upon hearing their story, the workman graciously hands his apron to the needy kangaroos. Katy, thrilled, dons the apron, tucks Freddy in the center pocket, and leaps home. In her new outfit, Katy has not only a snug spot for Freddy, but also pockets enough to shelter a play group of baby animals.

Listening to how Katy overcomes her biological flaw, children get a valuable lesson in persistence. In a most admirable manner, Katy is relentless in her search for a way to carry

Freddy. She demonstrates that adults will persevere until they solve problems, especially if solving those problems benefits their children. And she demonstrates that perseverance pays off, and you must not allow initial failures to hinder you.

Katy is as much a creation of H. A. Rey, the illustrator, as she is of Emmy Payne, the writer. Rey, best known as the creator of that rapscallion monkey Curious George, is one of the jolliest of children's book illustrators, and all his visual playfulness is on display in *Katy No-Pocket*. After a second or third reading, take time to study the illustrations with your child. Point out how the trees seem to grin, the flowers smile, and the cars chuckle. Look carefully, and you can find an amusing and clever detail in every drawing in the book.

Four games follow. None of them will take much time and only one requires you to hop.

WHO IS HIDING IN KATY'S POCKET?

Katy Kangaroo proved her educational worth to me the first day I met with a bright kindergarten student named David. David loved listening to stories, he loved thumbing through books and gazing at the pictures, and he loved carrying books around his house and classroom. Children who are this fond of books are usually eager to learn to read. But not David. The whole idea terrified him. During class lessons, when his teacher talked about letters and their sounds, David was miserable. He squirmed and fiddled, giggled and moaned. His behavior disrupted the class, but David's teacher sympathized with his problem. She understood, as did his parents, that David was not trying to make trouble. Instead, he was anxious, and he simply could not sit quietly and listen. Clearly, something had to change, and so I was asked to help.

I wanted to earn David's trust right from our first session. Unless he trusted me, he would not feel safe enough to do

GRADES

preschool, kindergarten, and first

SKILLS

listening to sounds in words

what he needed to do in order to learn—take a few risks. And I wanted to prove to him that taking those risks would produce satisfying results. *Katy No-Pocket* turned out to be perfectly suited to my purpose.

Immediately after David and I introduced ourselves, I held up the book. "Your mom tells me that you enjoy listening to stories. I have one here I hope you will like," I said.

David smiled and asked, "Can I see it first?"

I handed him the book, and he turned the pages, carefully studying each picture. When he was finished, he returned the book to me and, by nodding, indicated that I could start reading. When I finished the last page, David asked me to read it again.

"I will," I said. "But not until later. First, how about we play a game? I happen to know a guessing game that stars Katy Kangaroo."

David looked interested, and so I continued. "I went to visit Katy recently, and while we were talking, I noticed that she had a baby animal in each of her pockets."

"You did not!" David shouted.

"Oh yes I did. What's more, somehow she knew that soon I would meet a boy called David."

"Really?" he asked.

"Absolutely," I said, although the tone of my "absolutely" let him know this was make-believe. "And Katy told me that when I did meet David, I should challenge him to name some of the animals in her pockets."

After he finished laughing, David asked, "Is there a monkey?"

"Nope, there isn't. But wait, don't name another animal yet. You see, Katy told me to give you hints—one before each guess," I said.

"Okay, what's my hint?"

"In Katy's top pocket, there is a long skinny baby animal whose name begins with the sound *sss*. Can you tell me who it is? If you are wrong, don't worry. I will give you another hint, and you can guess again," I said.

"Is it a spider?" David asked.

"No, it's not a spider. That was a very good guess, because *spider* does begin with *sss*. Remember, though, the animal in Katy's pocket is long and skinny. For your next hint, I'll tell you a little more of the animal's name: *sss-nnnn-aaaa*," I said, stretching out the sounds and saying them as clearly as I could.

"Snake!" David yelled.

"Yes," I said. "You figured out one of the animals. Katy will be so happy when I tell her. Do you think you can figure out another?"

"Yup," he said.

"Great. There is an animal hiding in one of Katy's bottom pockets. This animal has black and white stripes. Its name begins with the sounds *zzzzz-eeee*."

"Zebra!" David shouted.

"Wow! You got it on your first try. That's amazing. Now, here is a third animal. This one has stripes, too, and its name begins with the sound *ttttt*."

"Skunk?" he asked.

"A skunk does have a big stripe, but its name begins with the sounds *ssskkk*. You need an animal that begins with the sound *tttt*. Do you want to hear more of the name? Would that be a helpful hint?" I asked.

"I think so," he answered.

"This animal's name begins with the sounds *ttt-iiii-ggggg*."

"It's a tiger," he declared.

"You are so good at this game!" I said.

"Can we play some more?" he asked.

"Not today, but we can play next time you come. That is, if you want," I said.

"I do," he quickly replied.

"And if Katy wants to play, too, of course," I added.

"Will you read the book again now?"

"Sure," I said, smiling.

I had every reason to smile. For over ten minutes, David had focused his attention on analyzing letter sounds in words. This was exactly the kind of activity he found so troublesome in school, but there was no anxiety now. David liked playing. Perhaps he would have found equal enjoyment playing a similar game without a link to *Katy No-Pocket*. But it is all too easy to imagine him shunning any activity, even a game, that called for concentrating so closely on letter sounds. WHO IS HIDING IN KATY'S POCKET? made it easier for him. The game was based on the lead character of a book he had just heard and thoroughly enjoyed. He knew that I had never actually chatted with Katy, but he happily suspended logic in favor of imagination and gave the game a chance. Almost immediately, he realized he was a good player. He could figure out the animals. He was triumphant, and that made him all the more willing to keep on playing.

*E*xactly how many pockets does Katy have in her magnificent apron? This is a logical question to ask your child after reading the book, and he can answer by counting. If he needs help to count accurately, go ahead and assist him. When he successfully counts Katy's pockets, you should reward his skill by appointing him your household's Official Master Pocket Counter. What does an Official Master Pocket Counter do? He counts pockets. Your child can start by counting his own pockets. How many is he wearing right now? Once he knows, he can tackle yours. Then he can count the number you and he have together. Are there other people at home? Are they wearing clothes with pockets? This might call for some extra counting.

No matter how enthusiastic your child is, do not overload him with duties on his first day in office. You want your child's appointment as Official Master Pocket Counter to last for a while, which means you must be cautious about exhausting the job's appeal. Tomorrow, after all, everyone will be wearing different clothes with a different number of pockets, presenting new opportunities for the pocket counter of the house.

BE AN OFFICIAL MASTER POCKET COUNTER

GRADES

preschool and kindergarten

SKILLS

counting

EAT THEM IF YOU CAN

GRADES

kindergarten and first

MATERIALS

jelly beans, raisins, or some other treat

SKILLS

counting, skip counting, adding, drawing a picture to solve a number problem

*I*f BE AN OFFICIAL MASTER POCKET COUNTER is too easy for your child, introduce him to a harder version of the game called EAT THEM IF YOU CAN. You begin the game by presenting your child with a bag of jelly beans (or a box of raisins, if you prefer). When he asks to eat some of the beans, say, "Sure, you can have a few—at least, you can if you win them."

When the child asks how he can win the beans, explain that he will have to count. First, he must find out how many pockets are on the clothes he is currently wearing. Then ask him to imagine your putting two beans into each of those pockets. Can he tell you how many beans you would need to accomplish that task? If he can tell you the right number, you will give him the same number of beans to eat. Would he like more candy? Then he must tell you how many jelly beans *you* would have if there were two beans in each of *your* pockets. Does he still want more candy? If he can figure out the number of jelly beans needed to put four in each of his pockets, he can eat those beans, too. If you think your child has collected too many beans for immediate consumption, you can insist that he save some of his winnings for later.

To solve these jelly bean problems, children usually count beans one by one. Even children who know how to do addition count the beans. That is fine with me. As children count, they are deeply engaged in matching beans and pockets, which is hard enough to do when they are in kindergarten or first grade.

After a few rounds, call a halt to the game. Your child might demand to keep playing—the game being so tasty—but don't give in. As with any game, if you stop the action while your child is still eager to play, he will be happy to play again—maybe tomorrow.

Before long, your child may find it extremely easy to solve the problems and collect his jelly beans, especially if he wears clothes with very few pockets. When that happens, here is a way to make the game more challenging. Tell your child to pretend that he just received an apron of his own, like Katy's, only his apron has five pockets. Next tell him to pretend that in each of the apron's pockets there are three jelly beans. If he can tell you the number of imaginary beans tucked in those imaginary pockets, you will take that many beans out of the bag and give them to him. After you've questioned your child about an imaginary apron with five pockets, you might try asking about an apron with six pockets, or three, or any number. Don't be surprised if your child has difficulty grappling with this new kind of problem. For young children, it can be very hard to count imaginary jelly beans in imaginary pockets. If your child finds the task too difficult, suggest that he draw a picture of the apron, the pockets, and the beans. The illustration should get him over the hurdle.

If, even with a drawing, he cannot solve the problem, it is best to return to real pockets, at least for a little while. Rushing a child's learning is always a mistake.

KANGAROO HOP

GRADES

preschool and kindergarten

MATERIALS

a CD player and a CD with a great beat

SKILLS

developing physical strength and muscle coordination, identifying with a character in a story

*I*n the 1950s, teenagers went to dances called sock hops where they spent the night jitterbugging. After reading *Katy No-Pocket*, you and your child, and any friends you care to include, can throw a special dance party, too—a KANGAROO HOP. A KANGAROO HOP can last ten minutes or half an hour, or longer, depending on your mood. The right music is an essential ingredient for a successful hop. Appoint yourself DJ and then select dancing songs with a wild and crazy beat. As soon as the music starts to play, everyone should dance the KANGAROO HOP. What is the KANGAROO HOP? Look at the drawings of Katy bounding from here to there. Her forearms bent up by her sides and her big legs springing in tandem—Katy is doing the KANGAROO HOP. Imitate her, and you will be kangaroo hopping, too. Hop for one song, or two, or three. Stop for refreshments and then, if you want, hop some more.

Why exhaust your child with hopping? Exercise is a good thing in itself as just about everyone knows. But by exercising in this way, you will help your child imagine the characters in a book more vividly, help the child *feel* those characters in his legs and arms. And you will help your child see a book as a starting point for fun. So, start the music and

FREDERICK

WRITTEN AND ILLUSTRATED BY LEO LIONNI

1967

CALDECOTT HONOR BOOK

GOOD READING FOR KINDERGARTEN AND FIRST GRADE

*I*n 1959, when he was fifty years old, Leo Lionni wrote and illustrated his first picture book, *Little Blue and Little Yellow*. Over the next three decades, in an astonishing outpouring, he published a children's book nearly every year. Connoisseurs of Lionni argue over which qualifies as his greatest work, but for me there is no contest. The honor goes to *Frederick*, Lionni's story of a uniquely gifted mouse.

The story begins in the autumn—a time of work for diligent field mice. The family of Frederick the mouse toils away gathering and storing corn, nuts, wheat, and straw for the cold months ahead. Frederick, however, occupies his time sitting quietly in the warm sun. He claims that he is at work collecting colors, words, and the sun's rays, but what can he mean?

We find out late in the winter when food supplies are running low. The mice, in their gloom, think of Frederick. They do not turn on him, though, or blame him for eating food that he did not gather. Instead they look to him for entertainment and inspiration, and Frederick gives them what they want. He feeds their souls with elegant, flowing descriptions of brighter times. He nourishes their hearts with word songs evoking joy and light. Frederick, in his artistic, poetic, and nonconformist way, sees to it that his little tribe of mice survives.

It is not easy being different from your friends—especially for children. There is great pressure to fit in with the group, and it is hard to resist that tug. What will the other kids think of me, a child might wonder, if I don't feel like playing catch right now? What if I hate using crayons and everyone else loves using them? What if I'm the only person who cannot remember the alphabet? Will I be accepted? Will anybody like me? For a questioning child, Frederick offers a wonderful role model. He goes his own way, and yet he is not rejected or scorned. On the contrary, by being different, Frederick becomes a hero.

Three of the four activities that follow are, not surprisingly, word games, for no mouse inspires a love of words and language more than Frederick. SECRET FRIENDS inspires love of a different sort—a love of friendship.

WORD COLLECTION

*F*rederick loves words. He understands their power and appreciates their splendor. Some words are delicious—not only for their meanings but also because of the way they fill your mouth when you say them. You can prove this to yourself by slowly pronouncing words like *daffodil*, *accolade*, and *kaleidoscope*. Other words evoke powerful memories or feelings. Most of the time we don't give any thought to the beauty and tastiness and power of words, and we have no reason to do so. But it's a good idea to encourage your child to think about these qualities occasionally—to become someone who not only uses language but notices its different traits, someone who can be reflective and shrewd about words.

After reading *Frederick*, for instance, you and your child might become word collectors in the tradition of Frederick, the poet. Frederick collected his words mentally, holding them in his mind until he burst forth with verse. I suggest, though, that you and your child start a written collection.

You should begin your collection with two words—one

of your choosing and one of your child's. Take a bit of time making your selections. Discuss your ideas. Consider your choices.

Once you have decided on a word and your child has picked his, write each one on its own index card. If your child feels comfortable writing, hand him a pen or pencil. If he does not want to write, you should do the job. No matter who writes, your child can decorate the cards using colored pencils or crayons.

When the cards are ready, tape them on a large sheet of poster board, turning the board into your WORD COLLECTION display poster.

After you both place one word on the poster, stop for the day. Your child may want to add more words, but don't do it. Instead, plan on adding new words in a few days and then again a few days after that. If you feel like it, invite family members or friends to contribute words. No one, though, should supply more than a single word a day. Choosing a word for your collection should be an event, and, by adding just one word per person every few days, you will keep up the excitement. You can, however, at your discretion, include phrases like *chocolate chip cookies*, *golden sunsets*, and *wild tigers*.

To encourage your child's love of words is one good reason to make a word collection. There is another reason as well. Most children are eager to learn to read and write, but the prospect often troubles them. Will they find the task too hard? Will they embarrass themselves? Will they disappoint their parents? Scary questions. Making a WORD COLLECTION can help a child overcome these fears. When making a collection, a child considers just one word at a time. He selects the word himself. He sees it in print. He might even print it himself. He sees it on his word poster every day. If you go over the words now and then, your child may notice, after a few days, that he can read some of the cards. That is exciting. It is better than exciting. It is reassuring. If the child can read words in his collection, and if he has even written a few of them, he already has concrete reasons to feel good about his abilities. With that good feeling, he can go forward learning to read and to write with a little less fear and a little less worry.

*F*rederick was one of Debbie's favorite literary figures. She loved that mouse. She also loved making her own WORD COLLECTION poster, especially after I pointed out that in doing so she was following in Frederick's footsteps. Debbie found this an enormously appealing notion. For several weeks, we made writing words on index cards and then sticking them on a large sheet of poster board the first item on our agenda. By the time we had twelve words—six of Debbie's and six of mine—on our WORD COLLECTION poster, I suggested a change of action.

"You know, Debbie, Frederick didn't just collect words. When the time was right, he used them to compose stories and poems."

"I remember. That was the best part," Debbie said enthusiastically.

"I have a way that you and I can use the words in our collection to make up stories, like Frederick did. It's a storytelling game," I said.

"How do we play?" Debbie asked.

"First you pick two or three words from the collection and tell me your choices. Then I have to use the words to make up a story. It can be a long story or a very, very short one. Go ahead, select some words, and I'll see if I can do something clever with them," I said.

Debbie studied the collection before announcing her choices: *mushroom*, *wizard*, and *manatee*.

"Oh dear," I moaned, "those three words don't have anything in common, do they? And I have to get them into one story. This will be difficult, but I'll try my best."

Debbie giggled, delighted with herself for giving me such a challenging task.

"Okay, I've got it," I said after a minute. "It is a very short story, but it is a story and it uses all of the words. 'Once a *manatee* gave a delicious *mushroom* to a friendly *wizard.*' "

USING YOUR COLLECTION

GRADES

kindergarten and first

MATERIALS

the words from your WORD COLLECTION

SKILLS

using specific words to make stories

"That's too short," Debbie complained.

"Well, I could make it longer, but to succeed at the game, I don't have to. Still a longer story might be fun. How about this? 'Once a *wizard* lost all his magic. Only a giant *manatee* could restore his powers. The *wizard* sailed all the seas hunting for a giant *manatee*. When he finally found the *manatee*, the *wizard* handed him a large *mushroom*. In exchange, the *manatee* gave the *wizard* back his magic.' "

"That's much better," Debbie said, smiling.

"Now I get to pick out three words for you," I said.

"Can I make a short, short story like you did?" she asked.

"Sure," I said, "those are the rules. Here are your words: *sunset*, *velvet*, and *pumpkin*."

Debbie thought for a bit, and then said, "Once upon a time a lady in a *velvet* dress got a *pumpkin*. Then she saw the *sunset*, and she was happy."

"Excellent job, Debbie. I love your story. Now it is my turn again, but this time you can pick out more words, if you want," I said.

"How many?" she asked.

"Up to six. Don't worry, though, I won't give you so many. I'll stick to three. Okay?"

"Okay," Debbie said. "I'm giving you six, and they will be really hard!"

When we had each taken another turn, we agreed that was enough for the day, but before putting the WORD COLLECTION away, we added two more words—one of my choosing and one of Debbie's.

Then I said, "I think Frederick would be proud of us."

And Debbie answered, "I think so, too."

Over the next few weeks, Debbie and I kept playing the game and continued adding words to our collection. Before long we had twenty-six tacked on the poster board—some cards overlapping others. Now when we made up stories, Debbie gave me as many as eight or nine words at a time. It wasn't always easy for me to make up a story, but Debbie didn't mind when I stumbled. It is good, once in a while, for a child to see an adult struggle with a task. It lets the child know that learning is sometimes hard and that results don't always come easily—even for grownups. I didn't want Debbie to struggle, though, not in this game. I wanted her to feel like a word expert. Initially, therefore, I only gave her three or four words, and I accepted any story she told, no matter how discombobulated. When she got stuck, I gave suggestions to get her going. The more we played, the better Debbie got at the game. She handled more words. Her stories made more sense. One day, she easily turned out a clever tale with half a dozen WORD COLLECTION words. Somewhere Frederick was smiling.

*F*rederick is lucky to belong to such a caring tribe of mice. His family is loyal and willingly shares a shrinking supply of food, even though Frederick failed to gather a single nut or seed. And Frederick is loyal in return. He does not keep his talent to himself. When the time is right, he offers his special gifts and, in the process, helps everyone live through the dark winter days. The mice never discuss their feelings or actions. They do their good deeds without being asked. These are highly civilized rodents, and your child could do worse than imitate their behavior. How can you encourage your child to think unselfishly of the needs of others? You might want to invoke morality and patriotism and all kinds of other good things. But then, too, you might want to play SECRET FRIENDS.

I learned about SECRET FRIENDS from a colleague when I was a classroom teacher. Every year, she held a SECRET FRIENDS week in her class and her students invariably enjoyed the event. When I tried the game, my students loved it, too.

At the beginning of SECRET FRIENDS week, I drew the stu-

SECRET FRIENDS

GRADES
kindergarten and first

SKILLS
developing an awareness of others

dents together for a class meeting. Every child wrote his name on a slip of paper and then dropped the slip in a big bowl. When all the names were in the bowl, I passed it around once again. This time each student withdrew a slip. The person whose name was on the paper, whether it was someone the student knew well and liked a lot, someone he had avoided all year long, or even someone who was a bit of an enemy, would be his SECRET FRIEND for the week.

The rest of the rules were simple. Each person had to keep the name of his SECRET FRIEND a secret. Daily, for the remainder of the week, everyone in the class had to do something special for his secret friend. You could help your secret friend at cleanup time. You could bring him a special snack. You could compliment his work or praise his thinking. In the morning, I reminded the children about their SECRET FRIEND obligations. During the day, I asked a few youngsters to whisper their good deeds in my ear. I offered suggestions to students who were wondering how to help their SECRET FRIENDS. At the end of the week, the class again sat together and each person revealed the name of his SECRET FRIEND. The students all agreed that during the week our classroom had been a friendlier place.

It is easy to adapt SECRET FRIENDS so that you and your child can play at home. After reading *Frederick*, spend a couple of minutes discussing friendship with your child. Then suggest that he pick someone to be his SECRET FRIEND. He might choose a sibling, a parent, a grandparent, a schoolmate, or a neighborhood playmate. You should pick a SECRET FRIEND, too. Then explain that every day for the next three days you will both do something special for your respective SECRET FRIENDS.

As soon as your child understands what it means to be a SECRET FRIEND, discuss possible considerate acts. Your child, for instance, could pick up his friend's toys, give him a piece of candy, or hug him for no reason whatsoever. If your child's SECRET FRIEND lives far away, suggest that he telephone to send his love. He could send his friend a drawing or a painting. Alternatively, he could write his friend a letter. He does not have to do the actual writing; instead, he could dictate his words to you. If possible, you should both choose at least one way to please your SECRET FRIENDS today and then either carry out your plans or figure out when and how to do so. Do the same thing tomorrow and the day after.

Just as I regularly reminded my students of their SECRET FRIEND obligations, you might need to remind your child about being a good SECRET FRIEND. It is important to do so without nagging, though. You can certainly ask if he needs assistance to carry out his friendly deeds. Your child might want to give his SECRET FRIEND a small gift, for instance. Offer to help him select the present. Maybe he would like to bake cookies for his friend. You can help with that job, too. At the end of the three days, your official SECRET FRIEND time will come to an end (not that your acts of friendship need to stop). Now you have a decision to make. Should you tell your SECRET FRIENDS all you did for them? That's a tough call. You and your child might consider what Frederick the mouse would do. I can't be positive, of course, but I think he'd keep the secret.

I DREAM OF FREDERICK

GRADES

kindergarten and first

SKILLS

developing vocabulary and an interest in words

*G*argantuan, *scrumptious, ominous*, and *lavish* are not part of any typical kindergartner's or first grader's vocabulary. But they are marvelous words, and they are fun to say. If you want to introduce your child to the many pleasures of using fancy words, I suggest playing I DREAM OF FREDERICK. Here's how: every few days you will present a new and amusing word to your child—*exquisite*, for example.

Tomorrow at breakfast, you might announce, "Last night I had the strangest dream. In it, Frederick, the mouse in the story, came to me and said, 'I want you to teach Vivian, your lovely child, a wonderful word.' I asked what word, and the mouse said, '*Exquisite*.' Then he said, '*Exquisite* means "beautiful." Vivian has an *exquisite* smile.' After that I woke up. But Frederick is right, you do have an *exquisite* smile."

A week later at lunch you might say, "Frederick came into my dreams again. He had a new wonderful word for you: *preposterous*. He said, '*Preposterous* means "very, very silly." It is *preposterous* to invite a blue whale to dinner.' And then I woke up."

That is all there is to I DREAM OF FREDERICK. After you share a word, leave the game behind for a few days. Then have another dream. What if your child forgets every word you introduce? It does not matter. Increasing your child's vocabulary is not the goal of this game. The goal is to help him have fun with the English language and its glorious abundance of splendiferous words.

MARTHA BLAH BLAH

WRITTEN AND ILLUSTRATED BY SUSAN MEDDAUGH
1996
GOOD READING FOR KINDERGARTEN AND FIRST GRADE

Susan Meddaugh is the author and illustrator of several books about Martha the dog. The first of these was *Martha Speaks*. But my favorite Martha book is called *Martha Blah Blah*.

Martha is different from other dogs. She speaks. She speaks perfectly—at least she does when she laps up proper quantities of Granny's Alphabet Soup. It seems that for Martha the soup's letters travel to her head instead of dropping into her stomach. Once the letters lodge in her brain, Martha can talk. Unfortunately, though, in *Martha Blah Blah*, something goes terribly wrong and Martha, who is normally so articulate, can now spout only gibberish. What is undermining the talkative dog's ability to communicate? The new owner of Granny's Soup, Granny Flo, in a price-cutting move, has reneged on the company's longtime promise to put every letter of the alphabet in every can of soup.

Before long, Martha discovers the cause of her problems, and she speeds off to deal with Granny Flo. Does our canine heroine convince the cost-saving CEO to reletter the soup? Of course she does. She's Martha.

Martha talks, but in every other way she is all dog—bouncing around, acting on impulse, expressing emotions without restraint. She behaves rather like a young child, which is probably why young children find her so irresistible. You can begin your Martha adventures with *Martha Speaks* or one of the other Martha books, but make sure you read *Martha Blah Blah* to your child at some point. After you have done so, you can help your child learn more about Martha's treasured alphabet by playing the following games.

MISSING LETTERS

GRADES

kindergarten

MATERIALS

uppercase and lowercase magnetic letters, large bowl, wooden spoon

SKILLS

learning letter names

Simon was in kindergarten and struggling to learn the alphabet. Some letters were easy for him to remember—the *S* that started off his name, for instance. The names of other letters fled his mind in seconds. His struggles led him to believe that he was just plain dumb. Not surprisingly, he hated alphabet time in school.

Simon was, in fact, a very bright little boy. He just needed more practice with letters. I could have given him workbook sheets and flash cards to drill him in the naming of letters. These materials probably would have helped. But Simon would have hated the work. So I tried to engage him, instead, in a Martha-derived letter game called MISSING LETTERS.

I read *Martha Blah Blah* aloud to Simon, and then I pulled out a large bowl that I had already filled with six magnetic alphabet letters: uppercase *T*, *M*, and *F*, and lowercase *d*, *c*, and *s*. I used the smaller-size magnetic letters, but the jumbo ones work, too. I lifted the letters out of the bowl one at a time, naming each as I did so.

This naming is especially important with letters like lower-case *p*, which, when flipped around, looks exactly like lower-case *d*. One by one, I dropped the letters back into the bowl, naming them again. Then I began stirring the letters around with a wooden spoon.

"Alphabet soup, Simon. I am making alphabet soup. But I might decide to be like Granny Flo and slowly eliminate letters from my soup. What do you think of that?" I asked.

"I don't like it," Simon declared.

"Well, you can stop me, but it won't be easy. I'll begin by taking one letter away. If you can name the letter I took, I will have to return it to the soup," I said.

"That's easy," he replied.

"Not all that easy. You see, you have to close your eyes while I'm removing the letter. If, after I tell you to open your eyes, you name the missing letter, back in the soup it goes. But if you cannot name the missing letter, I get to remove it permanently. We play six rounds. After the sixth round, if there are any letters left in the soup, you win the game. If the bowl is empty, I win. Do you think it's easy now?"

"Not so easy," he conceded.

"Are you ready to play, though?"

"I'm ready," Simon said, squeezing his eyes shut.

After taking the *M* from the bowl, I told Simon to open his eyes. He did, and set about examining the remaining five letters. He could not, however, figure out which was missing.

"I give up," he said after a bit.

"That means I keep this *M*," I said, showing him the letter.

"I'll never win," he groaned.

"Don't be so sure. There are still lots of letters in the alphabet soup. How about we study them together very carefully and you can try to memorize each one?" I suggested.

Simon nodded and began sifting through the remaining letters. Following my advice he held each one in his hand and repeated its name several times.

"I'm ready," he declared when he was done.

I made a big to-do of stirring the soup and then demanded that Simon once again shut his eyes so that I could remove a letter. On opening his eyes, he pushed the remaining four letters around and then confidently announced that the *T* was missing. He was right. With much pretend annoyance, I returned the letter to the soup. At the conclusion of the second round, therefore, there were five letters in the bowl. Simon's confidence soared, and we went on with the game. When we finished the fifth round, there were three letters in the soup. This meant Simon's victory was inevitable, since even if he lost a letter, two would remain.

"Only a single question left to decide," I said. "Will you keep all three letters in the soup or will you only have two?"

"Three!" he shouted and closed his eyes.

I removed the *T* and then told him to check the soup.

"You took the *T*," he said. "Hey, that's not fair. You took the *T* before!"

"I'm allowed. As long as a letter is in the soup, I can take it," I said. "And look, Simon, you do have three letters left!"

"I told you," he said.

You probably realize something Simon did not. It was virtually impossible for him to lose this game. Suppose that five times in a row he failed to name the MISSING LETTER. Come the last round, there would still be a letter in the bowl. If he could remember the name of that letter two seconds after seeing it and saying it, victory would be his.

Why did I rig the game in Simon's favor? Most children happily replay games they win, and I certainly wanted Simon to play MISSING LETTERS again and again. The more he played, the more opportunities he would have to name the twenty-six uppercase and twenty-six lowercase letters of the alphabet. This task, memorizing the alphabet, had been frightening for Simon. Now, however, it was an enjoyable pastime. That was well worth my chronic role as the game's loser.

In the course of the next several weeks, Simon and I played MISSING LETTERS repeatedly. Simon always enjoyed himself, but I was getting bored. So, in the middle of playing one afternoon, I decided to introduce FEEL THOSE LETTERS, a slight variation on the game. I began by placing six magnetic letters in a large bowl and naming each one. I told Simon to study them for as long as he wanted. Next I stirred the letters with a wooden spoon. Then I insisted that he close his eyes. So far, the new game was exactly like the old game. But after he closed his eyes, I said something surprising.

"Simon, I've decided to change the rules a little. This time, you have to tell me which letter I've stolen from the soup, but you have to keep your eyes closed."

"My eyes closed? How can I win with my eyes closed?" he asked.

"Good question," I said, "and I have the answer. But first, cup your hands together."

He did, while asking, "Now what?"

"Now I am going to put the letter I removed from the soup into your hands. True, you cannot look at the letter because you must keep your eyes closed tight, but you can feel it. You can touch it all over, and when you think you know which letter it is, tell me. If you are right, I'll return the letter to the bowl. If you are wrong, it stays out. At the beginning of the game, there are six letters in the alphabet soup. If I can eliminate all the letters, I win. If you keep even one letter in the soup, you win. And . . ."

"And we play six rounds," he said.

"Correct. And . . ."

"And I want to keep as many letters in the soup as I can."

"That's it. Are you ready to feel the letter?" I asked.

He was, and I plopped an *s* in his hand. He felt it, named it, and won the round.

FEEL THOSE LETTERS

GRADES

kindergarten

MATERIALS

uppercase and lowercase magnetic letters, large bowl, wooden spoon

SKILLS

learning letter names

"I like that. Give me another," he said.

"I will, but first close your eyes."

This time I dropped a *K* in his hands.

"It's an *R*," he said.

"Open your eyes and look," I replied.

"Oh, it's a *K*. I don't get to keep it," he said.

"There are still a lot of letters in the bowl. Are you ready to feel again?"

He was, and I gave him a *W*.

"Is it an *M*?" he asked.

"Open your eyes and find out," I said.

"It's a *W*," he said. "Oh, yeah, I forgot. There isn't an *M* in the soup."

"I'm going to let you keep that *W* anyway, since *M* and *W* feel so much alike."

"Thanks!" he said.

Simon thought I was being generous, but that wasn't exactly the case. When a child cannot see the letters, it is much harder to remember which ones are in the bowl. And since letters like *M* and *W* or *n* and *u* are so difficult to distinguish by touch, I always credit a child no matter which of the two letters he names.

When we finished the game, Simon, who had managed to keep four letters in the bowl, announced that he liked both versions. That was fine with me. Over the next couple of weeks, we alternated between the two games until he could recognize, by sight and by touch, each and every uppercase and lowercase letter in the alphabet.

*I*magine that you just heard me say these three sentences: I like my *'ike*. It is *'lue* and it has a ringing *'ell*. I think it is the *'est 'ike* ever.

Could you figure out what I am trying to say? Could you identify the sound that is missing from my words? And do you know which letter represents that sound? More important, could your child do any of that?

To figure out these odd-sounding sentences, you have to translate *'ike* to *bike*, and you have to understand that a single sound, *buh*, represented by the letter *b* accounts for the difference between them. A child who can derive *bike* from *'ike*, and *blue* from *'lue*, already understands that words are made up of individual sounds and that every sound is represented by a letter or combination of letters. It is a crucial understanding. And it is not easy to acquire.

If your child does not already appreciate the connection between words, sounds, and letters, don't be surprised and don't worry. Children can learn the connection and with practice can master it. One way to learn and to practice is to play WHAT DID I SAY?

Begin by picking a sound to eliminate from your vocabulary—the *g* sound in "go," for instance. Then solemnly announce that Granny Flo has been at it again, stealing letters. Only this time, you yourself, instead of Martha the dog, happen to be the victim. You know because you're having trouble speaking. Does your child require proof of your woeful state?

WHAT DID I SAY?

GRADES

kindergarten and first

SKILLS

learning to hear individual sounds in words

You can demonstrate your victimhood by uttering a few odd-sounding sentences.

"Nasty *'ranny* Flo better *'ive* back that letter. It is no *'ood* to talk without it. But we can *'et* it back, I think."

Quickly explain that you and your child can defeat Granny Flo, but it will take some work. First, your child has to figure out what you are trying to say. Assure him you will repeat the sentences over and over again until he knows. Second, after he has deciphered the sentence, he must identify the missing sound. The missing sound—not the missing letter. If he has trouble doing this, give him three choices.

"Did she take the *guh* sound or the *tuh* or the *nnn*? Which do you think?"

When he picks the right sound—and it could take him a couple of tries—you must do your part and name the letter that matches that sound. Accomplish all of this, and together you and the child will have outsmarted Granny Flo. But Granny Flo will not give up her selfish ways so easily. No, she will steal another letter, and you and your child must outsmart her again. Outsmart her twice, and you will win the game. Fail either time, and Granny Flo wins.

It can be harder than you might imagine to speak with missing sounds. For your first games you don't have to invent your own sentences. Instead you can use the following:

Little *'ed 'idinghood* took a walk in the woods. It was *'ain-ing*. She got wet and *'an* to the house.

I have *'oldfish* in a bowl. My *'randmother 'ave* it to me. It was a nice *'ift*.

My *'og* likes *'elicious 'og* biscuits. He gobbles them *'own*. Then he runs out the *'oor* to play.

My best *'riend* likes *'rench 'ried* potatoes. His mother *'ixes* them *'or* him every day.

The 'encil is on the desk. So is my blue 'en and a 'retty drawing 'ad. Can you 'lease bring them to me?

A 'ig 'rown 'ear lives in the woods. He likes to sit 'eside the 'eautiful 'rook.

In the summer, 'orn on the 'ob is so yummy. I 'an eat three ears and still 'all for more.

My family 'ook a long 'rip in our car 'oday. 'omorrow we will 'urn around and go home.

If you and your child 'ike the game a 'ot, p'ay it as 'ong as you want! It can on'y improve your chi'd's know'edge.

ALPHABET SOUP

Martha the dog uses letters from Granny's Alphabet Soup in order to speak. But if she had wanted to write, she could have used those same letters to spell words. That is what you and your child will do if you play ALPHABET SOUP.

You should begin by taking a collection of at least thirty magnetic letters and dumping them into a large salad or pasta bowl. Make sure that your collection includes at least two of every vowel: *a*, *e*, *i*, *o*, and *u*. You can put in more letters, as long as about a third of them are vowels. When all the letters are in the bowl, tell your child that you have just finished preparing a jumbo portion of Granny Flo's wonderful soup. Then hand him a large spoon and tell him to dip it once in the bowl and ladle out as many letters as he can. Depending on the size of the spoon, he will scoop up one, two, three, even four. Now he should try to use those letters to spell words. Some lowercase letters are reversible. Flip *p* and you get *d*, for instance. If your child gets a flippable letter, he can use it

GRADES

first

MATERIALS

two sets of magnetic letters, large bowl, large spoon

SKILLS

reading and spelling

Martha Blah Blah

either way. One-letter words are against the rules in this game. You can't point to an *a* or an *i* and call that a word. Two-letter words are acceptable, though. Your child can use all of his scooped-up letters or only a few. Chances are that, on his first turn, the child will not be able to make any words at all. Tell him not to fret. He gets to hold on to all of his unused letters. Then, on his second turn, he will ladle again, combine his new letters with his old ones, and, if he is lucky, have the right letters to spell a word or two. At some moment in the game, your child might want to dismantle words in order to use his letters to better advantage, but this is not allowed.

It is perfectly okay, however, to offer help. Suppose you see letters that your child can use to make a word. You could pull them aside and say, "Put these four letters in the right order, my dear, and you will have a word."

You can offer even more help by saying, "If you put these four letters together correctly, you will spell the word *milk.*"

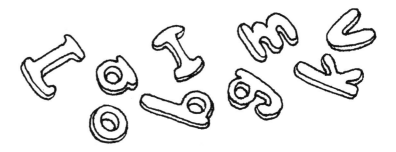

Of course, between your child's first and second turns, you get a chance to ladle your own letters and try to make words. You and your child should go on alternating turns until the bowl is empty. That is when the game ends. And who wins? The person with the most words—not to mention the person who is slowly learning how to read and write.

CROW BOY

WRITTEN AND ILLUSTRATED BY TARO YASHIMA
1955
CALDECOTT HONOR BOOK
GOOD READING FOR KINDERGARTEN AND FIRST AND
SECOND GRADES

Most children's books have a lighthearted tone, even when addressing serious issues like the nature of friendship. *Crow Boy* is different. In *Crow Boy*, Taro Yashima tells a poignant tale of a lonely child, and the tone of the book is solemn. Children don't find the book upsetting, though. On the contrary, they find it inspiring.

For five years, young Chibi attends school in his small village in rural Japan, and for five years, he is an outcast. Although he goes to school every day, he never makes friends and does not learn his lessons. Often, rather than listening to the teacher, Chibi studies the patterns on the classroom ceiling, the markings on the top of his wooden desk, and rain streaks on the windowpanes. The other children, even the youngest, tease Chibi and call him names.

Then, in his sixth and final year in school, Chibi's class gets a new teacher. This teacher, Mr. Isobe, notices things about Chibi that no one else has ever observed. Mr. Isobe discovers that Chibi has a special talent—he can imitate the voices of crows. He can mimic the sounds of newly hatched crows, father crows, and mother crows. He can copy the sounds of happy crows and of crows that are sad. With his teacher's encouragement, Chibi enters the school talent show. Standing before his fellow students and their families, Chibi gives a magnificent and passionate performance imitating crows. In that grand and totally satisfying moment, Chibi proves himself to everyone.

Any child who has ever felt misunderstood or underappreciated, as every child does at one time or another, will identify with Chibi's plight. Just as important, any child who has ever ridiculed a classmate, as nearly every child has done at one time or another, will recognize a bit of himself in Chibi's tormentors and will dislike what he sees. Hearing the book read aloud is not going to prevent your child from ever again being cruel or thoughtless. That is too much to ask from *Crow Boy*. But hearing Chibi's story and cheering his success might well encourage your child to be a little more tolerant of youngsters who are different from himself.

Without preaching or moralizing, Taro Yashima gives children a valuable lesson in ethical behavior. And here, in the form of games, are a few lessons, academic instead of ethical, derived from the book.

I SEE IT

GRADES

kindergarten and first

SKILLS

developing visual focus; identifying shapes, colors, numbers, and letters

*M*ost of us go about the day without closely inspecting the ordinary things in front of us. Not Chibi. To Chibi, the wooden planks of his classroom ceiling offer a fascinating terrain, the raindrops on a windowpane are endlessly interesting, even the patterns on a patch of clothing are worthy of scrutiny.

Using Chibi as inspiration, you can encourage your child to test his own powers of observation. The next time you both go out walking, invite him to participate in an I SEE IT contest. To begin the contest, you must first select an I SEE IT target. It might be a color, a shape, a number, a letter, or even a word.

Let's say you choose the color blue. During the next few minutes, you should walk down the street noting every bit of blue you see. Maybe you will spot someone wearing a blue sweater. You might pass a blue neon sign above the dry cleaners. Perhaps you will notice a blue dress in a window display or a blue pair of shoes on the feet of a fellow stroller, even a bluebird, not to mention the blue sky. The more alert you are, the more blue you will see.

After your child becomes a trained color observer, try looking for shapes. How many circles, triangles, or squares can you discover in your neighborhood? Next consider a letter hunt. During a walk around the block, ask your child to find as many *t*'s as he can—uppercase *T*, lowercase *t*, or both. Looking for letters is considerably harder than looking for colors or shapes. You might, therefore, set a specific goal—find five *t*'s between the supermarket and the hardware store, for instance. You can help your child succeed by pointing out a few places where an elusive *T* or *t* might be lurking.

This game will give your child a lot of experience identifying and naming colors, shapes, and letters. But there is a second, less obvious purpose to I SEE IT. As your child plays, he must work hard to isolate the targeted color, shape, or letter from everything else he sees. That is very similar to the specialized way of seeing you use whenever you read. Unconsciously, you focus your attention on a very small area—namely, a few words on the page of a book. You don't look at the rest of the words on the line, the other lines on the page, or the words on the facing page, and you certainly don't look at the room where you happen to be sitting, with all its patterns and colors. To be an efficient reader, your child must learn to narrow his eyesight in the same way you do. Playing I SEE IT, and working hard to be just as observant as Chibi, is a fine way to prepare a child to do just that.

COPY MY SOUNDS

"*W*asn't it neat how Chibi copied the sounds of crows so perfectly?" I asked Daniel after I finished reading *Crow Boy* to him.

"Yeah," he answered.

"I wonder if I could do that? Do you think I could?" I asked.

"Maybe," he answered.

"Do you think you could?" I asked.

"I don't know," he answered.

"I have an idea. Let's test ourselves, but not with crow sounds. Instead, I'm going to say a nonsense word made up of several different sounds and you have to copy me. Then you make up a nonsense word, and I will try to copy you. Does that seem like a good plan?" I asked.

Daniel nodded yes.

"Okay. Here is the word I want you to copy: *flum.*"

I immediately repeated the word, only this time I spoke very distinctly and stretched out all four individual sounds, so that I really said "*ffff-llll-uuuu-mmm.*" Daniel listened intently to both renditions, the quick pronunciation and the stretched-out version. Then, attempting to imitate me, he came up with something that sounded like *flsum.* Well, that was pretty good, for a first effort. I didn't correct Daniel. I congratulated him for being such a good listener. Why did I do that? Daniel had tried his best to reproduce my word, and I wanted him to feel good about that. If I corrected him or made him repeat the sounds until he got them right, I would have found myself facing a reluctant, resentful child instead of an enthusiastic one.

After praising Daniel and enjoying his smile, I said, "Now it is your turn. You say a weird word, and I will try to copy you."

"Okay," said Daniel, and he paused. Then he said something like "*Frishloostimicleruffamitalisacious.*"

Obviously, I could never replicate this outpouring, and I knew full well that Daniel was hoping I would fail. To please him, therefore, I loudly lamented the impossibility of the task before me.

"Oh, you gave me such a hard job. I don't see how I can ever copy you. I'll do my best, though: *frismeflisut.*"

Daniel and I both laughed because I was so far off the mark.

"I couldn't copy your word at all," I moaned. "But I did try. I can be proud of that. Now here's another word for you. Are you ready?"

"Ready."

We played a few more rounds. In each, I gave Daniel a nonsense word of three or four sounds, and he gave me a polysyllabic extravaganza. When it was time to stop, Daniel announced that he really enjoyed Chibi's copying game and hoped we could play it every week.

I was delighted to hear this, since COPY MY SOUNDS would help ready Daniel for the great tasks of learning to read and learning to write. Before children can figure out how any given word is spelled, they must understand, either implicitly or explicitly, that nearly every word is a blend of individual letter sounds. *Cat* has three sounds: *c-a-t. Dream* has four: *d-r-ea-m.*

When Daniel copied one of my nonsense words, he had to listen for the sounds in that word. To repeat *grut,* for instance, he had to hear four sounds: *g-r-u-t.* To repeat *plust,* he had to hear five sounds: *p-l-u-s-t.* Daniel did not realize that in mimicking me he was splitting words into individual sounds, but he was. Nor did he know that playing the game would contribute to his future success in reading and writing, but it would.

DID YOU HEAR MY SOUND?

GRADES

kindergarten, first, and second

MATERIALS

a jar with a lid, some dried beans or pennies

SKILLS

listening for specific sounds in words

Soon enough, Daniel was so adept at COPY MY SOUNDS that I decided he was ready for a greater challenge.

"Daniel," I said at the beginning of a work session, "I have a new game for you today."

"Is it like the copying game?" he asked.

"In a way, yes," I said, "only this game is much harder, and to be a successful player, you must be as good a listener as Chibi, the Crow Boy."

"I am that good," Daniel said confidently.

"I think you are. That's why I think you will like this game. Do you want to know another reason I think you will like it?" I asked.

"Yeah," he said.

"You play this game with a shaker, and it is so much fun to shake a shaker." I handed him an empty jam jar, which earlier in the day I had washed clean and then filled about a quarter of the way up with dried lima beans.

"Test it out," I said.

Daniel wrapped his hand around the jar and immediately started shaking. Delighted with the sound, he did not stop. I let him shake, knowing that I would have no luck getting him to focus on the game unless I did so. After a few moments, though, I held his hand still.

"You can use the shaker again," I reassured him, "but only when the time is right."

"When is the time right?" he asked.

"I'll tell you," I said, "but first I want you to listen to this sound: *mmmmm*."

"I hear it," Daniel said, grinning.

"Excellent. I'm sure you can copy the sound, too."

"Easy. *Mmmmmm*."

"Wonderfully done. Now comes the tough part. I'm going to say a word. If you hear the *mmmmm* sound in it, you can shake your shaker as loud as you want. But if you don't hear the sound, you must not shake, not even a little. Think about the word *monkey*." I pronounced it with a heavy emphasis on the initial sound. "Do you hear the *mmm*?"

Daniel nodded yes.

"Good. In that case you get to shake. But if I say the word *tiger*, you don't shake because there isn't any *mmm* sound in *tiger*. You got it?" I asked.

"Got it," he replied.

"Great. Here's your first word: *meatball*," I said, making sure to stress the *mmm* sound at the start.

Daniel giggled and began shaking the jar.

"Good job," I said, bringing an end to the shaking. "Now, how about *ketchup*?"

No shake.

"*Mustard?*"

Shake.

"*Game?*"

No shake.

"Listen again, Daniel, and I think you will hear *mmmm*. It isn't at the beginning of the word, but it's there. *Gammmmme*."

Loud shake.

"Great. How about *worm*?" I asked.

Daniel said the word to himself a couple of times, and when he was sure he heard the *mmm*, he put the shaker to work.

I presented him with several more words, some worthy of

shakes and some not, before the doorbell rang signaling the arrival of Daniel's father and the end of our work time.

The moment Daniel strode through the door for his next meeting, he declared, "I want to play that shaker game again."

"Sounds good to me, Daniel, but we have a problem," I said.

"What?"

"I dismantled the shaker. Here's an idea, though. How about you stand up during the game, and whenever you hear the right sound, you can jump up and down?" I asked.

"Great," said Daniel.

"You know, when Chibi listened to the crows, he didn't hear one sound, he heard many different crow cries."

"I remember. Mother crows and baby crows."

"I was thinking that if Chibi was playing this game, he would like to listen for a new sound today."

"Yeah."

"How about listening for the sound *sssss*? Do you think you can do that?"

"Sure, easy," he said.

"And if you hear it . . ."

"I get to jump!"

"Your first word is *spaghetti*. If you hear the *ssss* in *spaghetti* you can jump."

And jump he did.

He jumped again for *sofa*, *grass*, and *skating*.

He stood still for *book* and *run*.

And then, with Daniel's permission, I switched sounds again, to *fffff*. I told him, too, that if he heard the *ffff* sound in a word, he could either jump up and down or stamp his feet. It was up to him.

He stamped for *fingernail*, jumped for *puff*, and stood still for *toes*.

You may have noticed I never put the target sound in the

middle of a word. It is much easier to hear first sounds and last sounds than middle ones, and I didn't think that Daniel was ready to listen for sounds in the middle of words. If your child finds it very easy, though, to hear first sounds like the *nnnn* in *nifty* and last sounds like the *pppp* in *lap*, go ahead and see if he can hear the *nnnn* in *banner* and the *pppp* in *floppy*. If he can't, no problem. Just return to the easier way of playing.

DID YOU HEAR MY SOUND? helps children identify and isolate specific sounds in words. When a child is learning to read and write this is a very valuable ability. Consider the word *slip*. Children who can accurately distinguish the four sounds *sss-lll-iiii-pppp* are in a position to record those sounds with letters. Likewise, a child who appreciates that words are made up of individual sounds can look at the letters *s-l-i-p*, pronounce the sound of each letter in order, and then blend the sounds into a familiar word: *slip*.

By the way, if you want to make a shaker, but you do not happen to have dried lima beans in your cupboard, you can use pennies or paper clips or anything else that jingles and jangles in a jar.

IN SEARCH OF JAPAN

GRADES

kindergarten, first, and second

OPTIONAL MATERIALS

books about Japan, Japanese cookbook, a book of Japanese fairy tales

SKILLS

exploring another culture

*U*sing both words and pictures, Taro Yashima does a wonderful job of evoking life in rural Japan. After reading the book to your child once or twice, try leafing through it, and, without reading, focus your attention on the illustrations. In each illustration, you can discover a little bit of Japan. You will notice Japanese writing on the chalkboards and wall displays. In the corner of one classroom stands a large abacus. Children walk barefoot or wear thong sandals. Chibi wears a zebra-grass coat in the rain and lives in a thatched house in the mountains.

Having caught a glimpse of Japan in Taro Yashima's drawings, you and your child might want to learn more about this important island nation. If so, consider beginning your investigations in the library. You might look at nonfiction books about Japan—especially ones with lots of photographs. You might also borrow a book of Japanese fairy tales. If you have never read Japanese tales, you are in for a treat. These stories are similar in many respects to their European cousins, but Japanese tales have a wonderfully exotic quality that should engage both you and your child. Before leaving the library, you can stop off in the adult reading room and borrow a Japanese cookbook. Then tonight, or tomorrow night, try preparing a Japanese delicacy as a part of your dinner. If that seems a little much, you could take your child to a Japanese restaurant just to see what it is like.

You might take a little visit to Japan via the Internet. Surfing about, I have found photographs and maps of Japan along with reproductions of Japanese paintings and woodcuts. I even found one site that lets children design their own kimonos and assemble their own Japanese-style flower arrangements.

What if your child loves *Crow Boy* but has no interest in learning about Japan? Don't force it. To have enjoyed *Crow Boy* is good enough.

AND TO THINK THAT I SAW IT ON MULBERRY STREET

WRITTEN AND ILLUSTRATED BY DR. SEUSS
1937
GOOD READING FOR KINDERGARTEN AND FIRST GRADE

*I*magine a children's librarian who is allowed to stock his library with only a single author. Which author should that be? The answer is obvious. The librarian should choose the one, the only, the great, and the voluminously prolific Dr. Seuss. In 1937, the good doctor published his first children's book, *And to Think That I Saw It on Mulberry Street*. Over the next sixty years, he proceeded to produce a vast collection of wildly wacky and whimsical stories. Although his later books are wonderful and hugely popular, I am especially fond of his earliest works, and his first book is a particular favorite.

The book stars Marco, a young boy who, to please his father, must report on everything interesting he sees while walking to and from school. But Marco has a problem. Along the entire route, the only thing he notices is a horse and wagon on Mulberry Street. He certainly cannot report such a boring sight. A little adjustment is called for, and so Marco imagines that the horse is a zebra. Yes, that is much better. A zebra, though, should not pull a lowly wagon. No, a zebra should pull a chariot. Then again, is a zebra large enough for this task? No, a chariot must be drawn by a reindeer! As Marco heads home, the chariot switches into a sled and the reindeer evolves into an elephant. Moment by moment, Marco's fantasy becomes more and more elaborate, until by the time he reaches his front door, Mulberry Street, as he imagines it, is host to a spectacular parade complete with a magician, giraffes, a ruby-bedecked rajah perched upon the elephant, a brass band, and more. What a sight! What a story! And, oh, that Marco, what an imagination!

By the zillionth reading, and there probably will be a zillion readings, you will know the sequence of events, and so will your child. This could mean that now, as you turn the pages, your child will chant Seuss's rhymed lines as you read them aloud.

Applaud this pretend-to-be-reading impulse, since, for many children, make-believe reading is a big step toward doing the real thing.

Here are two useful games to play with your child. If you like them, you might end up playing them a zillion times—more or less.

YOUR OWN MULBERRY STREET

GRADES
kindergarten and first

SKILLS
developing auditory memory, encouraging an active imagination

*D*id you ever play the children's game IN MY GRANDMOTHER'S TRUNK? Players take turns filling an imaginary trunk with an odd assortment of possessions. The first player might say, "In my grandmother's trunk, I packed roller blades." The second player adds to the trunk, but only after repeating the first player's contribution. "In my grandmother's trunk, I packed roller blades—and a cucumber." The third player repeats everything packed so far and adds something new. "In my grandmother's trunk, I packed roller blades, a cucumber—and a pair of orange shoelaces." Players keep filling the trunk until one person cannot remember the complete list of items inside. Then the game is over—unless you want to play again.

One afternoon, I decided to play a Dr. Seuss variation on this traditional game with Natalie, a first-grade student. After reading *And to Think That I Saw It on Mulberry Street* to her, I announced boldly, "This morning on Broadway, I saw a tiger singing songs."

"No way!" Natalie shouted.

"Yes, I did. In fact, this morning on Broadway, I saw a tiger singing songs and a girl spinning ten yo-yos."

Natalie giggled.

"Now that I think of it, I believe you were on Broadway, too. I bet you saw some fabulous sights. But before you tell me what you observed, you have to repeat everything that I said. You have to begin, 'This morning on Broadway, I saw a tiger singing songs and a girl spinning ten yo-yos. . . .' When you have said all of that, you can add any crazy thing you want."

Natalie got the idea and declared, "This morning on Broadway, I saw a tiger singing songs and a girl spinning ten yo-yos—AND a green giraffe."

Then I said, "This morning on Broadway, I saw a tiger singing songs, a girl spinning ten yo-yos, a green giraffe—and an acrobat turning a cartwheel."

Our Broadway visions kept growing, until we had a dozen magnificent paraders. Much to my astonishment, neither of us had forgotten a single character. Still, we mutually agreed that our Broadway pageant was long enough, and that we had imagined sights no one could beat, not even Marco on Mulberry Street.

I had two practical reasons for playing this slightly odd game with Natalie. First, YOUR OWN MULBERRY STREET gave her practice remembering a long list of words. The ability to remember words is crucial to a child's success in school. Like it or not, rote memorization is a basic educational skill. Second, the game helped build Natalie's imagination. It takes considerable creativity to place green giraffes on Broadway. Many people believe that children are imagination machines, and that it is unnecessary to foster this childhood gift. But that isn't true. Children need opportunities to fantasize, and it helps when appreciative adults offer encouragement. Every time you say, "Let's pretend," you offer that encouragement. You might not use those exact words. Instead, you might give your child a stuffed dog and listen when the child tells you tales of his animal's adventures. Or you might provide costumes and dress-up supplies so that your child can pose as Superman or a fairy princess. Or you might make up stories about improbable parades traveling up and down the main street of your town.

THAT'S A MULBERRY STREET!

GRADES

kindergarten and first

SKILLS

fostering analytical thinking, encouraging an active imagination

*O*n Tuesday, I read *And to Think That I Saw It on Mulberry Street* aloud to Sara. On Thursday, I introduced her to a game based on the story.

"Sara, do you remember the Mulberry Street story, the one with Marco?" I asked to get her mind back on the book.

"I liked it. Can you read it again?"

"I will later, but right now I want to play a game with you."

"Okay."

"I am going to tell you something about my day, sort of like Marco told his dad about his walk home from school. I might tell you something that really happened or I might make something up. I could make up a really wild story, like Marco. Or I might say something believable; for instance, I took a long walk yesterday. Only I'd be fibbing, because I didn't take a long walk yesterday. If you think I am being honest, you say so. But if you think I am fibbing, you say, 'That's a Mulberry Street!' Here's an example: Yesterday I went to the zoo. What do you think? Is that true or is it a Mulberry Street?"

"True?" she asked.

"Nope, that's a Mulberry Street. Try another. Yesterday I had spider pie for breakfast."

"That's a Mulberry Street!"

"It sure is. How about this: Yesterday I had a banana and yogurt for breakfast."

"It could be true," she said.

"Yes, it could be. But it might not be. What do you think?"

"I think it's true," she said.

"Absolutely right! What about this: Yesterday I rode to my office on a hippopotamus."

"That's a Mulberry Street!" she said, laughing at the notion.

"You're right again. How would you like to test me? You could say something that really happened, you could say something that seems true but isn't, or you could say something totally strange. The choice is yours."

Sara thought for a moment and then said, "Yesterday I had apple pie."

"Hmm, that's a hard one. I remember your telling me that you love apple pie. I remember giving it to you as a special snack on your birthday. Since you love it so much, I'm going to say it's true."

"Nope, you're wrong. I had applesauce. I tricked you!"

"You sure did. Do you want to give me another chance?"

"Okay. Yesterday I played with Sally."

"Let me think. I know Sally lives in your building. I know you really like playing with her. But I also know you go to after-school on Wednesday. I don't think you would have time for after-school and a play date. So I think that's a Mulberry Street."

"You're right."

"It took a little thinking, but I like trying to figure things out," I said. "Now here's one for you. Yesterday I took a bath in root beer."

"Mulberry Street! My turn! Last night I could fly," she said.

"That's a Mulberry Street! I know you can't fly, not unless you've grown a pair of wings recently," I said.

"I haven't, but maybe I will someday," she said, and then laughed.

"Sara, you have as good an imagination as Marco! Speaking of Marco, are you ready to hear the book again?" I asked.

"Yes!" she said.

I picked it up and started reading.

Sara liked the game. She especially enjoyed the outlandish Mulberry Streets—my spider-pie breakfast and root-beer bath, for instance. I played this game with Sara to teach her about thinking logically, though that may seem odd given the absurd things we said to each other. You may have noticed that every time Sara made a statement about her day, I spent a few moments evaluating her words out loud. I weighed the possibilities. I considered facts that I knew about Sara's life. When I did pass judgment, I gave Sara specific reasons for my choice. Sara's method for judging my own claims was, by way of contrast, simply to guess. I didn't expect her to stop guessing. I only wanted to give her an example of how a person can think through a problem by means of logical analysis. That was enough for now.

What if your child only makes up wild stories and never says anything that could plausibly be real? You can still give good reasons for saying, "That's a Mulberry Street," in the same spirit I told Sara she couldn't fly since she doesn't have wings.

And the game has a second value, since every fantastical Mulberry Street fosters your child's imagination.

THAT'S A MULBERRY STREET! should take only a minute of your time. If you play for longer than that, the game will lose its appeal. You might try it out some evening after tucking your child into bed. And when you finish the game, what book should you read for a bedtime story? *And to Think That I Saw It on Mulberry Street*, of course.

THE 500 HATS OF BARTHOLOMEW CUBBINS

WRITTEN AND ILLUSTRATED BY DR. SEUSS
1938
GOOD READING FOR KINDERGARTEN AND FIRST AND SECOND GRADES

In 1938, a year after publishing *And to Think That I Saw It on Mulberry Street*, Dr. Seuss gave the world his second classic, *The 500 Hats of Bartholomew Cubbins*, a grand tale of hats, fools, and courage.

Young Bartholomew Cubbins travels to town hoping to sell a basket of cranberries—a perfectly ordinary thing to do. But something out of the ordinary happens. King Derwin, the monarch of Didd, comes driving through the city streets. The townspeople doff their hats, as they should. Bartholomew, too, pulls off his hat, but somehow, a new hat appears atop his head. When Bartholomew removes this second hat, another takes its place. A fourth hat replaces the third, and a fifth replaces the fourth. King Derwin is not amused. He orders the Captain of the King's Own Guards to carry Bartholomew off to the castle. There His Majesty tries, but fails, to find someone, anyone, who can rid Bartholomew's head of hats. Nadd, the Wise Man, cannot bare Bartholomew's head. Neither can the Father of Nadd, nor the Father of the Father of Nadd. Yeoman of the Bowmen is sure he can succeed, with his colossal bow and mighty arrow. As soon as he shoots hat number 155 off the terrified Bartholomew's head, though, a replacement appears.

Hat after hat shows up and every hat is identical, until number 451 materializes with two feathers instead of one. Hat number 452 is even more ornate, sporting three feathers. Hat 453 has feathers and a red jewel. Hat 454 is fancier yet. And then, just when the King's nasty nephew, the Grand Duke Wilfred, is about to toss poor Bartholomew off the top of the castle's highest turret, Bartholomew's 500th hat, an indisputable masterpiece, appears. King Derwin, astounded by its flowing plumes and gigantic ruby, is smitten. He must have Bartholomew's 500th hat for himself, and he gets it, in exchange for 500 pieces of gold. As soon as the King lifts off that 500th hat, Bartholomew's head is, at long last, bare.

Children love young Bartholomew Cubbins, and how could they not? He is a wide-eyed innocent who, although he finds himself in precarious circumstances, faces his travails with courage and nobility. As any child can tell you, it is never easy dealing with all-powerful but very foolish adults. Somehow, Bartholomew manages. Dr. Seuss must also have loved Bartholomew, for he made the boy the hero of a second and equally wonderful book, *Bartholomew and the Oobleck*.

The 500 Hats of Bartholomew Cubbins is an unusual book for Dr. Seuss. The story does not rhyme. But in every other respect, the book is typically Seussian. There are Dr. Seuss's wonderfully wacky characters: the ancient Nadd family, the softhearted executioner, and the howling, yowling magicians, to name just a few. The drawings, too, are immediately recognizable. No other illustrator has ever drawn such smug smirks, delighted smiles, astonished glances, and furious grimaces. And there is the most Seussian factor of all—humor. Dr. Seuss is always gloriously and outrageously funny. How do children develop a sense of humor? In part, a sense of humor comes from turning the pages of books like *The 500 Hats of Bartholomew Cubbins* at the side of an adult who cannot help giggling and smiling at the author's wit.

The next three activities, all based on those confounding hats, should produce a few giggles and smiles of their own.

A*fter* reading about Bartholomew and his reproducing hats, your child might enjoy making a hat of his own. And, with your help, he can do it. He can make a hat out of paper. It won't be a magical hat, although you can pretend it is.

To create a paper hat large enough to fit your child's head, you must begin with a very large sheet of paper. Art supply stores and some stationery stores sell 18″ × 24″ pads of newsprint. A sheet from one of these pads is perfect. Of course, you can make hats with smaller sheets of paper, but they will have to fit tiny heads—doll heads, for instance.

After you get your paper, your next job is to turn the rectangular sheet into a square. Fold one corner of the paper to form two overlapping triangles with a strip of paper at the top.

MAKE A HAT

GRADES

kindergarten and first

MATERIALS

large sheet of paper, scissors, transparent tape, crayons or colored markers

OPTIONAL MATERIALS

ribbon, feathers, stickers, glue

SKILLS

following instructions, working with basic geometric shapes

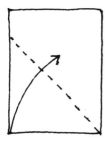
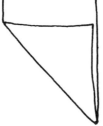

Cut off the top strip.

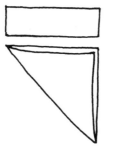

You can unfold the paper and show your child the square.

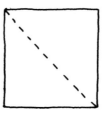

Then fold it back into a triangle again.

Take the left-hand point on the base of the triangle and pull it over so that it touches the right-hand point, and fold.

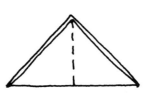

You still have a triangle, but it is a smaller triangle.

Hold the triangle so that the base is on the bottom.

One side of the triangle is closed, but the other side is open. Using transparent tape, seal the opening from top to bottom.

Look at the base of the triangle. You will see four layers of paper.

Hold the triangle upright and pull the front two layers and the back two layers of the triangle apart.

Now you have a hat. Your child can wear it like this:

or like this:

If the hat slips too far down your child's forehead, you can stick a bit of tape over both ends of the hat to shorten the opening.

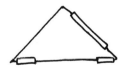

Don't leave the hat on your child's head, though. Instead, suggest that he decorate his creation. He can draw pictures on it with crayons or markers. He can cover it with stickers. He can tape on feathers or strips of colorful ribbons. Your child can make his hat as simple as Bartholomew's first 450 or nearly as extraordinary as his 500th.

What will your child do while wearing his magnificent hat? He might pretend to be Bartholomew, which could be great fun—especially if you pretend to be King Derwin of Didd. Then again, he may have other make-believe ideas in mind.

And if one hat doesn't satisfy his needs, feel free to make another, and another, and another.

Even if your child creates just one hat, he is bound to observe some interesting geometric truths while manipulating the paper. He will discover, for instance, that if you fold a square in half, you get a triangle.

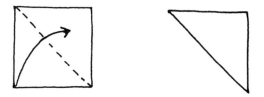

He may notice that he can divide a single triangle into two smaller ones.

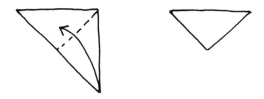

You can point out these geometric facts, but it is probably better not to. As your child folds the paper, he may make such discoveries on his own, which is always the best way to learn. And if your child fails to notice the relationships between triangles and squares right away, no need to worry. He is becoming familiar with these things anyway and will draw a few conclusions in due time.

HOW MUCH IS 500, ANYWAY?

GRADES

first and second

MATERIALS

lots and lots of pennies; paper cups; sandwich-size plastic bags; rubber bands

SKILLS

counting to high numbers, learning about the number system

*O*ne, two, three, four, five—it is easy to give a child real-life examples of these numbers. You can ask him to touch one spoon, hold two pencils, eat three cookies, hop four times, or kiss you five times. But when numbers get bigger, children run into trouble. Three hundred, three thousand, what's the difference? From a young child's point of view, not much, since the child cannot accurately imagine either number. For that matter, when numbers get truly enormous, adults run into trouble, too. A trillion, for instance. Who can conceive of a trillion?

With a little assist from Bartholomew and his hats, though, it is possible to help your child understand large numbers—up to 500, anyway. After reading the story aloud, tell your child that you've decided to let him make a 500 collection. His will not be a collection of 500 hats or, more regrettably, 500 pieces of gold. It will be a collection of 500 pennies. And when the collection is complete, he can spend the money any way he wants.

After making this announcement, dump the contents of your change purse on a table. Ignore the nickels and dimes, and pull out the pennies. These pennies will be the start of your child's collection. In a day or two, empty your purse again and add to your child's holdings. Needless to say, it will take time for your child to collect 500 pennies—a few weeks at least. While pennies amass, therefore, your child will need to store his increasing wealth. You could clump all the pennies together in a bowl or a jar. But that presents a problem. When your child wants to know how many pennies he has, he will have to count his entire collection one penny at a time—a cumbersome task, especially as the collection gets really big. There is one way to store pennies, though, that makes it easy for your child to keep track of his money. For this method to work, all you need are ten paper cups and five sandwich-size plastic bags.

As you give your child pennies, he will deposit them in the paper cups. Each cup will hold exactly ten pennies.

After loading his first cup, he should nest a second cup inside it and then start filling again.

When your child has a tower of ten cups loaded with ten pennies each, give him an empty plastic bag and have him dump the 100 pennies inside. Tie the top of the plastic bag with a rubber band to prevent the pennies from falling out.

Then he should start filling the ten paper cups once again. Before too long, he will have a second set of 100 pennies, which he will pour into a second plastic bag. Eventually he will have five full bags and, therefore, 500 pennies. On that glorious day, pour all the pennies out on the floor and let your child run his fingers through the coins. As he plays with his hoard, remind him of *The 500 Hats of Bartholomew Cubbins*. Ask him to spread his pennies out so that none of them overlap. Then tell him to imagine each penny suddenly turning into a hat. What a lot of hats that would be!

But, of course, your child does not have 500 hats. He has 500 pennies, and now he must decide what to do with them. He might like to trade his pennies in for a five-dollar bill and then go shopping. He might want to preserve his collection— at least for a while. If he is a patient sort, and you are willing, he could put these 500 pennies in a jar and leave them there while he starts a second 500-penny collection. Five hundred and five hundred—why, that's a thousand!

Every time your child adds pennies to his collection, help him tally his assets. At first, you will count by ones—the individual pennies in your child's first cup. As soon as your child fills one cup, though, you can start counting by tens and ones: one cup full and three extra pennies—that's ten, eleven, twelve, thirteen. Four cups full and two extra—that's ten, twenty, thirty, forty, forty-one, forty-two. What if your child does not know how to count by tens? That's okay. You do it for him. When he is ready, he'll join in. Load your purse with pennies every day, and by week's end you might be counting by ones, tens, and hundreds. As your child keeps track of his money, he may notice certain interesting characteristics in how we count. When he has three full paper cups, for instance, it means he has ten, twenty, thirty pennies. When he has two full bags and five cups, he has one hundred, two hundred and ten, twenty, thirty, forty, fifty pennies. Amazing! Three tens is thirty. Five tens is fifty. It's a system, and a very good system it is—the number system.

YEOMAN OF THE BOWMEN

Yeoman of the Bowmen was a skillful archer. With his mighty bow, he shot a tiny hat straight off Bartholomew's trembling head, and, fortunately for Bartholomew, he didn't miss. That's some fancy shooting. Would your child like to see how his ability to hit a target compares with the yeoman's? You merely need to make some creative substitutions in the way of archery equipment and hat. For a bow, let him use his finger. For the arrow, give him a cap from a soda bottle. For the hat, use a single eggcup that you can cut away from either a Styrofoam or a cardboard egg carton.

YEOMAN OF THE BOWMEN

GRADES

kindergarten, first, and second

MATERIALS

the plastic cap of a soda or water bottle, an egg carton, scissors

SKILLS

developing hand-eye coordination

Place the eggcup, hollow side down, on the floor and have your child sit about three feet away from it. Then put the bottle cap on the floor directly in front of him. Your child's job? He must try to hit the eggcup by flicking the bottle cap with his finger.

He can use any shooting method he prefers—the push, the shove with his finger, or the conventional finger flick. But the bottle cap must not leave the floor. You can award points to your child, if you want, one for every strike of the hat. You, too, can try your hand (or finger) at shooting. In fact, you might stage a YEOMAN OF THE BOWMEN contest. Take turns shooting and declare that the first archer to get six points is the bowman champion.

While playing, your child will be training his hand to obey instructions from his eyes. Good coordination between hand and eye helps children succeed at target games, certainly, which is a good thing. But that same coordination also helps a child with the difficult task of controlling a pencil.

All that and more. For when your child pretends to compete with Yeoman of the Bowmen, he will, simultaneously, increase his love of Dr. Seuss's book.

MANY MOONS

WRITTEN BY JAMES THURBER
ILLUSTRATED BY LOUIS SLOBODKIN
1943
CALDECOTT MEDAL BOOK
GOOD READING FOR FIRST AND SECOND GRADES

James Thurber was one of America's funniest writers. His tales and cartoons in *The New Yorker* magazine kept legions of fans laughing for many years. Thurber also wrote a few children's books. *Many Moons*, a delightful picture book, was written for his daughter in 1943.

Ten-year-old Princess Lenore is ill—the result of eating too many raspberry tarts—and is languishing in bed. Her father, the King, will do anything to cure Lenore, but what, exactly, must he do? The Princess knows. She wants, she needs, she must have the moon. But how can the King grant her wish? He calls for the Lord High Chamberlain and orders him to get the moon, but the Chamberlain objects. The moon is too far away—35,000 miles. And it is too big—bigger than the Princess's room.

The King demands that the Royal Wizard obtain the moon. The Wizard, too, explains that the moon is too far away—150,000 miles. And it is too big—twice the size of the palace. The King asks the Royal Mathematician. But the Royal Mathematician proclaims that the moon is 300,000 miles away and half the size of the kingdom.

The Court Jester, being an observant man, notices that the Chamberlain, the Wizard, and the Mathematician have differing notions of the moon. The Jester, who is wise as well as observant, decides to ask the Princess what she believes. He discovers that hers is a tiny golden moon, smaller than her thumb. Now the Court Jester knows just what to do. He arranges for the Royal Goldsmith to craft a little golden disk and string it on a golden chain. An overjoyed Lenore receives her moon, and the next day we find her skipping rope in a sun-filled garden.

Many Moons, a modern fairy tale, has all the delights any child could desire. But Thurber knows that children compose only half his audience. The way he plays with language is clearly intended for his adult readers. True enough, children will enjoy listening to the Mathematician explaining all he has done for the King. But adults will take special pleasure in hearing the Mathematician say, "I have computed how far is Up, how long it takes to get Away, and what becomes of Gone. I have discovered the length of the sea serpent, the price of the priceless, and the square of the hippopotamus."

Louis Slobodkin won the Caldecott Medal for his *Many Moons* illustrations. They are wispy drawings, vague enough so that children will use their own imaginations when picturing Thurber's fairy-tale world.

The next four activities will, I hope, delight moon lovers— both adults and children—and push children to use their imaginations in still other ways.

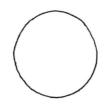

The many moons in *Many Moons* had one thing in common—they were full moons. But the moon is full just once a month, usually—although there are occasional months with two full moons, and rarely, very rarely, February has no full moon at all. Seen from Earth, the moon is always changing shape. Astronomers have named eight points in this cycle, which we call the eight phases of the moon.

There is the new moon, which is invisible to the eye:

The waxing crescent:

The first quarter:

The waxing gibbous:

The full moon:

The waning gibbous:

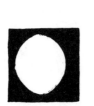

The last, or third, quarter:

The waning crescent:

And then it is back to the new moon:

To complete this cycle takes 29 days, 12 hours, 44 minutes, and 2.8 seconds. Well, call it a month. After reading *Many Moons*, you might spend some time discussing the night sky with your child. You could make drawings such as those on page 127 to illustrate the moon's eight phases. You might spend a few moments every day for the next month (or as many days as you can) gazing up at the moon. Observe how it waxes and wanes. You might enjoy tracking the moon's daily state on your computer. There are several Web sites on the Internet that will let you moon-gaze from your own desk. This is especially helpful on cloudy or rainy nights when the moon would otherwise be impossible to see.

One evening, while MOON GAZING, your child may ask why the moon changes shape. Good question. Don't answer right away, though. Instead, remind your child of the Court Jester and how he asked Princess Lenore to explain her ideas about the moon. Then suggest that your child imagine his own explanation for the moon's phases. You might get him started by proposing fantastical theories of your own. Maybe the moon begins the month really skinny and then every day it eats a little more light. Eating light makes it get fatter and fatter until it is completely full. Then the moon goes on a diet until it is skinny again. Or maybe the moon changes shape because it is too boring to look the same night after night.

Making up stories with your child is a good idea. As children get older, they often become reluctant to use their imaginations. This is a shame, since imagination is at the heart of creative thought. An excellent way to keep children imagining is to imagine along with them.

So let *Many Moons* lead you to MOON GAZING for a month. And let your gazing lead you to invent tales about the moon's ever-changing shape. At some point, though, you might want to stop imagining and tell your child the scientific reason for the moon's waxing and waning. Perhaps you know the facts already, but in case you are unsure, you will find a simple explanation of the moon's cycle on page 345.

FULL MOON BOOK

GRADES

first and second

MATERIALS

paper, pen, crayons or colored
pencils, saucer, stapler, list
of Indian moon names at
the end of this activity

SKILLS

learning the months of the year

*O*ne afternoon I asked Nora, a second grader, to name the current month. She looked embarrassed and shrugged her shoulders. I told her it was March, the third month of the year. Then I asked if she knew the name of the upcoming month. Another shrug. A second grader should know the months of the year and know them in order, more or less, and so I decided to help Nora master this piece of basic knowledge.

I began by reading *Many Moons* aloud, and Nora loved the book. This gave me an excuse to talk about moons—especially full moons. Talking about full moons evolved into a discussion of months.

"Did you know that there is a full moon every month of the year?" I asked.

"Every month?" she asked back.

"Just about every month. Sometimes, although it's a very unusual occurrence, February does miss a full moon. On the other hand, now and again months have two full moons. Some people call the second full moon in a month a blue moon. I like that. I like the idea of naming moons," I said.

"Me too," agreed Nora.

"Did you know that Indian tribes named the full moons for every month? In fact, I have a list here of a whole bunch of the Indian moon names. Can you guess what some tribes called January's full moon?" I asked.

"No," she said.

"The Wolf Moon. Isn't that neat? It makes me imagine a wolf howling inside the moon—you know, instead of the man in the moon," I said.

Nora smiled.

"Here's an idea. Why don't we create a FULL MOON BOOK. The book will have a page for each month of the year, and each page will show a full moon. We can make up a name for each moon. Or, if we want, we can borrow names from Indian tribes. When we have a page for each month, we can make a cover and bind the pages together into a book. What do you think?" I asked.

"Good idea," she answered.

I pulled out a few sheets of paper, a pen, a box of colored pencils, and a saucer. After gathering these supplies, I said, "We should start with the first month of the year—January."

I took one sheet of paper and, before doing anything else, picked up the pen and drew a margin of about half an inch down the left-hand side of the page. We would need this margin in order to bind the book properly. Then, using the saucer rim as a template, I drew a circle and wrote *January* underneath.

"What do you want to name this moon?" I asked.

"I don't know," Nora replied.

"As I said, some tribes called January's full moon the Wolf Moon, and, according to my list, other tribes called it the Hoop Moon. Which do you like best?"

"Hoop," she said.

"Well, we could certainly call it that, but it might be more fun to make up our own name. Can you think of any cold, January-feeling words?" I asked.

"How about snow?"

"I love it. Let's call it the Snow Moon. Why don't you write that on top of the moon," I said.

When she finished writing, I suggested that she draw a snowy picture in the center of the moon. Nora, who enjoyed drawing, thought this was a fine suggestion and, using the colored pencils, proceeded to draft a snowman.

"That takes care of January. Now we need February. First month, January—second month, February," I said as I presented Nora with a fresh sheet of paper. This time Nora drew the moon's circle, and she wrote the month under it.

"What are the Indian names for February?" Nora asked.

"There are several, actually," I said, looking at the list. "There is Hunter Moon, Opening Buds Moon, Big Hoop Moon, and—what do you know?—Snow Moon."

Nora laughed at that, proud of herself for thinking of the name first. She did not like any of the other Indian names, though.

"What is special about February? I know, Valentine's Day— a great February holiday," I said.

"Love Moon? Can we call it Love Moon for Valentine's Day?" she asked.

"Sure we can," I said.

And with that Nora got back to work.

She designated March's full moon as Happy Moon because it was currently March and she was happy.

Having completed three pages, we stopped for the day. We took up the task again at the very beginning of our next session. Before working on new pages, we took a few minutes to admire Nora's work for January, February, and March. Then we polished off the next three months: April, May, and June. A third work session got us through July, August, and September. In our fourth session, we finished the year. That completed our work on the innards of the book.

It took one more session to make the cover,

and staple the pages together—taking care that all the staples were inside the margin lines.

After pounding the final staple in place, Nora and I studied the book—looking through it month by month.

By the time we made this final run-through, Nora had spent a considerable amount of time concentrating on the months of the year. She still had not memorized all twelve months in chronological order. She could recite the names from January to June, though, and that was a good start.

Here is the list of Native American moon names I shared with Nora. You and your child might want to use some of them. Or you could let the Indian names inspire you when making up names of your own.

JANUARY: Wolf Moon, Hoop Moon
FEBRUARY: Hunter Moon, Opening Buds Moon, Big Hoop Moon, Snow Moon
MARCH: Maple Sugar Moon, Worm Moon, Drying Up Moon
APRIL: Frog Moon, Pink Moon, Leaf Moon, Dusty Face Moon
MAY: Flower Moon, Budding Moon
JUNE: Strawberry Moon, Planting Moon, Fattening Up Moon
JULY: Blood Moon, Buck Moon, Summer Moon
AUGUST: Moon of the Green Corn, Sturgeon Moon, Breeding Moon
SEPTEMBER: Fall Moon, Cool Moon, Harvest Moon, Corn Moon

OCTOBER: Hunter's Moon, Moon of Falling Leaves, Starting to Freeze Moon

NOVEMBER: Beaver Moon, Hard Face Moon

DECEMBER: Midwinter Moon, Big Hard Face Moon, Cold Moon

When you finish your FULL MOON BOOK, keep it available so that each month when the moon is full, you and your child can pull it from a shelf and look at your own many moons. Then, if you can, wander outside and enjoy the moon's glow.

MOON FACTS

GRADES

first and second

OPTIONAL MATERIALS

books about the moon

SKILLS

learning facts about the moon, developing an interest in astronomy

*T*he Chamberlain, the Wizard, and the Mathematician in Thurber's *Many Moons* are all sure they know the correct facts about the moon. They are wrong, of course. Terribly wrong. But your child can discover some correct facts. Indeed, your child might like learning lots and lots of moon facts and thereby become a moon expert, ready at a moment's notice to spout amazing data that will astound the world. Below you will find a variety of moon facts—including the genuine size of the moon and its true distance from Earth.

The Facts

None of the characters in *Many Moons* knows the actual distance from Earth to the moon. In fact, the moon's distance from Earth varies. It can be as close as 221,449 miles (356,371 kilometers). This is about the same as making forty-five round-trip flights between New York and Los Angeles. The moon can be as far away as 252,736 miles (406,720 kilometers). This is about the same as making fifty-one round-trip flights between New York and Los Angeles.

The moon is much bigger than the Chamberlain, the Wizard, or even the Mathematician thought. Imagine putting a belt around the middle of the moon. The belt would be about 6,782 miles (10,913 kilometers) long. That's a big belt! It is approximately the distance of a round-trip flight between New York and London, England. The Earth's belt would be even bigger, of course. It would be about 24,863 miles (40,004 kilometers) long.

The moon controls the tides of Earth's seas. The moon is always tugging on the Earth due to a force called gravity. But the force of the tug is not the same all day long. When the tug is at its strongest, it is high tide. When the tug is at its weakest, it is low tide. The tug is strongest twice a day. That is why there is high tide twice a day. The same is true for low tides. Two times a day the moon's tug is weakest, and so two times a day the tide is low.

The moon travels a little more than three-fifths of a mile (or one kilometer) every second. This means the moon could travel from New York to Los Angeles in about one hour and six minutes.

The moon circles around Earth, but no matter where the moon is in its orbit, the same side always faces Earth. This means from Earth we always see one side of the moon, and we never see the other side.

The moon is slowly drifting away from Earth. It moves about $1\frac{3}{8}$ inches (3.5 centimeters) every year. In one hundred years it will be about $11\frac{1}{2}$ feet (3.5 meters) farther away from Earth than it is today.

You weigh about one-sixth of your Earth weight on the moon. This means if you weigh sixty pounds on Earth, you will weigh only ten pounds on the moon. If you weigh ninety pounds on Earth, you will weigh fifteen pounds on the moon.

The first people to walk on the moon were United States astronauts. They traveled on a spaceship called *Apollo 11*. It took three days for them to get from Earth to the moon. They landed on July 20, 1969.

One day on the moon lasts about fourteen Earth days. This means that if you were an astronaut living on the moon, you would have two full Earth weeks between the moon's sunrise and sunset. Of course, you'd have about two weeks of nighttime, as well.

If you want to learn even more about the moon, you can search out books in the library or bookstores. Or you can stay at home and look for moon facts on your computer. Traveling about the World Wide Web, you can find outstanding astronomical sites, many of which include sensational pictures of the moon in all its phases.

After listening to *Many Moons*, Jessica had just one thing to say: "I want a moon necklace, too."

I loved this response, and so I said, "I wish I could give you a golden moon necklace. Sadly, I can't do that, but there is something I can give you that you might like almost as much."

"What?" asked Jessica.

"Well, *give* isn't the right word, exactly. I should have said, 'There is something I can help you make that you might like almost as much.' "

"What? What?" Jessica shouted.

"AN ALMOST GOLDEN MOON NECKLACE," I answered.

"What's that?" she asked a little less excitedly.

"It's a necklace, and we can make it together. It will be shaped like the full moon, and, although it won't really be gold, it will be almost golden. Does that sound like something you'd like to make?"

It did, and so we got to work.

First, I took a blank index card and, using a half dollar as a guide, drew a circle on it. I could have used a quarter, but a half dollar is a little larger, which makes the final necklace a bit more impressive.

I gave the card to Jessica, and carefully, carefully, she cut out the circle. Then I gave her a gold metallic marker and told her to color one side. We waited several minutes to let this

AN ALMOST GOLDEN MOON NECKLACE

GRADES

first and second

MATERIALS

index card, half dollar or quarter, pencil, scissors, gold metallic pen, gold gift-wrap ribbon, pushpin

SKILLS

bringing a story to life

side dry. If you don't let the ink dry, you will get a smudgy moon, and that would be a shame. Next Jessica turned the circle over and colored the reverse side with gold. When she finished and the ink was dry, we held the golden disk up to the light and admired its moonly glow.

"It's beautiful," Jessica said.

"Yes, it is. But we still have tasks before it's finished."

"Like what?" she asked.

"Well, you can't have a necklace without a chain, can you? I'm afraid your chain can't be a golden one, like the Princess's. But I think I have some gold ribbon left over from wrapping a birthday gift. We could use that."

"Yeah," she said.

After fetching the roll of ribbon, I asked Jessica, "How do you think we should attach the ribbon to the moon?"

"I don't know," she answered.

"How about we make a small hole in the moon just large enough for the ribbon to slip through?" I asked.

Jessica nodded. I took out a pushpin and using its point stabbed a hole halfway between the middle of the moon and its circumference. I wiggled the pin around to make the hole larger. When Jessica saw what I was doing, she asked to help, and so I gave her the pin and let her wiggle.

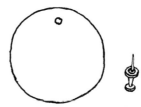

Then we needed to cut the ribbon from its roll. The chain had to be long enough so that Jessica could easily slip it on and off over her head. To get the right length, I asked Jessica to sit still while I swung the ribbon around her neck. I pulled the cut end down the right side of her chest and the roll side down the left.

When the two sides were at the middle of her chest, I snipped the roll side.

With only a little help from me, Jessica pushed the ribbon through the hole and tied the ribbon's ends.

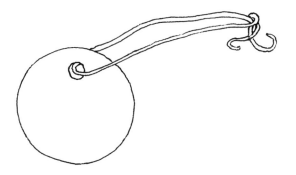

As soon as the knot was secure, she dropped the necklace over her head. I led her to a mirror so that she could admire herself.

"Why, you look like a princess bedecked in gold," I said.

Jessica smiled.

Why did I make this necklace with Jessica? Children who love stories have something in common: they use their imaginations to make narratives come to life. These children have a marvelous time picturing themselves playing with Princess Lenore in the palace garden or joining her for a romp with the Court Jester. Not all children, though, have this ability. Such was the case with Jessica—at least until she listened to *Many Moons*. Somehow Princess Lenore's necklace seemed real to her, and not only that, she wanted one just like it. I knew I had to take advantage of this situation. Nothing I had planned for our hour together was nearly as important.

Boys as well as girls are usually happy to make a golden necklace. If a boy seems reluctant, suggesting he give the necklace away as a special gift generally creates enthusiasm for this project.

PART TWO
HOW TO PLAY WITH CHAPTER BOOKS

A BEAR CALLED PADDINGTON

WRITTEN BY MICHAEL BOND
ILLUSTRATED BY PEGGY FORTNUM
1958
GOOD READING FOR KINDERGARTEN AND FIRST AND SECOND GRADES

*T*here are many endearing bears in children's literature, and so only a very special animal can stand out sufficiently to become a classic. But Paddington is a rare bear.

When Mr. and Mrs. Brown stumble upon a young and very sweet-looking creature sitting forlornly in Paddington Station, they are instantly charmed. The little wide-eyed bear, they discover, has no home, no family, no friends, no one to care for him, and so he has parked himself in the train station. Within minutes, Mr. and Mrs. Brown invite him to live in their house.

It is soon apparent that Paddington, as the Browns call him, has a knack for getting into sticky situations. During his first meal with the Browns, in the station restaurant, Paddington manages to smear himself with strawberry jam, somersault into his tea, and cover himself with cream.

"You wouldn't think," said Mrs. Brown, "that anyone could get in such a state with just one bun."

The Browns escort their food-stained bear home and send him upstairs to take a bath. Not a good idea, for, as anyone could predict, leaving a bear alone in a bathroom invites chaos. You cannot really hold Paddington responsible, therefore, for the resulting flood.

The next day, Paddington nearly decimates the window display of Barkridges Department Store. And that is nothing compared to the uproar he causes when he attends a theatrical performance or the bedlam he incites at the beach. In every chapter Paddington has a new adventure, and in every chapter he finds himself in new difficulties.

If, after hearing *A Bear Called Paddington*, your child craves more of the bear, there are multitudinous sequels to satisfy his longing. Before starting a second book starring Paddington, though, take a little time to play one of the following games.

SHAVING-CREAM WRITING

GRADES

kindergarten, first, and second

MATERIALS

large plastic garbage bag, shaving cream, large baking tray, bowl of water, paper towels, food coloring

SKILLS

practice with the alphabet, practice writing words

*B*illy did not want to write. Not ever. Not nohow. The moment a pencil touched his hand, it went flying, and often Billy and his chair went flying, too. With a little effort, I could get him seated again. With more effort, I could get a second pencil to stay in his hand. And, if I put on enough pressure, I could get him to write a few words—ones he sounded out letter by letter. Actually, Billy was fairly accomplished at sounding out words, which should have given him pleasure. Instead, his commotion and my resulting irritation made the whole experience of trying to write unpleasant for both of us. My goal was to help Billy feel relaxed and confident when writing. Obviously, I was not succeeding.

What to do? I was stumped until Paddington, that clever little bear, provided a solution. Billy was a fan of Paddington the bear and of the book series. He enjoyed every Paddington book he'd ever heard, but the original volume was still his favorite. I was sure, therefore, that he would remember the day Paddington used shaving cream to write on the Browns' bathroom floor. It occurred to me that I should let Billy write with shaving cream, too. If he was amused enough by this odd way of inscribing words, perhaps he would gradually become less resistant to writing in the ordinary way. It was worth a try.

The next time Billy walked through my office door, he was surprised to see a large plastic garbage bag covering my worktable. Resting on top of the plastic was a bowl of water, an aluminum baking tray, an aerosol can of shaving cream, a four-color set of food coloring, and a roll of paper towels.

"I have a new activity for us today," I said in answer to Billy's confused look. "We are going to write like Paddington."

"Write like Paddington?" he asked.

"Yes, just like Paddington. Do you remember when he used shaving cream to write his name on the bathroom floor?"

"Yeah," Billy replied.

"I thought it would be fun for us to imitate him and write with shaving cream, too."

"Shaving cream?" he asked.

"Yup, shaving cream. Want to try?"

"Okay," he replied.

"We can't write all over the bathroom floor," I said as Billy laughed, "but we can write on this baking tray."

With that, right in the center of the tray I spurted a glob of cream and started spreading it around. I wanted to end up with a thin, even layer of white cream which we would then use as a writing surface. A moment later, Billy joined me in spreading cream. Soon a blanket of white covered the tray. Our fingers were covered with white, too, until we cleaned them in the bowl of water and dried them with paper towels.

"Now that the tray is ready," I announced, "you can say any word you please, and I'll write it in the cream."

"*Antidisestablishmentarianism!*" exploded Billy. And then he burst into a fit of giggles.

"I'll write it, even though I'm not sure how to spell it. I doubt it will fit on the tray, but let's see what happens."

Lowering my index finger to the tray, I pushed away cream and exposed lines of aluminum in the shape of the lowercase letter *a*.

Then, one by one, I added letters.

"Neat," Billy said over and over as *n* and then *t* and then *i* appeared.

By the time I got to *antidisest* the tray was jammed.

"*Antidisestablishmentarianism* is definitely not going to fit. We need a shorter word. Can you think of one?" I asked.

"*Tiger*, my favorite animal," he announced.

"*Tiger* it is," I said.

I smoothed over the cream and wiped away *antidisest*, then added extra shaving cream, smoothed some more, and, when I had a clear white surface, began writing.

A moment later, no doubt to his own amazement, Billy blurted, "Let me try. I want to write."

"Sure," I said, trying to sound casual, although I felt like cheering. "As soon as I finish."

I completed *tiger* as quickly as I could and let Billy prepare the tray for his word.

"Since you picked a word for me, I should get to pick one for you," I said.

Billy grumbled, but agreed.

"*Tag*," I said. "You have to write *tag*."

"Oh, that's cinchy," he said. Confidently, his fingers slid through the cream, producing a *t* and then an *a* and then a *g*. He didn't flip his chair or flop on the floor. He wrote. He even smiled while writing. Thank you, Paddington.

Billy and I each wrote two more words, and when it was his turn, he wrote willingly—even eagerly. I was concerned, though, that if the novelty wore off, Billy's resistance to writing might reemerge. To keep the game fresh, therefore, I suggested that we use food coloring to create tinted words.

"I want red words," Billy said immediately.

"Sounds good to me. Go ahead, squeeze a couple of drops in the cream and use your fingers to mix. Then you can write any word you want," I said.

Billy needed no further encouragement. He whirled the food coloring around, producing red swirls and then red swirls in a pinkish base, and when he couldn't wait any longer, he wrote his own name, *Billy*, and immediately afterward he wrote *red* because the cream was red. One color looked so fine he decided to add another. He squeezed yellow drops, got a glowing orange, and wrote *Pad*, short for Paddington, and *Felix*, the name of his favorite stuffed animal. Next he added blue, which, mixed with the orange, resulted in a murky gray, and wrote *pizza*, his favorite food. We agreed that the shaving cream was now too yucky, and so I declared clean-up time.

Billy and I wrote with shaving cream a lot over the next several weeks. As he made letters appear on the tray, I complimented his writing. I praised his selection of interesting words. I applauded his skill in spelling. I admired the care with which he formed his letters. After about a month, I noticed a difference in Billy's attitude toward writing, even when we were not elbow deep in colored shaving cream. On days when I pulled out a pencil and paper and insisted that Billy write in a more standard fashion, his chair, for the most part, stayed upright. True, he still did not love writing, but at least he was willing to try. Why the change? The game proved to Billy that he could write words, even hard words, with a considerable degree of ease. This gave him the confidence he needed to trade his finger for a pencil and shaving cream for paper. Even after we moved on to other activities, Billy and I did, on occasion, return to SHAVING-CREAM WRITING. When he had to study for a particularly difficult spelling test, for instance, I let him practice the toughest words by writing them over and over again, Paddington style, in shaving cream.

Billy was in the second semester of first grade and ready to write words. If your child is younger and just mastering the alphabet, SHAVING-CREAM WRITING can help him with the job. Begin by drawing a letter in the cream, having your child name it, and then, if he can, say its sound. Next, name a letter and ask your child to write it. Or make a sound—*mmm*, for instance—and challenge your child to draw the corresponding letter. If these tasks are very easy for your child, you can make things harder. Say a word, such as *top*, and ask your child to name its first letter. If he can, he gets to form a *t* in the cream.

What if your child is able to write words but makes spelling mistakes when doing so? Should you correct him? Should you let the mistakes slide? The answer depends on your child. Some children get upset when you tell them they have misspelled a word and become less willing to write. When that is the case, I don't correct. Other children are happy to fix mistakes—especially when it means getting an extra chance to mess around in shaving cream.

A SIMPLE CARD TRICK

GRADES

first and second

MATERIALS

deck of cards, a person to trick

SKILLS

learning how to learn

*I*n the last chapter of *A Bear Called Paddington*, the Browns celebrate Paddington's birthday with a party. The highlight of the celebration is a magic show, performed by Paddington, complete with a disappearing act and a nifty card trick. Of course, because it is Paddington's show, almost everything that can go wrong does go wrong. Nevertheless, children envy Paddington. He knows a card trick, and almost all children think that possessing such knowledge is totally neat. Unfortunately, most tricks are too hard for young children to learn. Here, though, is a trick that is simple enough even for first and second graders to execute and yet dazzling enough to impress family and friends.

Before teaching the trick, I suggest that you learn it yourself. When you think you understand how it works, try it out on your child.

Begin by shuffling a deck of cards. When you are done, peek at the bottom card and remember it.

Be sure your child does not see you sneak that look. Next, tell him to pick a card, any card, and memorize it. Then tell him to place his card—his mystery card—on the top of the deck. Cut the deck in half and put the bottom section on the top. Your child will think his mystery card is lost in the deck. It is not lost, though, because you know which card rests directly above. It is the card *you* memorized—the one that was formerly on the bottom of the deck.

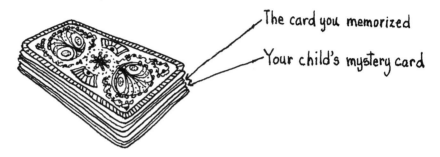

The card you memorized

Your child's mystery card

Cut the deck again. This time, though, transfer only a small number of cards—about six—from the bottom to the top. The additional cut will make your child doubly sure that his card is beyond discovering.

Now comes the astonishing part. Place the deck on a table. Turn over the top card, look at it a moment, and then say, "That's not your card." Flip the next card and say, "No," again. Keep turning; keep saying no. After you've flipped through several cards, don't be so fast to say no. Instead say something like, "Could this be your card? Magic, help me decide. Help me, magic. My magic tells me this is not your card." Keep dismissing cards until you see the one you memorized. You will reject that card, too, of course. But as soon as you turn over the next card, say, "Oh, magic, magic, yes, yes, this is it! This is the card!" Wave the card about victoriously, then lean back, and wait for your child to cry out, "How did you do that?"

You will answer his question, but first put up a minor

protest, citing the magicians' code of secrecy. After a bit, give in to his demands, and show him how the trick is done. Let him practice on you until he perfects the routine. When you think he is ready, arrange for him to give a performance. His first audience (preferably a single individual) should be someone who will root for him no matter what—just in case anything that can go wrong does go wrong.

After his first performance, you can arrange for others. I suggest that you give the trick a name. Call it Paddington's trick. Then, next week, when a family friend comes to dinner, ask your child to do Paddington's trick for the evening's entertainment. He can do Paddington's trick again when his grandmother comes to visit or when a neighbor drops by for coffee.

To master this card trick, or any other, your child must be patient. Learning to flawlessly execute a trick takes time. Your child will not perfect even this simple one on his first try. He will need to rehearse, and he must be willing to make mistakes as he practices his moves. He must keep focused on the long-range goal and not be overly concerned with little failures along the way. This is the exact attitude a child must have to learn anything, including reading, writing, and arithmetic. And if that isn't a good enough reason to teach your child this card trick, just imagine the look of pride on his face when his audience cries out, "How did you do that?"

ANYTHING AND EVERYTHING CAN GO WRONG

GRADES

kindergarten and first

SKILLS

encouraging an active imagination

*P*laying *Anything and Everything Can Go Wrong* will take less than three minutes of your time. It is such a quick and easy game you can play it every day—at least every day while you are reading *A Bear Called Paddington* to your child. You might begin this afternoon, during lunch.

Before your child takes a first bite of his tuna sandwich, interrupt him by saying, "Imagine if Paddington joined us for lunch today. I bet lots of things would go wrong. Why, even without Paddington, there might be problems. Here's an idea. While eating, we can take turns thinking of things that might happen. For instance, I could spill milk all over my lap and get soaking wet. Now it's your turn. What do you think could go wrong?"

Most children will jump in with an idea, but if your child has trouble doing so, make a suggestion (he could get mayonnaise in his hair) or two (the kitchen table might collapse). After your child announces his choice, you go again. This time, though, make a preposterous contribution.

"Maybe the rye bread will call out, 'I beg you, please, don't eat me!' "

When your child complains that this is too silly, explain that too silly is totally acceptable in this game. Why, things can get even sillier. A giraffe could come barging through the door, snatch the tuna sandwiches, and hide them in the chandelier.

Now that your child realizes that absolutely ANYTHING AND EVERYTHING CAN GO WRONG with this lunch, you just might hear some wild imaginings. And that is the point of this game. ANYTHING AND EVERYTHING CAN GO WRONG gives children the chance to fantasize. Many adults believe that children use their imaginations in the same way they use their lungs—without thought or effort. But that is not the case. Children need lots of opportunities to imagine and lots of adult support for doing so. ANYTHING AND EVERYTHING CAN GO

WRONG offers one opportunity. Don't overdo it, though. Most children enjoy the game, but if you play for too long, it gets boring. Two or three imaginary calamities at lunchtime are plenty. You can always play again tomorrow—while walking to school, for instance. What could go wrong on the way to class? You could lose a glove. You could lose a shoe. Or you could encounter a two-headed, polka-dotted boa constrictor who steals your book bag.

MY FATHER'S DRAGON

WRITTEN BY RUTH STILES GANNETT
ILLUSTRATED BY RUTH CHRISMAN GANNETT
1948
NEWBERY HONOR BOOK
GOOD READING FOR KINDERGARTEN AND FIRST, SECOND, AND THIRD GRADES

*E*lmer Elevator, the hero in *My Father's Dragon*, is a resourceful and daring child. After a stray cat tells him about an imprisoned baby dragon, Elmer sets out to rescue the entrapped creature. True, the dragon is held captive by frightful untamed beasts on the very distant Wild Island, but that does not stop Elmer.

Armed, at the cat's suggestion, with lollipops, hair ribbons, chewing gum, and a few other select items, Elmer stows away on a ship bound for the port of Cranberry on the Island of Tangerina. From Tangerina, it is a hop, skip, and somewhat perilous jump to Wild Island. Elmer, though, is not intimidated by a whale that looks like a rock. Nor later, on Wild Island, is he rattled by fearsome boars, hungry tigers, a ferocious lion, an enormous gorilla, or a river full of crocodiles. And, thanks to the cat's excellent advice, he has the exact equipment needed to outsmart these intimidating animals. Elmer is the intrepid master of each and every hair-raising situation.

Wouldn't it be wonderful to be as surefooted in the face of danger as Elmer Elevator? Wouldn't it be terrific if we could handle our worst crises with lollipops and rubber bands? Children slip happily into the fantasy world created by Ruth Stiles Gannett, the book's author. They enjoy hearing about Elmer's willingness to face alarming (but not really scary) situations. They delight in his cleverness, his imagination, and his success. For, of course, Elmer does free the dragon, and in doing so proves that intelligence, creativity, and determination can overcome brute animal strength. Hurrah for Elmer Elevator!

As the book ends, the baby dragon, with Elmer sitting safely on his back, flies away from Wild Island. Where will the young boy and baby dragon go now? To find out, you can read *Elmer and the Dragon* and then *The Dragons of Blueland*. Neither sequel is as beguiling as the original, but that does not stop Elmer lovers from insisting on hearing them.

Between reading the first and second books, though, why not try out one or another of the following activities?

*C*ould Elmer have survived his travails on Wild Island without a stash of sweet, juicy tangerines? Not likely. After reading the book, then, consider honoring the tangerine for its crucial role in helping Elmer. How do you honor a tangerine? You preserve it—at least for a time—by turning it into a SPICE BALL. What is a SPICE BALL? It is a tangerine encased in cloves. The balls do not look pretty, but they do give off a pretty fragrance.

It is easy to make a SPICE BALL—although the process takes time. All you need is a tangerine and an ample supply of whole cloves. If you can't get a tangerine, you can use an orange—preferably a navel orange.

SPICE BALL

GRADES

kindergarten, first, second, and third

MATERIALS

tangerine, jar of whole cloves

SKILLS

developing control over finger movements

One by one, you press cloves into the tangerine until every bit of the skin is covered with clove heads.

The closer together you place the cloves and the less rind you leave exposed, the longer your SPICE BALL will last.

It can be difficult for children to push the clove points through the tangerine skin. When you push too hard or in the wrong direction, the points tend to break off before the skin gives way. That is why you need teamwork. If you get the clove point into the tangerine, your child can finish by pushing the clove until only the head shows. I suggest, too, that you purchase high-quality cloves. Their stems are stronger than those of cheaper varieties, which means the heads are less likely to snap.

While you work, some juice will seep out of the tangerine. Do not let that worry you. Leaking juice will not affect the final product. Just wipe (or lick) your fingers and keep poking.

It takes about an hour, all in all, to cover a tangerine with cloves, but you do not need to tackle the task in a single sitting. You can work on it over four or five days. I do not advise taking more than a week to finish, though, lest the tangerine dry out or, worse yet, rot. To move the project forward at a more rapid pace, consider sticking in a few cloves when your child is not around.

After the tangerine is completely cloved, it will continue to dry out and, in the process, shrink. This brings the cloves closer together, which is exactly what you want.

Your SPICE BALL should exude a lovely scent for many months. I met someone who kept a SPICE BALL for three years, although I cannot say whether it still had any odor or not. No matter how long your ball lasts, every time your child looks at it, every time he sniffs it, he will be reminded of the greatest tangerine eater of them all—Elmer Elevator.

SPICE BALLS make wonderful gifts, by the way. After cloving his own tangerine, your child might like to clove another for his grandmother or a special uncle.

*L*ook at the front or the back flyleaf of *My Father's Dragon*, and you will find a detailed map of the Island of Tangerina and its neighbor, Wild Island. The drawing pinpoints every crucial location in Elmer's adventure.

If before you begin reading for the day you and your child turn to one of the maps, you can spend a few moments going over the story so far. "There's Tangerina, the island with all the tangerines. Here are the rocks linking Tangerina to Wild Island. Look, that's the whale Elmer stepped on. Do you see the tiger? It sure is lucky Elmer thought of that chewing gum trick." And then you can use the map to wonder what will happen next. "I'm sure Elmer will meet that lion, but what will he do when he does? Will he have to fight the gorilla? How will he get across the river to the dragon?"

You can do more than just talk about the map in the book. You and your child can make your own map and use it to imagine new experiences for Elmer and the dragon. That is exactly what I did with Molly, a young student of mine. Our map did not show Tangerina and Wild Island. Instead we created a new island—one we could use to continue Elmer's adventures with the dragon.

MAPMAKING

GRADES

kindergarten, first, second, and third

MATERIALS

sheet of 22″ × 28″ poster board (it's best to use the rough side), pencil, colored pencils or markers, 3″ × 5″ index cards, scissors

SKILLS

understanding the structure of stories

I began the map by outlining an island in the center of a 22″ × 28″ sheet of poster board.

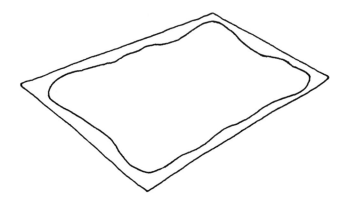

Then Molly and I took turns using colored pencils to draw interesting places for Elmer and the dragon to visit. Molly drew a river; I drew a beach. Molly drew a waterfall; I drew a swamp. Molly drew a cave; I drew a quicksand pit. Since we both wanted magic in the story, I drew a witch's hut and Molly added a magic mountain. To make sure we remembered all our ideas, we labeled everything.

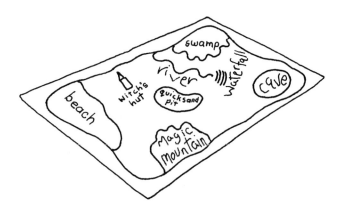

That was enough to get our story started. If we wanted more locations later, we could always add them.

Now we needed characters for our drama. We had to have Elmer and the dragon, of course. It took a bit of discussion, however, to decide who else to include. We agreed on a witch to go with the hut and a giant bear who would live on the mountain. Later we added a sea monster, a bat family, and several other interesting beings. How did we make the characters? We used 3″ × 5″ index cards. To create the witch, for instance, I cut an index card in half lengthwise, and then folded that half in half. Now I had a tentlike shape that could stand up without my help.

On one side of this tent I drew a witch.

"It's sort of like a puppet," Molly observed when I finished my work.

"Yes indeed. And you can move the witch around the island anytime you want," I said.

Seeing the witch, Molly said, "I'll make Elmer, if you help draw."

"I'll help if you need me. But I bet you can draw an elegant Elmer all on your own," I said.

Molly began by forming a tent using the half piece of index card left over from the witch. Because Elmer needed to be smaller than the witch, she cut her tent to make it shorter.

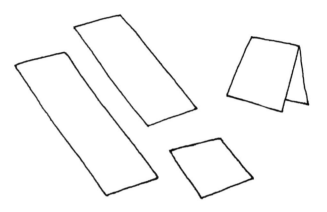

Then she drew Elmer—an excellent Elmer.

To make the dragon, I changed the shape of the index-card tent.

Molly used yet a different shape for the giant bear.

Next we had to divvy up our cast. I told Molly she could pick any two characters she wanted. She should consider her choices carefully, since she would have to think for that character and speak for that character throughout the entire story. Molly nodded and then took dibs on the witch and the dragon. That left me with Elmer and the giant bear.

We agreed to begin our tale by having Elmer and the dragon make a crash landing on the beach. Before their bumpy arrival, though, I put the bear on top of the magic mountain, and Molly placed the witch beside the hut. Then Molly held up the dragon so that it appeared to be flying and I held Elmer on top of the dragon's back.

"Look," I said in a squeaky Elmerish voice, "there's an island. I think we should stop and rest."

"Good idea," said Molly in her own voice.

"Let's land on the beach," I said in my Elmer voice.

Molly guided the dragon toward the map.

"Watch out! There's a big rock on the beach! Oh, no, you slammed into it! Are you all right? Your wing looks hurt."

"It hurts. I think I broke it. I can walk, though," Molly said.

"That's good. Let's explore the island. It looks like an interesting place," I said.

With that, I started sliding Elmer across the map while Molly moved the dragon.

"I see some mountains. Do you want to walk to them?" I asked.

"Okay. But I wish I could fly," Molly said.

At that moment, I let go of Elmer and took hold of the bear. I guided the bear off the mountain and plopped him next to Elmer. "I've got you, whoever you are, and I am going to eat you for dinner!" I said gruffly.

Then I switched voices and yelled, "Help me, dragon!"

And the dragon did help. He fought the bear and rescued Elmer.

But then the witch appeared, so Elmer and the dragon ran to the beach to escape her. When they reached the water, they met a multiheaded sea monster. That is, they met the sea monster after Molly finished making a new puppet.

At this point the doorbell rang, signaling the arrival of Molly's mother and the end of our work session. Molly was indignant. She did not want to stop the story. I assured her that our tale had only just begun, and we would certainly continue with it next week.

Why did I create this map with Molly and then use it to make up adventures? Giving children opportunities to invent stories is always a good idea. It fosters their imaginations. It develops their creativity. But in Molly's case, I had a special reason. Molly liked telling stories, but her tales rarely made any sense. Adults would listen attentively as she talked, they would nod their heads, but they did not follow her train of thought. Children were less patient. They'd interrupt her with, "I don't get it," and, "What are you talking about?"

The map was a way to help Molly form a more coherent narrative. By taking the lead, I could make sure our tale was organized and that the plot was logical. In this manner, I could help Molly appreciate how stories work. I didn't expect an instant transformation in Molly's ability to spin yarns, but it was a starting point. Of course, Molly did not know I was giving her a lesson in storytelling. She thought we were playing, and that was true, too.

*J*anet was in kindergarten and struggling mightily to learn the alphabet. She had a hard time naming both the uppercase and lowercase letters and a still-harder time attributing the correct sounds to those letters. Janet's parents were concerned enough to ask for my help.

During one of our first sessions, I asked Janet about her favorite books. *My Father's Dragon* topped her list. Her father had just finished reading it aloud to her, and she could not wait to hear the second book in the series.

"Would you like to search for a dragon?" I asked.

"I wish I could," she said.

"I have a way you can. You can't hunt for a real dragon, naturally, or go to Wild Island. You can hunt nevertheless."

FIND THE DRAGON

GRADES

kindergarten, first, second, and third

MATERIALS

paper, pen or pencil, scissors

SKILLS

working with the alphabet, spelling

My Father's Dragon
163

I took a piece of blank paper and held it lengthwise. Then I cut a strip from the top that was about two and one-half inches high.

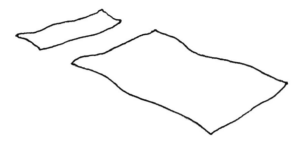

Next I divided the strip into six more or less equal boxes. In each box, I wrote one of the letters in the word *dragon*.

As I wrote each letter, I said its name, and Janet, even without my prompting, imitated me. When I finished writing all the letters, I said, "*Dragon*. These letters spell *dragon*."

Then I cut out each letter. When I was done. I placed the six letters in front of Janet and asked her to name them one by one. With a single exception, *g*, she was able to do so.

"Here's the baby dragon, Janet. But he is in trouble again. He is all divided up, and something worse is about to happen to him," I said.

"What?" she asked.

"The beasts of Wild Island are on their way here, and they plan to hide all the letters. They will scatter them about this room. But you can rescue the dragon, if you can find his letters and put them together so that they spell the word *dragon* once again. What do you think? Can you save the dragon?"

"I can!" she shouted.

"Well, then, shut your eyes, because the beasts are coming, and your eyes must be shut, or it will be too awful!" I said.

Janet giggled at the notion, but obediently closed her eyes tight. I took all six letters and hid them here and there. Each letter was in sight, just not in plain sight. After placing the last letter beside a sofa cushion, I told Janet to open her eyes. She was ready to jump up and start hunting, but I held her back.

"Wait a second, Janet, while I write something," I said. I wrote the word *dragon* on a fresh sheet of paper. "Here are all the letters you must find. I'll keep this paper right on the table so that you can look at it whenever you want."

Now Janet did start hunting. It took her about five minutes to locate all the letters and place them on the table.

"Time to put the dragon back together," I said.

"Can I look at *dragon* on the paper?" she asked.

"Sure," I said.

"This will be easy. I can copy," she said. Within a minute Janet was staring down at the reassembled *dragon*.

"Hurrah, Janet! You hunted for the dragon, you found the dragon, and you saved the dragon!" I shouted.

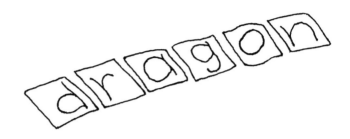

"That was fun," she said. "I want to save the dragon again."

"How about this time you save Elmer? I hear he is in a lot of trouble since leaving Wild Island," I said.

"Okay," she replied.

With that okay, Janet's second hunt was afoot.

After this rescue, I told Janet that the animals on Wild Island had hidden Elmer's toothbrush. Unless Janet found the letters in *toothbrush* and put them together in the correct order, Elmer wouldn't be able to escape the rhinoceros, and all was lost.

When Janet hunted for the dragon, she had a sheet with the word *dragon* on it. This was her guide. It let her know exactly what letters she needed to find. It showed her how to spell the word once she had all the letters in hand. This was appropriate for a child who was learning the alphabet. If you believe your child is ready for a greater challenge, have him look for all the letters and spell the word without a written guide. *Elmer* might be easy to find and reassemble, but finding and reassembling *magnifying glasses* will be a harder task.

Your child should start by rescuing the dragon and then

Elmer. After that, assuming the game is a hit, he can save Elmer's *toothbrush* or his *magnifying glasses* or anything else on the list below. Every item here was crucial to Elmer's success.

grain bag	knapsack	rubber boots
chewing gum	rubber bands	tangerines
compass	tooth paste	toothbrush
hairbrush	lollipops	hair ribbons
jackknife	comb	magnifying glasses

After three or four rescues, end the game and congratulate your child for defeating the animals of Wild Island. He might want to continue playing, but it is always better to stop a game while a child is enthusiastic. Tomorrow, though, or the next day, the terrifying beasts of Wild Island might return, compelling your child to heroically rescue Elmer's *comb* or his *chewing gum* or his *rubber boots*.

WINNIE-THE-POOH

WRITTEN BY A. A. MILNE
ILLUSTRATED BY ERNEST H. SHEPARD
1926
GOOD READING FOR KINDERGARTEN AND
FIRST AND SECOND GRADES

*T*here is an enchanted place. You can find it between the covers of A. A. Milne's masterpiece *Winnie-the-Pooh* (as well as in its sequel, *The House at Pooh Corner*). And in that enchanted place, you will meet the all-knowing and all-loving Christopher Robin, the brainier-than-he-can-ever-imagine Winnie-the-Pooh, gloomy Eeyore, timid Piglet, wise Owl, rational Rabbit, and all the other unforgettable residents of Pooh Corner.

Of course, Pooh and company do not live in a perfect world—they confront a variety of problems. Pooh gets stuck in Rabbit's hole for an entire week—his own fault, really, the consequence of eating too much honey. But it is not easy dieting his way out of such a tight spot. And there is a Woozle to track down and a Heffalump to avoid.

Some of the trials and tribulations will be completely familiar to children: taking a bath when you would prefer not to, trying to find a food you like to eat, or getting enough of the foods you truly love.

Open either *Winnie-the-Pooh* or *The House at Pooh Corner* to any page and start reading. Within a few lines, you are sure to be entranced. Milne never hits a false note. Every sentence, every phrase, every word is perfect, and this perfection makes you smile. That is, unless you happen to turn to the last chapter of *The House at Pooh Corner*. That last chapter, "In Which Christopher Robin and Pooh Come to an Enchanted Place, and

We Leave Them There," always makes me cry. I imagine Christopher Robin growing up and leaving Pooh, and my heart aches.

In general, though, there is no reason to leave the enchanted world of Pooh for very long. Children who hear the stories once usually want to hear them twice, three times, and more. Many memorize favorite parts. I did as a child, and I can still recite certain passages.

If you want still more of Pooh, Christopher Robin, and the delights of Milne after finishing *Winnie-the-Pooh* and *The House at Pooh Corner*, there are a couple of things you can do. First, you can, and certainly should, read Milne's wonderful books of poetry, *When We Were Very Young* and *Now We Are Six*. Second, you and your child can entertain yourselves with one or another of the following activities—each of which will keep your mind on Pooh even when you are not reading the books.

THE HUM GAME

GRADES
kindergarten, first, and second

SKILLS
learning to rhyme,
playing with language

*W*hat is the most Poohish thing about Pooh? Is it the fact that he is a Bear of Very Little Brain? His love of honey? His loyalty to Piglet, Christopher Robin, and all the others? For me, hums are the most Poohish thing about Pooh. What are hums? They are Pooh's made-up poems, and they always rhyme, except when they don't. And sometimes Pooh calls them poems and sometimes he calls them songs, but I like it best when he calls them hums. Pooh makes up hums about friends, honey, even snowy days. Every aspect of Pooh's life is material for a hum. Spurred on by the bear bard, you and your child can become hummers, too, by making up your own rhyming verses.

Pooh rarely plans a hum. Instead, he relies on sudden inspiration, which strikes as he strolls through the woods or when he sits down for a lick of some sustaining sweet. As

Pooh notes, "It is the best way to write poetry, letting things come."

Pooh's relaxed approach is a fine one, and you and your child should consider adapting it for your own poetic purposes. If you are not overly particular about the quality of your work, you can, like Pooh, compose mini-poems almost anytime and about nearly any topic.

Tomorrow at breakfast, for instance, you might hum your praise for cereal:

> I love my crispy cornflakes.
> A little milk is all it takes
> To turn them into a delicious meal,
> And I say that's a super deal!

This is a perfectly dreadful poem, but as a spontaneous ditty, it's not so bad—which is precisely the point. To create a Pooh-type poem, you do not need a great poetic mind. As long as you can rhyme, you can hum. There are several approaches to creating hums, but I suggest you begin by inviting your child to play THE HUM GAME.

To play, you think of a hummable topic. It might be birthdays. Then your child has to make up a two-line hum about this topic.

> Birthdays are so much fun.
> I hate it when they are done.

Next your child thinks of a topic for you—secrets, for instance. Now you must compose a two-line hum.

> Secrets are hard to keep.
> I might say them in my sleep.

And then you pick a new topic for your child—rain, maybe.

I hate the rain.
It is a pain.

Your child gives you a new topic, perhaps the beach.

Going to the beach is mighty grand.
I can build castles in the sand.

None of these are works of art. But each has two lines and each rhymes. That's all you need for a successful hum in this game.

What if your child can't think of a hum for one of your topics? It is perfectly fine to offer ideas. You might propose a theme: "Rain is awful—you could hum about that." You might even compose the first line: "I hate rain," then let your child think of the second: "It is a pain." And if you have trouble with your topic, ask your child for help. He might have some good ideas.

When your child plays THE HUM GAME, he will spend time rhyming, and since the ability to rhyme with ease is helpful for beginning readers, this will be time well spent. Look at this list: *nap, cap, lap, tap, map, gap, rap, sap*. Read the first two or three words to a child who is a good rhymer and he can usually finish the list on his own. A child who finds it difficult to rhyme, on the other hand, does not appreciate how the words in the list connect. Reading a few to him, therefore, will not do much good. How do children learn to rhyme? Usually the knack comes in three ways: hearing rhymes, making up rhymes, and getting lots of adult admiration for rhyming, even when the rhymes are silly. All three happen when you play THE HUM GAME.

What should you do if your child finds it hard to rhyme during the game? Making suggestions often works: "Let's see, when you jump rope you hop. *Hop* goes with *top, pop*, and *stop. Hop, top, pop, stop*—they rhyme. You can use them in your hum, if you want." What if your child thinks *cap* rhymes with *cab*? Don't dismiss his idea. Instead carefully consider the words: "*Cap, cab, cap, cab*—they are a little alike, *cap* and *cab*, but they don't rhyme like *cap* and *lap*."

You can think of your own topics, if you want, or you can take ideas from this list:

crayons	birthday cakes	Halloween
poison ivy	pizza	computers
sunsets	jump rope	school
baseball	rainbows	the number 10
bubbles	telephones	secrets
spiders	nail polish	best friends
witches	snakes	bobcats
oatmeal	kisses	peanut butter sandwiches
beaches	full moons	soccer
snow	thunder	slime
car rides	roses	tickles
stomachaches	marshmallows	balloons
butterflies	picnics	popcorn

THE HUM GAME does more than give your child opportunities to rhyme. It also encourages him to play with words, to invent with words, to create with words, to fall in love with words.

So, heed my sage advice, and hum this morning once or twice.

*T*he author A. A. Milne modeled Pooh on an actual stuffed bear owned by his young son, Christopher Robin Milne. Clearly, Milne, the father, understood that few things are as precious to a child as a stuffed friend. It is easy to buy such a friend for your child. It is even relatively easy to buy replicas of Pooh, Piglet, and Eeyore. Let me suggest, though, that instead of heading for the toy store, you and your child work together to sew a homemade bear—one that will be unique in all the world.

Making a stuffed bear does demand a commitment of time. It might take several days or even longer to finish the project. You will have to sew. You do not, however, need special talent with a needle and thread. Even tiny inexperienced fingers can manage a good part of the job.

Before you begin work, you need to get hold of a sturdy piece of cloth. I like making bears out of T-shirts. T-shirts are soft and flexible, which is what you want for a stuffed animal, but any strong cotton will do. Since you will be drawing on the cloth, it is best to choose a cotton T-shirt in white or a light solid color.

Next you need a pattern for the bear. You can make your own pattern, but it might be easier to photocopy the one on page 181. The pattern is designed to make a bearish kind of creature about seven inches tall. If you want a bigger bear, a good photocopy machine should be able to enlarge the drawing by 125 percent or even 150 percent.

When you have the pattern, you must pin it to a double layer of cloth, or, in the case of a T-shirt, the front and back of the shirt. First pin all four corners of the photocopy in place. Then run a row of pins directly inside the lines of the paper bear. With a little guidance, your child can do this work.

MAKE A BEAR

GRADES

first and second

MATERIALS

a T-shirt or a piece of soft but sturdy cotton material, cotton balls, permanent marker, scissors, thread, needle, straight pins, photocopy of page 181

SKILLS

developing control over finger movements, learning to be patient when completing a project

To avoid dealing with extra material, tell your child to cut out an area around the bear.

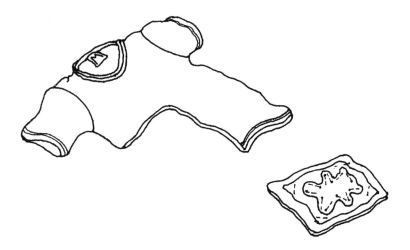

Next he can cut out the bear itself. This is not an easy task, in part because you must make sure that the fabric does not slip, which it tends to do even if you pin it together very carefully. If your child has too much trouble cutting, offer help, but as soon as possible, let him take over again. Don't worry

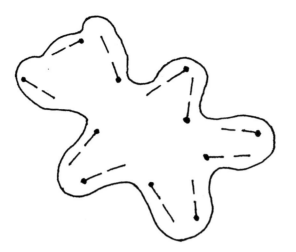

if the lines are raggedy. A few rough spots will personalize the bear.

After you cut out the bear, remove the paper pattern by pulling away all the pins. When you do so, be careful to keep the two pieces of fabric aligned. If the two pieces drift out of place, you will have to realign them after the paper is gone. Now pin the two pieces of cloth together so that they stay put as your child sews.

Cut a length of thread about 20 inches long. Push one end of the thread through the eye of a needle, bring the two ends of the thread together, and tie a knot.

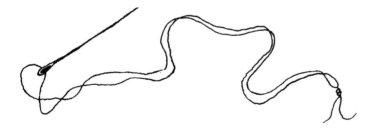

If your child has never sewn before, take a couple of pieces of scrap material and show him how to do a simple stitch. The needle goes down from the top

and then turns around and comes up from the bottom.

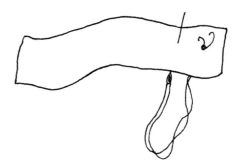

Then down and up and down and up again.

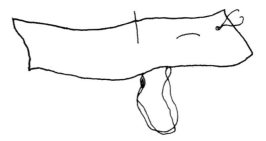

Once your child has the idea, hand him the bear. He should try to sew small stitches that are close together about a quarter of an inch from the edge of the fabric. His first needleful of thread will not take him all the way around the bear. At some point, therefore, you must snip the thread off the needle and make a knot. Rethread the needle and have your child start sewing again. As your child makes his way around the bear, he can remove any pins he passes.

Your child can begin stitching wherever he wants, but I suggest that he start here:

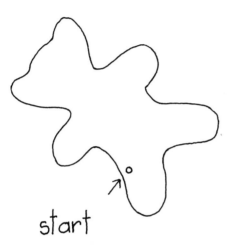

start

and travel around the the bear in this direction.

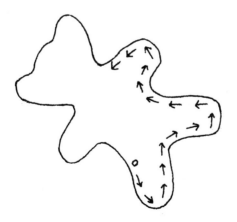

When he is about here, he should stop sewing.

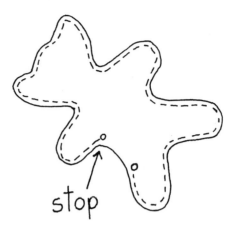

stop

Now comes a slightly tricky part. Your child must turn his mostly sewn animal inside out. He should be especially careful as he turns the arms, legs, head, and ears. His small fingers are a big advantage for this work.

Stuffing the bear comes next. I find that cotton balls make excellent stuffing. The balls are soft and you can easily push them into small crevices. Your child should fill the arms, legs, and head before working on the body.

The more cotton balls he shoves inside, the firmer his bear will be. Once the bear is as stuffed as your child wants, he can stitch up the opening. Then he should check for gaps in his sewing and patch anything that needs patching.

Afterward your child can draw the bear's features. Using a permanent marker, let him define the head and then draw ears, eyes, nose, and mouth. He can use dots to show paws.

If your child cares to, he can add clothes. He can draw a bow tie, a striped shirt, a belt, polka-dotted pants, or anything else that appeals to him and in any color he likes. Do not forget to work on the back of the bear as well as the front. Your child may ask you to help with the drawing, and that is okay, but the bulk of the work should be his.

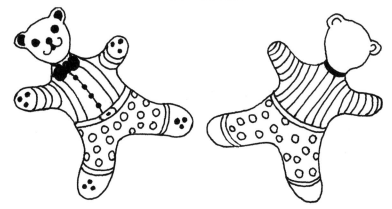

It takes a lot of finger control to pin, cut, sew, stuff, and draw a bear. To do a good job, your child must be as precise as possible with all the small movements he makes with his hands. He will need to exercise exactly such control and exactly such precision when forming letters and numbers. In a certain sense, therefore, making a bear is a lesson in penmanship—a fact which would certainly please Winnie-the-Pooh.

It requires patience to make a stuffed animal, and your child is bound to get frustrated along the way. Whenever a child sets out to master something new—from learning to sew to learning to solve quadratic equations—he must tolerate moments of frustration. Patience does not come naturally to children; it develops with experience. If your child gets upset occasionally while making his bear, comfort him. If necessary, help him with the work. But also view such times as opportunities to teach him the importance of sticking with a job even if the task is hard. When he finally hugs his finished bear, he will know that you were right.

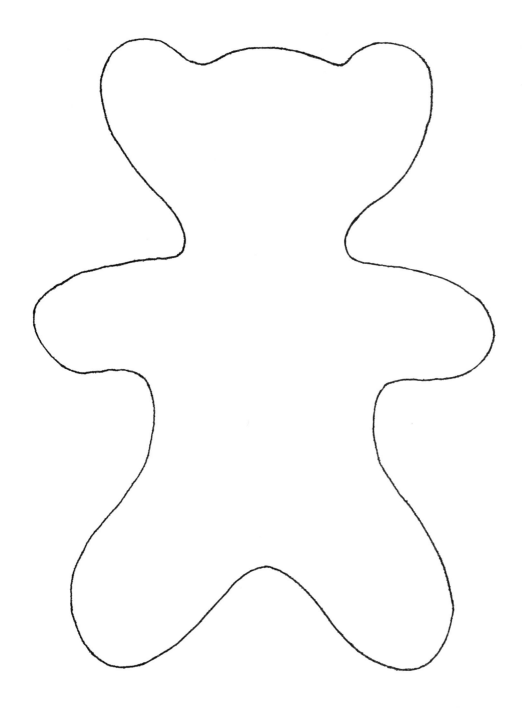

WOBBLY LETTERS

GRADES

first and second

MATERIALS

paper, pencil

SKILLS

improving skills in spelling

*E*mily was a terrible speller. Although she was in third grade, her writing resembled a first grader's, judging by spelling alone. Unlike many poor spellers, Emily did not let her problematic way with words inhibit her writing. She was justifiably proud of her very long stories, happily presenting them whenever asked. This was wonderful, but she still needed to learn to spell more accurately.

I knew that Emily was a big fan of the A. A. Milne books and that Pooh was one of her favorite fictional characters. One day, therefore, when Emily was complaining about how hard it is to spell words correctly, I pulled out my copy of *Winnie-the-Pooh* and read her this passage:

> "*That* was what I wanted to ask you," said Pooh. "Because my spelling is Wobbly. It's good spelling but it Wobbles, and the letters get in the wrong places."

Emily loved the quote, understanding all too well how letters insist on misplacing themselves. She was very receptive, therefore, when I suggested playing WOBBLY LETTERS, a game based on Pooh's description of spelling.

The game began when I wrote this sentence for Emily:

"I misspelled one of the words. Can you pick it out?"
"It's this one," she said, pointing to *anwts*.

"Do you know what word it is supposed to be?"

"I'm not sure," she said.

"It's supposed to be *wants*. The sentence should read, 'Pooh wants to eat some honey.' But my *wants* wobbled. All the letters are there, except they are mixed up. If you can put the letters in the right order, you earn two points."

"What if I make a mistake? Will you help me?" she asked.

"I won't help you, but I will give you a second chance. If you spell the word correctly on your second try, you earn one point. You need ten points to win," I said.

Emily smiled. "That sounds easy."

"It isn't all that easy, because I am only going to give you eight wobbly words. If you get all eight words right on your first try, you will have sixteen points and win the game. But if you get all the words right on your second try, you will only have eight points, and I will win. That means you must get at least some words right on your first try," I said.

Emily frowned.

"Here's the good news. You can take as long as you want to figure out the right spelling. I'll give you a sheet of blank paper, and you can test the letters this way and that way until you think the word looks correct," I said.

Emily smiled again. "I think I can get two points for *wants*," she said. "I know *w* comes first."

"Write it down, then," I said.

W

"Maybe the rest is like this," she said.

Whats

She looked carefully at her writing and then shook her head. "No, that's not it. Let me try something else."

"I've got it! I think I've got it. Do I have it?"

"Yes, you do, and you just earned two points. Here's your second sentence," I said.

"I see the wobbly word," she said, pointing to *elkis.*

"That's the one," I said. "The sentence is supposed to read, 'Piglet likes to smell flowers.' "

"I thought so," Emily said.

"Can you unwobble *likes*?" I asked.

"Easy. I know that word. It's *l-i-k-e-s.*"

"You just earned two more points. I better give you some harder words or else I'm sure to lose the game," I said. "Here, this is really a tough one."

Emily picked out the misspelled word.

"It is supposed to be *cloud*," I said, "and I meant to write, 'Pooh saw a cloud in the sky.' Can you fix my *cloud*?"

"I'm not sure," she said.

First she tested

Colud

and then

Culod

before announcing her choice.

Cluod

"That's almost right, but not quite. *Cloud* is a very hard word to spell. You get a second chance, though. And if you succeed, you rack up another point," I reminded her.

Emily went back to work. In a moment, she handed me her results.

"Is this it?" she asked.

Cloud

"Absolutely. That means you already have five points. You only need five more to win," I said.

We kept playing. At the end of the game, Emily had a total of fourteen points—a decisive victory.

It was a victory for me, too, given that Emily had just spent over fifteen minutes working as hard as she could to spell words correctly.

POOH PICNIC PARTY

GRADES
kindergarten, first, and second

MATERIALS
stuffed animals, food, party decorations

SKILLS
listening to the first sounds in words, understanding the importance of writing

*I*n the last chapter of *Winnie-the-Pooh*, Christopher Robin gives an outdoor party in honor of Pooh. Everyone has a wonderful time. Even gloomy Eeyore enjoys himself, at least as much as he is able. You and your child might want to throw a party in honor of Pooh, too. You don't need to wait until you've read about Pooh's party. You can have yours anytime you want. It won't be an ordinary party, since Pooh is not an ordinary bear. It will be a POOH PICNIC PARTY.

How is a POOH PICNIC PARTY different from other social events? First, it should be a very small affair. You might invite only a single child, and I do not advise including more than three. Second, to attend, guests and host must be accompanied by a favorite stuffed animal. Third, in homage to Pooh, your party menu must consist solely of foods that begin with the *p* sound. You can serve pizza, pasta, peanut butter cookies, pink lemonade, and a fruit salad made with pears, pineapples, plums, and peaches. It is impossible to imagine a POOH PICNIC PARTY without honey, and so honey will be an exception to the *p*-sound rule. In fact, consider giving each human guest a plastic bear filled with honey—the kind you can get at most supermarkets. Then partygoers can drip honey on peach ice cream, on pieces of pita bread, or even on potato chips and pretzels. Honey on pretzels sounds awful to me, but I know six- and seven-year-olds who feel differently.

Traditionally, picnics are outdoor events. If that is impractical, though, you can spread a tablecloth on the floor and have an indoor picnic. You might decorate the picnic area with pink ribbons and purple balloons. After the children finish eating, play a few games—pick up sticks or Parcheesi, for instance.

Include your child in all the preparations for the party. Let him help write the invitations. Maybe he can only scrawl a wobbly _POOH_ on each one. That is fine. Maybe he can also write the date, time, and request for a stuffed animal. That is fine, too. Any writing your child does, a lot or a little, is a good thing, for it will let him see how important writing is in life. After all, how can you send party invitations if you cannot write? Your child should also help select the menu. Call on him to evaluate each food for its _p_ sound. It might take considerable thought to arrive at a good combination of treats. Your child can join you in putting up decorations before the party begins and cleaning up after everyone leaves. In other words, do everything possible to make this his event, his party, his Pooh picnic.

If your POOH PICNIC PARTY is a big success, you might want to plan other special meals. These can be strictly family affairs. Tell your child that you will allow him to bring a stuffed animal to dinner or to lunch. If he brings a small animal, it can sit on top of the table. A larger animal can sit on a chair at the table. Then your child can prepare a plate of food for his guest. But he can only give his animal foods that begin with a letter you select. To pick that letter, think about your meal and think about the food you have in your kitchen. If you are serving chicken with rice and rolls and you know that there is a box of raisins in your cupboard, you will probably pick the letter _r_. Then your child can place a snip of roll, a spoonful of rice, and few raisins on a plate and present it to his stuffed friend. If you are having a cream cheese and tomato sandwich on toast, then _t_ is your letter. And when the meal is over, you, your child, and his stuffed animal can snuggle up with _Winnie-the-Pooh_ and enjoy a chapter or two.

PIPPI LONGSTOCKING

WRITTEN BY ASTRID LINDGREN
TRANSLATED BY FLORENCE LAMBORN
ILLUSTRATED BY LOUIS S. GLANZMAN
1950
GOOD READING FOR FIRST, SECOND, AND THIRD GRADES

*I*n all of children's literature you will not find a character as joyful and anarchic as nine-year-old Pippi Longstocking.

Pippi lives in Villa Villekulla, a tumbledown house with an overgrown garden, unaccompanied by mother, father, or any other adult. Pippi does not live alone, however. She shares her house with her pet monkey, Mr. Nilsson, and her spotted horse. Living without adult supervision has distinct advantages, as any child can imagine. In Pippi's case, "there is no one to tell her to go to bed just when she was having the most fun, and no one who could make her take cod liver oil when she much preferred caramel candy." Pippi has no money worries; she's got a suitcase full of gold. She does not fear dangerous predicaments. She knows she is the strongest girl in the world and will always come out on top.

Actually, Pippi rarely faces real danger. She confronts a variety of perils, to be sure, but she is never fazed and is always courageous. One day a pair of policemen attempt to remove her from Villa Villekulla. The officers chase her through the house, across the roof, over the balcony, and down the chimney. Is Pippi scared? Not a bit. For her, this is an enjoyable game of tag. When she gets bored, she grabs the exhausted policemen by their belts, lifts them into midair, and carries them off her property.

No wonder that children adore this irrepressible little girl. For when you read about Pippi, you somehow feel a little braver, a little more willing to take risks, a little surer of yourself. For eleven wonderful chapters, the author, Astrid Lindgren, describes Pippi's raucous adventures. And if that is not enough for you and your child, you can read about Pippi's further escapades in *Pippi Goes on Board* and *Pippi in the South Seas*.

Few characters in children's literature enjoy playing more than Pippi. Nothing could be more natural, therefore, than to play a few Pippi-inspired games in between reading chapters of the book or shortly after you finish it. Skim through the next four activities and pick the ones that seem best suited to you and your child.

HOW LONG CAN YOU BE STRONG?

"**P**ippi is so strong," said Elizabeth. "I wish I was that strong."

"She is amazing," I agreed. "I love how she lifts her horse up in the air."

"Yeah, that is neat," said Elizabeth.

"I know you're not as strong as Pippi. Who could be? But I bet you are stronger than you think. How would you like to test your strength?" I asked.

"Will it be fun?"

"I hope so. If it isn't, we can stop. Want to try?"

"Okay," she said.

"Great. Now, I have three tests in mind. Each one will tell us how long you can be strong. The first is the tiptoe event. It is easy to stand on your toes for a short amount of time, but if you try to stand on them for a long time, it gets very, very hard. This test will show how long you can be strong on tiptoe," I said.

"I'm ready," she declared.

GRADES

first, second, and third

MATERIALS

paper, pencil or pen, a stopwatch or any watch with a second hand

SKILLS

making estimates, comparing numbers, charting information

"Not quite. First we need a record sheet so that we can remember how strong you were in each event," I said while taking out a sheet of paper. Elizabeth watched while I wrote.

Elizabeth's Strength Record			
Date	Event	Estimated time	Tested time
March 4	tiptoe		

"I've included today's date and the name of the event. Now I want you to estimate how long you think you can stand on your tiptoes, and I will write that number. Before you estimate, though, think about this. You will take off your shoes and stand in your socks. You can't balance yourself on furniture or anything else. And you cannot move your feet around—even though it will be hard not to wiggle. If you move, I will stop the clock. So, knowing all of that, how long do you think you can stay on tiptoe?" I asked.

"I'm not sure, but maybe two minutes," she said after thinking about it.

"Two minutes. Let's see, one minute equals 60 seconds, and 60 plus 60 is 120. I will write down 120 seconds," I said.

Elizabeth's Strength Record			
Date	Event	Estimated time	Tested time
March 4	tiptoe	120 seconds	

"Go ahead and take off your shoes while I find my stop-watch," I told her. When we were both prepared, Elizabeth raised herself onto her toes, and I started the watch. A few times I had to remind her not to move her feet, although I did not stop the clock. She stayed on her tiptoes past 120 seconds . . . 121 . . . 122. After 127 seconds, she collapsed.

"That was fantastic, Elizabeth. You were strong for so long! I doubt Pippi could have done better. Your estimate was amazingly accurate, too. Look at how close the numbers are: 120 and 127."

Elizabeth's Strength Record			
Date	Event	Estimated time	Tested time
March 4	tiptoe	120 seconds	127 seconds

"You next," Elizabeth insisted.

"You want me to stand on my toes?" I asked.

"Yeah, do it," she said.

And so I did, but first I made my own record sheet and estimated my time. I did not think I could stay up as long as Elizabeth, and that was the case.

Peggy's Strength Record			
Date	Event	Estimated time	Tested time
March 4	tiptoe	80 seconds	84 seconds

"On to the second event," I said. "But I warn you, it's hard."

"I'm ready," Elizabeth said, full of confidence.

"This time, you must stand with your back against the wall and then slide down until you're in a sitting position. You have to stay in this seated position, without a chair, for as long as you can."

"Can I try it first before I estimate?" she asked.

"Good idea. Then you will know how hard it is to do."

I showed Elizabeth the right position. She quickly agreed it would be a tough pose to hold and made her estimate, 50 seconds, with that in mind.

Much to her delight, Elizabeth stayed in this odd position for a full 57 seconds.

Elizabeth's Strength Record			
Date	Event	Estimated time	Tested time
March 4	tiptoe	120 seconds	127 seconds
March 4	Wall sitting	50 seconds	57 seconds

That was longer than I could. I gave up after 32 seconds.

"Do you know how much longer you wall-sat than I did?"

Elizabeth shrugged her shoulders.

"Do you know how to find out?"

"I'm not sure. Add, maybe."

"If we add, we would combine our times. It would be as if you sat against the wall and then as soon as you gave up, I sat against the wall, and we kept the clock going until I gave up. But we don't want to combine our times; we want to find the difference between them. To find the difference between two numbers, you subtract. When I subtract 32 from 57, I get 25. That means you beat my time by 25 seconds."

I had explained how to use addition and subtraction to Elizabeth many times before, but these are difficult concepts, and I was not surprised that it was taking time for her to understand them. I was prepared, therefore, to be patient. Suddenly, though, something clicked, at least for a moment, and Elizabeth announced, "Yeah, if you added, the number would be bigger than my time and bigger than your time. That couldn't be right."

"Good thinking, Elizabeth," I said enthusiastically.

Our third event was the book strength test. By way of introduction, I told Elizabeth to hold her arm out directly in front of her with her palm facing up. Then I placed a children's dictionary in her open hand.

"In the book event, you hold this book right here for as long as you can. I'll take the dictionary away now, so that you can estimate how long you can be strong with a book in your hand," I said.

Even a brief trial run convinced Elizabeth that this was the hardest task so far. Her estimate, 30 seconds, reflected her realization. In actuality, she held the book for just 29 seconds.

"What's the difference between your estimate and your clock time?" I asked after her arm dropped.

"One second," she replied without hesitation.

"Good thinking again, Elizabeth."

After this, Elizabeth begged for more. I had other contests in mind, but we were almost out of time, and so I promised her more strength tests next week.

If, like Elizabeth, your child begs for more, here are a few extra events you can try.

Swing your arms in large circles for as long as you can.

Do jumping jacks until you must stop.

Sit on the floor with your legs stretched out in front of you in a V shape. Keep your hands in front of you, too. They can be on the floor but not on your legs. Then lift up one leg, and keep it in the air until it topples.

Stand straight with your feet shoulder-width apart and your arms straight out in front of you. Squat down until your thighs are at a 90-degree angle to your calves. Stand back up, and then squat down again. How long can you keep doing these squats?

You can have as many contests as you want and repeat the events whenever you like. You can compare old scores with new. And if you tire of these events, you can make up others.

As you carry out strength tests, talk about the numbers. It is not necessary to pull out paper and pencil and perform calculations. In fact, it is much better to keep your numerical discussions casual. You might note how close your child's estimate was to his official time or that he beat you by more than a minute in the jumping jack event. Children should feel that the numerical world is both interesting and enjoyable, and they are more likely to do so if they perceive their parents as number enthusiasts. You may feel a little foolish standing on your toes or sitting against walls, but remember that you are helping your child develop a positive attitude toward math, and there is nothing foolish about that.

SOUND TAG

GRADES

second and third

MATERIALS

a coin

SKILLS

isolating individual sounds in words

*P*ippi plays a wild game of tag. Her uproarious romp with the two policemen is one of the high points of the book. After reading this chapter to Carolyn, I decided to engage her in a game of tag—not the running, scrambling type of game that Pippi played, but a more sedate version called SOUND TAG.

I began the game by picking a word. I could have chosen any word at all, but, wanting to keep the book in our minds, I selected *Pippi*.

I announced my choice and told Carolyn that her job was to tag my word.

"How do you tag a word?" Carolyn wisely asked.

"You do it with another word," I answered.

Carolyn looked puzzled.

"You can tag a word from the front or from the back. You tag *Pippi* from the front by saying a word that begins with the first sound you hear in *Pippi*, the *p* sound. *Pin* or *poem* or *post*, for instance, can all tag the front of *Pippi*. You tag *Pippi* from the back by saying a word that begins with the *last* sound you hear in *Pippi*—the sound *ee*. *Easy* or *evening* or *eat* are good words for tagging *Pippi* from the back," I explained.

"But *Pippi* ends in *i* and *easy* begins with *e*," she observed.

"True, but it is the sound that matters in SOUND TAG, not the letters," I replied. "Do you understand what I mean?"

"I think so," she said with some hesitation.

"Let's take your name: Carolyn. It begins with the letter *c* but the letter *k* makes the same sound. If I wanted to tag your name from the front, I could use the word *candy*, which begins with a *c*, or *kite*, which begins with a *k*. Can you think of a word that can tag *kite* from the back?" I asked.

"Would I use the *e*?" she asked in return.

"Say the word and tell me the last sound you hear. Don't think about the spelling. Just concentrate on the sound," I said.

"Kite. *T*, I hear the *t* sound," she said.

"Absolutely. That means you can tag *kite* with *tickle* or *tummy* or *terrific*," I said.

"I get it. But how do I know whether to tag *Pippi* from the front or the back?"

"Excellent question, and the answer lies in this coin," I said, taking a quarter out of my pocket. "I toss the quarter. If it lands on heads, you tag my word from the front. If it lands on tails, you tag my word from the back."

Carolyn nodded. I tossed the coin, and it came up tails. "That means you must tag the last sound in *Pippi*."

"I need an *ee* word," she said.

"That's right," I agreed.

"I guess I'll take *eat*," she said. "What happens next?"

"Next I have to tag your word. This time, you toss the coin. If it lands on heads, I need a word that begins with the sound *ee*. If it lands on tails, I need a word that begins with the sound *t*."

After I tagged *eat* with *eel*, Carolyn asked how she could win the game.

"Another excellent question. We keep taking turns trying to tag words. If you get stuck and can't tag one of my words, you automatically lose. The same for me. If you manage to tag me ten times, though, you win. For me to win, I have to stop you before that happens. But I'll be nice. If you have trouble figuring out the beginning or ending sound, I'll help. Oh, one more thing, you cannot use the same word twice. That means you cannot tag *eel* with *eat*," I explained.

"I've already tagged you once," she said.

"Nine more, and you win. Are you ready to tag *eel*? If you are, I'll flip the quarter," I said.

"I'm ready!" she answered.

It took about ten minutes for Carolyn to beat me. She enjoyed herself thoroughly and walked away from our work time giggling.

I was happy, too. Carolyn had listened intently to a series of words and had managed to isolate either their initial or their final sounds. Not only that, she was able to think of new words beginning with specific sounds. It is not always easy for children to identify the particular sounds that make up words, but it is important to do so. Identifying the particular sounds helps children with both spelling and reading. Identifying the sounds in words is an essential skill.

Thanks to *Pippi Longstocking* and SOUND TAG, I always had a valuable way to spend a spare few minutes during Carolyn's tutoring sessions. If your child enjoys the game as much as Carolyn did, you can play it at home, in the pizza parlor, in the Laundromat—anytime, anywhere that you can flip a coin.

In the last chapter of *Pippi Longstocking*, Pippi throws a birthday party for herself. She invites Tommy and Annika, her neighbors and best friends. The three children share presents and eat cakes. And they play a party game—Pippi's own invention—called Don't Touch the Floor. In Pippi's game, the children must make their way around the kitchen without letting their feet, or any other part of their bodies, come into contact with the ground. There is only one way to do this. They must climb over counters, crawl along shelves, and leap to neighboring chairs as they traverse the room. Virtually all the children I know wish they could enter the book and join the fun. Short of that, they'd like to play the game in their own homes with their own friends.

Naturally, being a responsible parent, you cannot sanction a climbing, crawling, and potentially tumbling-from-counter-to-floor game. You can, however, safely and responsibly engage your child in a less dangerous version of Pippi's birthday fun.

To begin with, you need six game mats and six game cards. For the mats, use six sheets of 8½″ × 11″ paper. For the game cards, use six 3″ × 5″ index cards. Hand your child the mats and keep the cards for yourself. On each card, write a word or words that have special significance in *Pippi Longstocking*. On the first card, you might write *Pippi*. As you do so, your child will inscribe *Pippi* on one of his papers. On your second card, you could write *Villa Villekulla*. Then wait for your child to copy the words. Continue picking other people, places, or events to fill in the remaining cards and matching sheets. You could include *Tommy, Annika, schoolhouse, giving tree, Mr. Nilsson, robbers, policemen, Mighty Adolf, horse, ringmaster, teacher, Mrs. Settergren, pluttifikation*, or *coffee party*.

Next you must create a playing field. The field must have a hard surface. You might play on a wooden or linoleum floor, for instance. And you need an empty area large enough for

GRADES

first and second

MATERIALS

sheets of 8½″ × 11″ paper, 3″ × 5″ index cards, two pens or pencils, masking tape

SKILLS

developing a willingness to read and to write

your child to jump from here to there. This may mean pushing a chair or an intrusive table up against the wall. When you have cleared a space, take the paper mats and, using masking tape, secure them to different spots on your playing field.

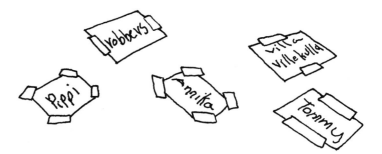

Tell your child to slip off his shoes, since this game is best played in stocking feet. Take the index cards, shuffle them, and hold the deck so that you do not see the words. Pick the first card and read it. If it says *Annika*, your child goes and stands on the *Annika* mat that lies somewhere on the floor. His feet must be on the paper—since the idea is not to touch the floor. But if a toe slips over the edge, do not be too strict.

Pick the next card. If it says *robbers*, your child must try to leap, or jump, or otherwise transport himself in a single bound to the corresponding mat. If he avoids the floor and lands on the mat—or mostly on it—all is well. If you read every card and your child makes every jump, he wins. If, however, he misses a mat and winds up on the floor, he automatically loses. Either way, you can feel free to play again. And since you will mix up the cards, thereby changing the order of jumps, your child faces a new physical challenge with each game.

After a bit of play, some of the mats will tear apart. When this happens, you or your child can make replacements. If you want, you can also add mats (and matching index cards). Depending on the size of your playing field, you can have eight, nine, ten, or more sheets taped to the floor.

Your child might insist that you try jumping, and you should not hesitate to comply.

This game is fun to play, but it also does something useful. It gets children writing as they label game mats, and gets them reading as they leap about the room. Younger children might not be able to handle so much writing, and they may need help reading some of the words. Give as much assistance as necessary. With some children, I do almost all the writing. With others, I write the words in light pencil strokes and let the children trace my letters. Over the years, I have found that making cards and mats, and adding new ones as needed, can get even the most reluctant writers putting at least a few words on paper. Once a child has a positive experience with writing—any positive experience at all—he is usually a bit more willing to write again on future occasions.

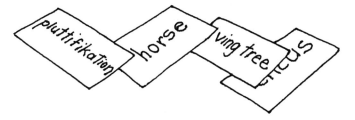

THING-FINDERS

GRADES

first, second, and third

MATERIALS

a variety of things

SKILLS

encouraging an active
imagination

*O*ne fine day, Pippi takes her friends Annika and Tommy on a thing-finding walk. Pippi, you see, is a Thing-Finder. What is a Thing-Finder? Here is Pippi's explanation: "The whole world is full of things, and somebody has to look for them. And that's what a Thing-Finder does."

But Pippi does not just find things, she also dreams up clever ways to make use of her discoveries. She sees an old can and announces that it will make an excellent cookie jar. She spots an empty spool of thread and envisions it as a bubble blower.

Could you come up with such an innovative use for a spool of thread? How about your child? Here is a way to find out. Start by searching your house for some little thing—a paper clip, a bottle cap, or a sock. Whatever you pick, challenge your child to think of the most unusual way he can imagine to use your found object. After sharing his idea or ideas, have your child hunt down a thing for you to contemplate. You each make three searches, present each other with three found things, and think up three ingenious uses. If along the way you fail to come up with an inventive use for one of your child's discoveries, you lose the game. The same holds true for your child. But if neither of you loses, you can proudly declare yourselves THING-FINDERS in the truest Pippi tradition.

While you play this quick game, you foster an important aspect of your child's intellect—his imagination. When a youngster observes that a sock could make an excellent sleeping bag for one of his action figures, he is stretching his imagination by looking at a familiar object and seeing it in a new way. It is not easy to give a fresh look to familiar objects, but ingenuity lies at the heart of thinking creatively and imaginatively.

MR. POPPER'S PENGUINS

WRITTEN BY RICHARD AND FLORENCE ATWATER
ILLUSTRATED BY ROBERT LAWSON
1938
NEWBERY HONOR BOOK
GOOD READING FOR FIRST, SECOND, AND THIRD GRADES

Mr. Popper is a house painter in the pleasant city of Stillwater, where he lives a quiet life with his wife and two children. But Mr. Popper dreams of wilder things. He wants to be a daring global adventurer—a Himalayan trekker, a diver for pearls in the South Seas, a lion hunter in India, and, most glorious of all, a partner in one of Admiral Drake's grand polar expeditions. Until now, Mr. Popper could only read about other people's adventures or catch glimpses of their exciting lives in newsreels. Everything changes, though, when a huge carton arrives on his doorstep.

What is inside the carton? A penguin, an honest-to-goodness live penguin. This splendid animal, arriving directly from Antarctica, is a gift from the great Admiral Drake himself. Thrilled, Mr. Popper names his new pet Captain Cook in honor of the world-famous explorer.

It is soon apparent that caring for Captain Cook will present Mr. Popper with a wide assortment of problems. Where can he find a sufficiently cold place for his penguin to nest? What will he feed Captain Cook? How does one take a penguin out for a walk? And, most troubling of all, how can an underemployed house painter pay for the upkeep of his new and demanding pet? Then the challenges multiply. Captain Cook gets a mate, Greta, and, shortly thereafter, Greta gives birth to ten baby penguins. But Mr. Popper never fails his penguins. Somehow he manages to come up with clever, humorous, and unforgettable ways to solve each and every predicament.

Mr. Popper has an inventive mind, and that is a wonderful advantage. As you read the book, you might stop once in a while to praise his ingenuity. If you hold the creative way he solves problems in high esteem, your child will, too.

In between chapters, why not try out the following activities with your child?

MR. ASTOR'S ANTS

GRADES

first, second, and third

OPTIONAL MATERIALS

a children's dictionary

SKILLS

analyzing sounds in words

Mr. Popper's Penguins is a wonderful book title because of the amusingly alliterative repetition of the letter *p*. The goal of playing MR. ASTOR'S ANTS is to come up with your own name-and-animal-sound repeating combinations. Using the letter *a*, you might choose any of quite a few names: *Astor, Acevedo, Acker, Allen, Adams* . . . And you might choose any of several animals: *ant, antelope, alpaca, alligator* . . . Link names with animals and you can get *Mr. Astor's ants, Mr. Acevedo's antelope, Mr. Acker's alligator,* or *Mr. Allen's alpaca.* When you are satisfied with your name and animal combination for the letter *a*, move on to *b*. Now you might end up with *Mr. Bellow's beagles, Mr. Berman's butterflies, Mr. Boswell's bats,* or *Mr. Bigalow's bison.* Go on to *c* and you could have *Mr. Caruso's caterpillars, Mr. Carlyle's canaries,* or *Mr. Carmichael's chameleons.* You cannot use *Mr. Culpepper's centipedes,* though. *Centipede* does begin with the letter *c*, but the *c* in *centipede* doesn't represent the same sound as the *c* in *Culpepper.* In this game, both the first letters and the first sounds must match. You could, therefore, use *Mr. Cesar's centipedes.*

There are two ways to play this game. In the first version, you pick any letter of the alphabet. Then come up with a certain number of name and animal matches. You could aim for two, or three, or five.

In the second version, you go straight through the alphabet

making matches for as many of the twenty-six letters as you can. You start with *a: Mr. Astor's ants*. Follow with *b: Mr. Berman's butterflies*. Next you'll work on *c* and then *d*, and so on until *z*.

If you have a children's dictionary, it can be fun and helpful to look through it for animals. I came up with *ant* and *alligator* on my own. It was only by flipping through the dictionary, though, that I thought of *alpaca*.

A children's dictionary will not offer much assistance with *q*, *u*, *v*, *x*, *y*, and *z*. To help you out, therefore, here are some exotic animals that you and your child might enjoy using when you play.

Q: (aside from quail)
    quetzal, a bird from South America
    quokka, a marsupial from Australia
U: (aside from unicorn)
    Ulysses butterfly from Australia and Indonesia
    umbrella bird from South and Central America
V: (aside from vulture)
    vampire bat from Central and South America
    velociraptor, a small meat-eating dinosaur
X: (aside from X-ray fish)
    xenops, a bird from South America
    Xenopeltis unicolor, the sunbeam snake from southeast Asia and India
Y: (aside from yak)
    yellow mongoose, a mammal from South Africa
    yellowhammer, the state bird of Alabama
Z: (aside from zebra)
    zorilla, a skunklike mammal from Africa
    zorro, a doglike fox from South America

You can make either version of the game harder by joining a person with an animal and then giving the animal something to eat—*Mr. Astor's ants eat anchovies*.

While considering the three words *Astor*, *ants*, and *anchovies*, your child will focus his attention on a single sound in each word—the first sound. And when he tries to think of an animal to match with Mr. Berman, he will mentally sort through bird, beast, insect, and fowl, until he finds one that begins with the sound he needs. These may seem like easy tasks, but for children, paying such close attention to individual sounds in words can be a challenge. It is a challenge they must master, though, in order to become fluent readers and writers.

What should you do if your child has trouble thinking up a name, an animal, or a food for a specific sound? Make suggestions. Should *Mr. Victor's vultures eat vinegar or violets*? Then let your child decide. Whichever delicacy he picks, congratulate him on choosing such an inspired combination of clever words.

MR. VICTOR'S

VULTURE

May I have the violets, please?

VIBRANT VINEGAR

"**L**ook at what I got," Allie said on entering my office. Then she handed me a small, soft, cuddly stuffed animal shaped like a penguin.

"How sweet! Look at its little flippers and adorable eyes," I said.

"I got it from my mom. She's reading *Mr. Popper's Penguins* to me. I like Captain Cook so much my mom gave me my own penguin," Allie explained.

"It's an excellent gift, and it gives me an idea," I said.

"What?" Allie asked.

"We could write our own book about penguins."

"I don't feel like writing," Allie said immediately.

I was not surprised by her response. Allie never felt like writing.

"But this book will be very special and very unusual," I said.

Allie looked a little interested.

"This book will be not only about penguins, but shaped like a penguin."

"Can we really make a book that looks like a penguin?" she asked.

"I think we can. It is certainly worth trying, don't you agree?" I replied.

Allied nodded her head and smiled. Permission granted, I took out two sheets of poster board. These sheets measured 11″ × 14″. My first job was to cut both pieces down to 8½″ × 11″.

PENGUIN BOOK

GRADES

first, second, and third

MATERIALS

two sheets of white poster board, four sheets of 8½″ × 11″ paper, scissors, pencil, black marker, stapler

SKILLS

developing skill and confidence in writing

Mr. Popper's Penguins

We would use the shortened sheets for the front and back covers of the book. On the rough side of one sheet, I drew the outline of a penguin.

I started with a rectangle. This was the penguin's body.

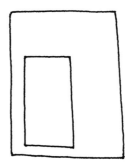

Then I drew an oval on top of the rectangle.

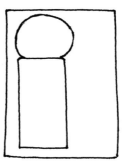

Next I drew the beak.

I drew a curved line from the top of the rectangle to the bottom. This was the penguin's belly.

Alongside the curved line, I drew a wedge shape for the penguin's feet.

I added a flipper to the body and an eye to the head.

Then I gave Allie a black marker so that she could color in the penguin's black feathers.

When she was finished, I pulled out four sheets of 8½″ × 11″ plain white paper. Next I made a pile of sheets. The penguin drawing was on the top of the pile. The four plain sheets of paper came next, and the second piece of poster board was on the bottom. I took the scissors and very, very carefully cut along the outline of the penguin. When I was done, we had two pieces of poster board and four sheets of paper—all penguin-shaped.

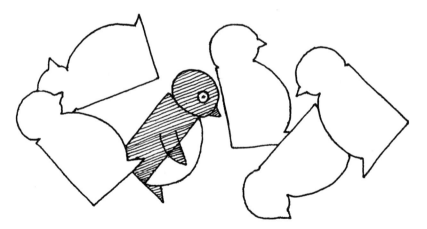

I held the pages together while Allie took a stapler and ran a row of staples down the left-hand side of the penguin.

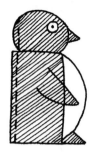

"*Voilà*, a penguin-shaped book. How do you like it?" I asked Allie.

"It's neat," she said, "but I don't have anything to write."

Ignoring her protest, I said, "First you need a title page. Do you have a good idea for a title?"

"*Penguin,*" she said.

"Excellent. Here's a pencil. You can begin by writing the title, *Penguin*, and your name, *Allie*, since you're the author. You'll write on the first page," I said as I opened the book.

"How do you spell *penguin*?" she asked.

I told her, and she started writing.

As soon as she was done, I turned the page. "What do you like about penguins?" I asked.

"I like the way they waddle," she said.

"That's perfect. You can write 'I like the way penguins waddle.' I'll help you spell *waddle*, if you want."

"Okay," she said.

"You can fit another idea on the right-hand side. Can you tell me what penguins look like when they waddle?"

"They look silly," she said.

"Write that. 'They look silly.' "

"Now what?" she asked.

"You can draw a picture if you want," I said.

She wanted.

Time to turn the page.

"What would you like to do with a penguin?" I asked. Allie's answer filled up two pages.

Allie had her own idea for the next two pages.

When I turned the page again, we were at the end of the book, and so Allie put down:

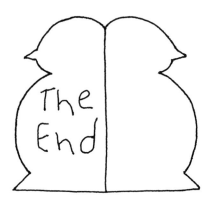

"Allie, you wrote a whole book!" I said.

"Can I take it home? I want to show my mom."

"You sure can."

"I didn't think I could write a book so fast," she said.

"It is a wonderful accomplishment. Too bad Mr. Popper can't read it," I said, and we both laughed.

Producing her PENGUIN BOOK was an important event for Allie. It was the first time that she was truly proud of her writing, and she enjoyed the feeling.

If you like the idea of making a PENGUIN BOOK and think your child will, too, it is easy enough to gather the necessary materials and begin. Allie wrote individual thoughts about penguins in her book. Your child might want to do the same. It is possible, though, that he would prefer writing an imaginative story about penguins. Or he might like to learn a few true facts about penguins and write one fact on each page. That would make an interesting book.

No matter what your child chooses to write, after he completes his PENGUIN BOOK don't put it on a shelf and forget about it. Instead, display it in some prominent spot, snap a photo of it for the family album, invite grandparents and other relatives over for a public reading. It is a big accomplishment to write a book, even a very short one, and so your child's creation warrants special attention.

*L*aura was in second grade and a very shy child. Her teachers complained that since she never spoke up in class, they were not sure she understood what they were teaching. Even working one-on-one with me, Laura was reluctant to express her ideas. On the rare occasions she did open up, I discovered that she was a creative and imaginative thinker. But when I complimented Laura on her perceptions, she was surprised. For some reason, she believed that her ideas were of little interest or value.

How could I persuade her otherwise? The game YOUR SOLUTION turned out to be, at least in part, the answer to this question. I introduced YOUR SOLUTION after reading about the blizzardy day Mr. Popper transformed his living room into a snow-filled playground for penguins and children.

"Imagine tobogganing in the living room! That wonderful Mr. Popper, he certainly figures out excellent ways to take care of his penguins. I think he must be one of the world's greatest problem solvers," I said.

"I wish I could toboggan in my living room."

"But you live on the eighteenth floor," I noted.

"We could move."

At that we both laughed.

When we stopped giggling, I said, "Laura, do you know what a clever thinker you are? You came up with such an interesting idea just now. Why, you're another world-class problem solver, just like Mr. Popper. In fact, your smart thinking just gave *me* an idea. I'm going to make up a problem—a problem starring Captain Cook, the penguin. It

YOUR SOLUTION

GRADES

first, second, and third

SKILLS

encouraging creative thinking
and an active imagination

will be a hard problem, and you will have to think of a solution, just the way Mr. Popper had to think of solutions to his problems. If you solve the problem, you win the game, but if you don't, I win. What do you say? Do you want to play?"

"What if my solution is bad?" she asked in return.

"That doesn't matter. If you can think of any solution, even a very strange or silly solution, you still win," I said.

"Okay, I'll try," she agreed.

"Pretend it's Halloween and Captain Cook wants to go trick-or-treating. What costume should he wear to disguise himself?" I asked.

Laura cocked her head, a quizzical expression on her face. Now I got nervous. What if she failed to think of a solution? Before my worries got out of hand, Laura broke into a smile and said, "I know! He could be a penguin."

"A great solution! A penguin disguised as a penguin," I said, much relieved that she'd come up with an answer.

"Give me another," she insisted.

"Okay, here it is: Captain Cook likes to eat fish. What happens, though, if there are no canned or fresh fish at the market, and there is no place to go fishing nearby? How can Mr. Popper feed Captain Cook?"

"He could go to a neighbor," she said without hesitating.

"Fine answer!" I cheered.

"Give me another!"

"I will, next time."

"Good," she said.

For several weeks, I greeted Laura with a new problem at the beginning of each work session, and Laura managed to devise a solution every time. I was impressed; better yet, so was Laura.

In the following list you'll find the first two problems I posed for Laura plus four more. Use them with your child if you want.

- Pretend it's Halloween and Captain Cook wants to go trick-or-treating. What costume should he wear to disguise himself?
- Captain Cook likes to eat fish. What happens, though, if there are no canned or fresh fish at the market, and there is no place to go fishing nearby? How can Mr. Popper feed Captain Cook?
- Mr. Popper lets you take Captain Cook to a swimming pool so that he can go swimming, but you must have the penguin back home by five o'clock. It is four o'clock now, and you can't get Captain Cook to come out of the water. What will you do?
- You want to give Captain Cook a present, but it can't be food. What will you get him?
- Imagine that Mr. Popper offers to let you keep Captain Cook at your house for a week, but your mother does not think this is a good idea. What three things could you say to convince your mother to change her mind?
- Captain Cook can *gork* and *ork*, but it is hard to know what he means by these sounds. Mr. Popper thinks he understands his penguin, but he is not always sure. He wants your help communicating with Captain Cook. How can you help?

Every time your child comes up with a solution to one of these problems, even if the solution is illogical or appears simplistic, he is thinking creatively and using his imagination. How did Laura decide that Captain Cook should be a penguin for Halloween? First she had to imagine Halloween. Next she had to imagine Captain Cook going from door to door. Then she had to think about what he could wear. Finally, in a burst of inventive thought, Laura realized that Captain Cook was already in costume. There was a lot of intelligent thinking behind Laura's seemingly simple answer. Any game that encourages intelligent thinking is definitely worth playing.

STUART LITTLE

WRITTEN BY E. B. WHITE
ILLUSTRATED BY GARTH WILLIAMS
1945
GOOD READING FOR FIRST, SECOND, AND THIRD GRADES

Stuart Little is my favorite mouse. Oh, I love Frederick in Leo Lionni's *Frederick*, and I love Chrysanthemum in Kevin Henkes's *Chrysanthemum*—excellent books about adorable mice—but Stuart Little is my best beloved.

Mr. and Mrs. Frederick C. Little are two perfectly ordinary human beings, and so is their firstborn son, George. But their second child, Stuart, looks exactly like a mouse. Stuart stands two and a quarter inches high, and he has a tail, a pointy nose, and whiskers. But Stuart can talk, and walk on two legs, and he enjoys the finer things in life. Had they wanted, Mr. and Mrs. Little could have mailed their newborn son anywhere in the country for the cost of a three-cent postage stamp. But, as E. B. White, the book's author, explains, "his parents preferred to keep him." And it is lucky for us they did. In my opinion, every child should have the pleasure of sharing in Stuart's many adventures. There is his unforgettable trip down the bathtub drain; his unfortunate tour on a city garbage barge; and his travels in his own mouse-sized car as he searches far and wide for his true love, Margolo the bird.

Stuart often finds himself in odd or difficult circumstances, but whatever the situation, he invariably keeps his wits and maintains his decorum. Stuart is far more mature than his older brother, George, and a bit more sophisticated than his parents. It is not always easy to be small in the big world, as any child can tell you. But Stuart manages quite well. When a child reads about Stuart's successes, therefore, he can assure himself that although the world may be daunting, it can be conquered.

The following activities offer your child the chance to make his own boat, to write his own laws, and to defeat you in a measuring game.

*T*wo of the most memorable scenes in *Stuart Little* involve boats. Toward the beginning of the book, Stuart offers to take command of the *Wasp*, a model sailboat cruising its way around the lake in New York's Central Park. With Captain Little at the helm, the *Wasp* races against the unmanned sloop, the *Lillian B. Womrath*. It is a grueling contest for our brave captain. Despite the dangers and setbacks, though, the valiant mouse heroically pilots his craft to victory.

Things do not go as well later in the book when Stuart purchases a tiny birchbark canoe named *Summer Memories*. *Summer Memories* is a lovely boat, but it leaks. Stuart works hard to get the vessel into seaworthy condition so that he can take the very, *very* tiny Miss Harriet Ames out for a paddle on the river. When the boat is ready, Stuart hides it under some leaves. Later in the day, he returns only to find *Summer Memories* in shambles. The boat is ruined, and so is Stuart's dream of a perfect afternoon with Harriet Ames.

After reading about either of Stuart's boating adventures, your child might like to make his own miniature sailing ship— one he can guide, if not actually board and command. Making a sailboat requires a good bit of work. It is one of the few activities in this book that demands more of the adult than the child. Your child might get impatient watching you do so

MAKING A BOAT

GRADES

first, second, and third

MATERIALS

wine bottle cork, a sharp knife or an X-Acto blade, pen, acrylic paint, small paintbrushes, pushpin or thumbtack, toothpick, white paper, colored markers

OPTIONAL MATERIALS

large bowl or roasting pan of water

SKILLS

learning to think scientifically, completing a complicated project

much of the job, but the results should make up for any vexation experienced along the way.

You need a wine cork to make the base or hull of the boat. I suggest you plan a lovely supper for yourself, open a bottle of wine, and when you are done drinking, take the cork and put it in a safe place. Then some Saturday or Sunday, get the cork, get your child, and get started making your boat.

First you must change the shape of the cork. Using a sharp knife or an X-Acto blade, flatten one side like so:

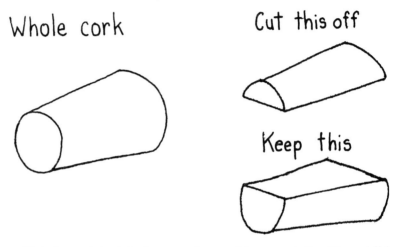

This is a tricky job, best performed by an adult with a child cheering from the sidelines. The second job is equally tricky and should also be done by an adult. Using a pen, draw lines that divide the flat side of the boat into three equal sections.

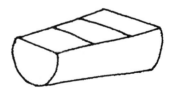

Then cut out a portion of the middle section. You should end up with an indent approximately the height of an eraser at the end of a pencil.

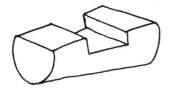

Don't be concerned, by the way, if the hull lacks elegance. Even if the lines are crooked, the boat will float, and that is the essential point.

Your child might be happy with a cork-toned boat, which is fine. On the other hand, he might prefer a more colorful vessel. If so, get some acrylic paints along with a couple of small paintbrushes, and let him liven up the boat with whatever colors or designs he chooses. Acrylic paints, which you can purchase at any art supply store, are best for this job because when they dry, they are waterproof.

To prevent the boat from wobbling as it sails, stick a pushpin or thumbtack into the bottom of the hull. This underside weight, or ballast, will keep your craft upright.

You must now make the mast and the sail. With guidance from you, your child can manage most of this work. To make the mast, he must first take a toothpick and snap about half an inch off one end.

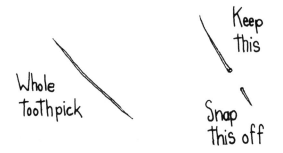

Next he needs to push the broken end of the toothpick into the hull. Since the broken end is not sharp, you might want to dig out a little hole first, using a pushpin or the sharp end of another toothpick. Then push the blunt end of the mast into the middle indented section of the cork, and twist until your mast is secure.

For the sail, cut out a rectangular piece of paper about the size of a large postage stamp. Then give your child colored markers and let him decorate the sail in any way he wants.

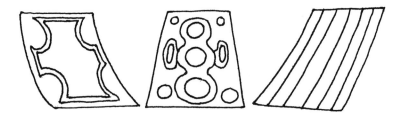

Pierce two holes in the colored sail, like so:

Slide the toothpick mast through the holes in the sail. Then roll the paper slightly so that the sail has a nice curve.

Your boat is now seaworthy.

You can sail it in a water-filled bowl, large roasting pan, sink, or bathtub. Blow gently on the sail and watch the ship lurch forward through the briny waves.

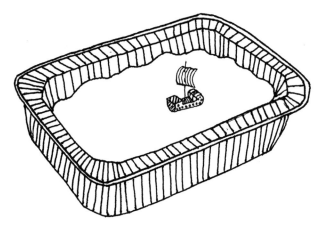

When your child has played with his boat for a time, ask him if he'd like to test a design change or two, just to see what will happen. He might cut out a new sail in the shape of a triangle, for instance.

Or he might try a trapezoid-shaped sail.

What happens if he puts two small sails on a single mast? How about if he adds a second mast and sail?

Will changing sails improve his boat? Or will the new sails cause his boat to wobble or even to tip over?

When you encourage your child to test different sails, you are also encouraging him to think scientifically. What, after all, does a scientist do when confronted with a problem? He thinks of alternative ways to address the issue, he tests his ideas, he considers the results, and he decides which solution works best. And your child will, in all probability, enjoy experimenting with sails. What could be better?

CHAIRMAN OF THE HOUSE

GRADES

second and third

MATERIALS

paper, colored markers

SKILLS

encouraging a sense of fun
with writing

*T*oward the end of *Stuart Little*, Stuart agrees to take temporary charge of the children at School Number Seven. There never has been and never will be a substitute teacher like Stuart Little. His first decision is to abandon arithmetic. Next, he nixes spelling, vetoes writing, and cancels social studies. But Stuart does have a lesson plan. First he declares himself Chairman of the World. He concedes that he is a rather small chairman, but wisely notes, "Size has nothing to do with it. It's temperament and ability that count." Then, being the world's chairman, he declares the need for world rules and cleverly engages the class in a lively discussion of good laws for his new regime.

After reading this chapter with my student Zach, I thought it would be an excellent idea to find out what rules he would call for if he were Chairman of the World.

Zach, it turned out, wanted to ordain world peace and end pollution. Those are worthy responses, but not very imaginative. Hoping for more originality, I suggested that, in our fantasies at least, I declare Zach Chairman of His House instead of Chairman of the World. Zach looked puzzled.

"Let's say that, for a time, I could put you in charge of your mother, father, and sister. During your term in office, you get to declare house laws—ones your whole family must obey. You might proclaim that, from now on, kids determine bedtimes. Or you could decide to eat nothing but ice cream all day long. Or you could . . ."

"I get the idea," said Zach. "How many laws can I make?"

"I think six or seven would be a good number."

"I can come up with more than that," he said.

"Excellent. Of course, you must write your ideas on a piece of paper to make them proper laws," I said.

I knew that, given the chance, Zach would object to writing his laws. He would propose all sorts of clever reasons why a written code was totally unnecessary. Before he could argue, therefore, I grabbed a sheet of paper along with a package of colored markers and suggested that he write each law in a different hue. Zach, having something of an artistic streak, liked the idea of colorizing his legal system. To my delight, and somewhat to my surprise, he picked up a red marker and, without a word, started writing.

True, his dictum, *Lots of candy*, does not express a great amount of legalistic eloquence. His dictum is not even a sentence. Nevertheless, for Zach, writing these three words was an important accomplishment. To my knowledge, this was the first time he had written words on paper without a fight. I wanted to applaud, but I contained myself. Applauding might have overwhelmed rather than encouraged him. I did, however, chuckle in appreciation of Zach's first law. My understated but authentically pleased reaction bolstered his confidence and led him to write a second law, in blue, followed by a third, in green.

After this initial burst of lawmaking, Zach bogged down. We chatted for a few minutes about possibilities, and soon enough he had a new idea.

Writing four laws in a row was all that Zach could comfortably handle, and so we stopped working on the list and took up other matters. In our next session, though, Zach continued writing legislation, and soon he had eight laws in eight different colors. He was very proud of himself—as he should have been.

lots of candy
no bedtime
no clean up
no bath
no toothbrushing
any food I want
no chores
no turning off TV

After reading about Stuart's morning at School Number Seven, you might ask your child if he would care to be CHAIRMAN OF THE HOUSE. If he would, ask him to write laws he believes should govern your home. Knowing your child's grievances in life, you will probably anticipate most of his ideas. But there could be a surprise or two, and those surprises might give you new insight into your child's thoughts and feelings. "Live and learn," as Stuart Little once said.

CHAIRMAN of the HOUSE

*A*ccording to Stuart, he is two and a quarter inches tall. Can you envision two and a quarter inches? Can your child? No need to imagine. Find yourself a ruler, a sheet of paper, and a pencil and then draw a line that is JUST STUART'S SIZE.

GRADES

first, second, and third

MATERIALS

ruler, paper, pen or pencil, scissors

SKILLS

learning to estimate size, learning to use a ruler accurately

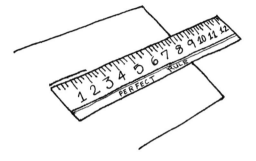

After spending a moment looking at Stuart's size and considering what it would feel like to be so small, you can play a game based on those two and a quarter inches. Before you can begin, though, you must use the line you drew to make a rectangle.

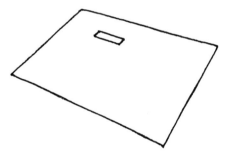

And then cut out the rectangle. This strip of paper is exactly Stuart's height.

Next make a second strip identical to the first. Give your child one strip and take the other.

Now for the game. The rules are simple. You and your child search the house until you find something JUST STUART'S SIZE—or as close to it as possible. You can set limitations: no sharp objects and no climbing on furniture to reach high shelves, for instance. You and your child have exactly five minutes to search. After five minutes (tracked either with a stopwatch or with your wristwatch) reconvene and present your finds. The one who has discovered something closest to Stuart's size wins the game.

If you don't feel like traipsing about your house, try this variation. You and your child should both study your Stuart-sized strips for about a minute. Then place both strips out of sight. On a fresh sheet of paper, draw a line—trying your best to make the line JUST STUART'S SIZE. Your child follows suit. When you are done, compare your results with the strips. The one who drew a line closest to Stuart's size wins.

While playing JUST STUART'S SIZE, your child will measure two and a quarter inches with a ruler; will hunt for a Stuart-sized object around the house; will draw a line close as possible to Stuart's height; will compare the found object or the drawn line with the rectangular strip to see how well he estimated; and will then compare his results with yours. That's a lot of measuring and estimating. If you and your child enjoy yourselves, you don't have to stop playing. You could, for instance, find objects or draw lines that are twice or even triple Stuart's size. Or you might try cutting the rectangular strip in half, which will leave you with Stuart Very Little.

CHARLOTTE'S WEB

WRITTEN BY E. B. WHITE
ILLUSTRATED BY GARTH WILLIAMS
1952
NEWBERY HONOR BOOK
GOOD READING FOR FIRST, SECOND, AND THIRD GRADES

*O*ne literary triumph was not enough for E. B. White. A few years after he published *Stuart Little*, White presented the world with *Charlotte's Web*, a magnificent tale of friendship and sacrifice. The story stars Wilbur, a lovable young pig with a terrible problem: he faces certain death. As soon as the weather turns cold, Farmer Zuckerman will slaughter Wilbur and turn him into bacon. It is inevitable—unless someone intervenes. Charlotte, an outstanding spider in every way, is that someone. But how can a spider save a pig? By doing what a spider does best—weaving webs. To save her friend, Charlotte weaves webs, exceptional webs, interlaced with words in praise of Wilbur-the-pig. Thanks to Charlotte and her mastery of words, Wilbur lives.

Sadly, though, Charlotte cannot escape her own spider's destiny. After creating her egg sac, Charlotte herself dies, bravely and alone. Spiders don't stay alive forever, after all. So, yes, Wilbur lives, but without Charlotte—"a true friend and a good writer."

Of course, Charlotte is more than a true friend. She is closer to being a perfect mother. She sings Wilbur lullabies and tells him bedtime stories. She is a willing and patient teacher to her young charge. At a crucial time in her own life, when she should be making her egg sac in the warmth of the Zuckerman barn, she travels to the county fair with Wilbur—just in case the pig should need her help. It is a great sacrifice, which Charlotte makes without complaint and without boasting of her good deed. But readers and listeners know and are filled with admiration for such a staunch and loving spider.

Wilbur outlives Charlotte by many years, but he never forgets her. Perhaps the following three activities will help you and your child remember Charlotte (and Wilbur, too) long after you've read the last page of *Charlotte's Web*.

FRIENDSHIP MEDALLION

GRADES

first, second, and third

MATERIALS

cardboard, drinking glass, pencil, scissors, newspaper, bowl of water, plastic container, paintbrush, acrylic paint, colored markers

SKILLS

appreciating the importance of books in our lives

*B*onnie charged into my office twice a week demanding to hear more of her favorite book, *Charlotte's Web*. I was happy to comply, and we spent ten minutes or so, I reading and Bonnie listening. It was an excellent way to begin our work sessions. While listening, Bonnie relaxed; she was quiet and attentive, and she retained this mood, which is most conducive to learning, even after I closed the book. Bonnie was in third grade and could barely read. This frightened and embarrassed her. As a result, she hated nearly everything having to do with reading. There was only one exception. Bonnie loved listening to books. This was good—very good. It meant that although learning was difficult, Bonnie understood that when she finally could read, the world was full of wonderful books for her to enjoy. I knew Bonnie's parents read to her every day. But with a child like Bonnie, listening to stories wasn't only a nice way to spend time; it was crucial. Thus the minutes that I spent with her reading aloud from *Charlotte's Web*. Of course, in ten-minute spurts it took us many weeks to finish the book. When we finally did, I felt we needed to commemorate the event.

Often while reading *Charlotte's Web*, Bonnie and I talked about friendship. We agreed that Charlotte was an exceptional friend to Wilbur and that Wilbur was a good and reliable friend in return. Given that friendship is such an important theme in the story, I wondered if there was anything Bonnie and I could do to salute friendship—the friendship between ourselves, as well as the friendship between Charlotte and Wilbur—as a way of memorializing the book. I asked Bonnie if she had any ideas.

"We could buy friendship necklaces," she said.

"Friendship necklaces? I've never heard of friendship necklaces. Can you explain them to me?" I asked.

"It's like this. A jeweler makes a silver heart. But then he cuts the heart in half and puts each half on its own chain. That makes two necklaces each with half a heart. You would take one necklace and I would get the other. Then when we meet, we can put the heart together and it will look really pretty. I know because that's what my sister and her best friend do with their friendship necklaces," she said.

I liked the idea of creating some sort of matched friendship token, but ours would have to be different from her sister's. After giving alternative possibilities some thought, I suggested that we make, not buy, a FRIENDSHIP MEDALLION.

"What's a medallion?" Bonnie asked.

"It's a large circular medal. You can wear it as a pendant on a chain, but you don't have to. It can just be a wonderful piece of decoration. We can make our FRIENDSHIP MEDALLION out of cardboard. First we'll paint the cardboard white so that it will look pretty. After we paint it, you can draw a picture on the front side with colored markers and I'll write words about friendship on the back. Then we'll cut the circle in two parts. I'll take one part and you'll take the other. I know that whenever I look at my part, I'll think of you, and the wonderful time we had reading *Charlotte's Web*."

Bonnie liked this idea and she was eager to get to work. To begin the project, we needed a sheet of cardboard. Lying on my desk was a yellow legal pad. The cardboard back, I realized, would be perfect for making a FRIENDSHIP MEDALLION.

After ripping the cardboard away from the paper, I went to the kitchen and got a drinking glass.

"What is that for?" Bonnie asked.

"It will help us draw a circle," I said.

I turned the glass over, placed it on the cardboard, and started drawing a line around the rim. As soon as Bonnie understood what I was doing, I gave her the pencil and let her finish the job.

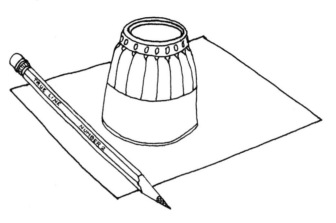

Next we had to cut out the circle. Bonnie insisted on trying, and so I let her. She did a fine job. True, the circle was not perfectly round, but neither of us cared.

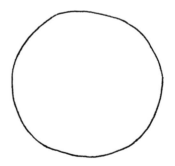

Our next step was to paint the medallion a pure white, using acrylic paint. Acrylic white is very bright and it does a good job of completely covering the cardboard gray. You can buy acrylic paints at any art supply store. Preparing everything for painting took a little time. First I covered my table with newspaper and got a bowl of water, an empty plastic container, a paintbrush, and a tube of paint. After putting all of the supplies on the newspaper, along with the cardboard circle, I squeezed some paint into the container and gave Bonnie the brush. I told her to moisten the brush by dipping it in the water.

Then she painted one side white, and when it was dry, I turned the circle over and told her to paint the back. While the back was drying, Bonnie and I cleaned up the mess.

When we returned to the table, I placed the bright white circle in front of Bonnie and handed her a set of colored markers. Without hesitation, she started to draw. In about five minutes, she completed her side of the medallion.

"Your turn," she said, pushing the circle in my direction.

"I'd like to start with the words *friendship is*, but I don't know what to put next. Do you have a suggestion?" I asked.

"Friendship is giving," she said.

"I like that. I also like *friendship is caring*. How about I write *friendship is giving* on one half of the circle and *friendship is caring* on the other? That way, after we cut the medallion in two, we will both get a friendship thought," I said.

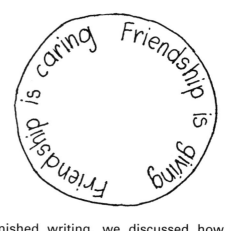

When I finished writing, we discussed how to cut the medallion. We could cut in a straight line or a wiggly one. Bonnie preferred wiggles. Using a pencil, I drew a snakelike line across the circle. I drew on the side with words to make sure that both parts of the medallion got a full friendship sentence.

"Would you like the honor of cutting the medallion?" I asked.

"I would," she replied.

"Go ahead, then," I said.

Bonnie snipped away, and when she was done, so was our medallion. We were both delighted with the results.

Before Bonnie left for the day, she selected one side of the medallion to take with her, and I kept the other.

It has been several years since Bonnie and I made our FRIENDSHIP MEDALLION, and several years since she was one of my students. I still have my part, though. I keep it in a box of mementos collected over my tutoring career. Every time I see it, I do indeed think of Bonnie, and of Charlotte and Wilbur, too. I wonder if Bonnie ever stumbles upon her half and, if she does, what thoughts come to her mind.

SINGLE-LINE
WEB GAME

GRADES

first, second, and third

MATERIALS

paper, pencil

SKILLS

learning to analyze a problem
thoughtfully

Charlotte's miracle webs are responsible for saving Wilbur's life. Of course, as Dr. Dorian, the wise physician in *Charlotte's Web*, points out, any spiderweb is a miracle of nature. Only spiders have the ability to create silken threads from their own bodies and then weave those threads into intricate designs. This task cannot be accomplished by man, woman, or child. But any man, woman, or child can play this web-making game. The rules are quite simple, but the game can prove rather challenging.

Take a look at this drawing:

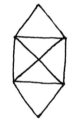

I drew it—my web—with a single line. I crissed and crossed, but I never retraced a line, and I never lifted my pencil from the paper. It's a lovely web, don't you think? Now here is a job for you. Copy my web. Draw it with a single line. Don't work alone, though. Instead, hand your child a pencil and let him work alongside you, copying the web for himself. If you both get stuck, below is one among several possible solutions.

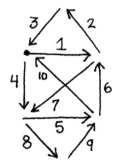

If you and your child enjoyed copying that web, here are four more you can try. You will find solutions on page 240.

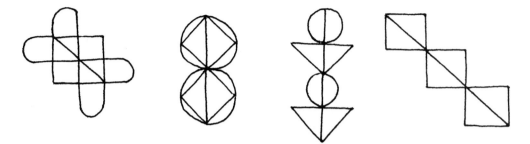

After mastering these webs—or giving up in frustration—you can design your own single-line web and let your child reproduce it. Then give your child a chance to make an original one-line web for you to copy. Do not expect him to make your life easy. Jon, a student of mine, once gave me this web to copy.

Not all webs, by the way, can be created in a single line. This very simple one, for instance, cannot.

Amazing, no?

You can avoid giving your child an impossible web like the one above by drawing all of your webs with a single line.

After a few webs, you will tire of this game, but, assuming you and your child had fun, you can return to web-making another day. This is a fine game to play while waiting for food in a restaurant or passing time in a doctor's office.

When your child first attempts to copy a web, he will probably forge ahead impulsively. He will begin drawing without giving much consideration to why one line should come before another. Soon enough he will notice that this approach has limitations. Reflecting a little, your child will realize that it is much better to slow down, analyze the drawing, think about the relationships between the lines, and consider possible ways to proceed. Discovering the value of making a thoughtful, considered effort when trying to solve problems is an important lesson for every child to learn.

When you are not in the mood to draw, you could always pull your copy of *Charlotte's Web* off the shelf and spend a few minutes admiring the amazing webs that Garth Williams, the book's illustrator, drew for Charlotte, the spider.

Here, in case you need them, are solutions to the four webs on page 239. There are other ways to complete each web. If you and your child want to give yourselves a superchallenge, you might try finding a second or even a third solution to your favorite web.

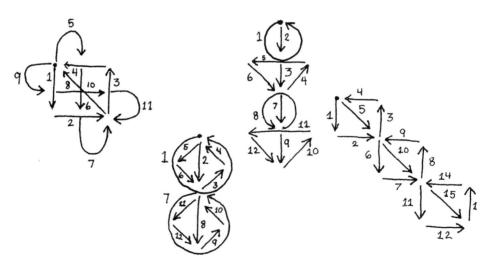

BLEND THE FRIENDS was Rachel's favorite game. We started playing while reading *Charlotte's Web*, but months after finishing the book, when I let her choose any activity she wanted, she invariably called out, "BLEND THE FRIENDS."

You begin the game by taking two or more names of people or pets or fictional characters who are good friends. The first time I played with Rachel, we used Charlotte and Wilbur. Then you divide the names into their individual syllables and write each syllable on a 3″ × 5″ index card.

Now you BLEND THE FRIENDS. How? By mixing up the syllables in an interesting way, and thereby making a single, long, nonsensical name. Perhaps you like

GRADES

first, second, and third

MATERIALS

3″ × 5″ index cards, pencil

SKILLS

learning to isolate the syllables in words, practice reading multisyllabic words

But you might prefer one of the following.

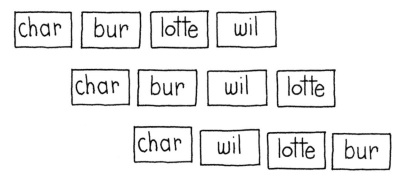

Rachel's favorite was

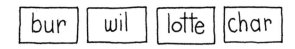

After Rachel and I created a blended name for Charlotte and Wilbur, we did the same for our own names. To make things more interesting, we used both our first and last names.

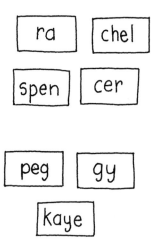

Soon we had a blend we liked.

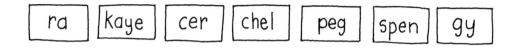

It was quite a mouthful and we both enjoyed saying it again and again—even though we stumbled over the syllables while doing so. But *rakayecerchelpegspengy* was not enough for Rachel. She wanted to add Sammy, her dog's name. After making cards for *sam* and *my*, I needed to explain something to Rachel. At the end of Sammy the letters *my* sounded like *me*. When the letters stand alone, though, they rhyme with *pie*. Since we wanted this to be a blended name, we needed to pronounce the *my* on the card the way it sounded when it was part of *Sammy*—no matter where we put that syllable in the word. Rachel immediately accepted this idea, and so we set about blending the three names.

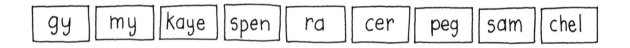

Every time we played, Rachel picked a new set of names to blend. She used family names. She used friends' names. She used the names of pets. She liked the list of names to get long and then longer. Once she included her name, her mother's name, her father's, her sister's, her best friend's, her dog's, and her cat's and ended up with a seventeen-syllable extravaganza. It was not easy for Rachel to sound out this very long word, but with my help she managed and, better yet, she was eager for more.

THE ENORMOUS EGG

WRITTEN BY OLIVER BUTTERWORTH
ILLUSTRATED BY LOUIS DARLING
1956
GOOD READING FOR FIRST, SECOND, AND THIRD GRADES

*C*hildren are fascinated by dinosaurs. It's an indisputable fact. Some children are so entranced they become expert paleontologists before leaving second grade. Other children are less engrossed, but I have yet to meet a child who is totally indifferent. No surprise, then, that children love *The Enormous Egg*, a book that tells the story of a dinosaur—a living dinosaur of today.

The story begins in Freedom, New Hampshire, where one summer's morning twelve-year-old Nate Twitchell's hen lays an enormous egg. The egg is 15 inches around and weighs 3¼ pounds. The poor hen cannot tend such a monstrosity without help, and so Nate lends a hand by turning it several times a day. Weeks and weeks go by, and it seems that all of Nate's labors have been in vain. But then the egg hatches, and a very strange lizardy creature crawls out of the shell. Later that day Nate learns that his unusual hatchling is a dinosaur—a triceratops, to be exact.

It isn't easy for Nate to feed his growing dinosaur. And the triceratops, christened Uncle Beazley, certainly grows. At birth he is 13½ inches long and weighs 3 pounds. Two and a half weeks later, Uncle Beazley is 5 feet 6 inches and weighs 144 pounds. Growth like that calls for a lot of grass.

At summer's end, it is clear that the dinosaur can no longer stay at the Twitchells'. Accompanied by Nate, Uncle Beazley moves to Washington, D.C., where he winds up at the National Zoo. There Dr. Ziemer, a kind and amiable paleontologist, can weigh and measure the triceratops every day. It is a good plan, or it is until United States senator Granderson discovers who is residing at the zoo. Senator Granderson thinks Uncle Beazley is an unnatural, un-American beast who should be exterminated. Don't worry: before the book ends, Nate saves Uncle Beazley. Virtue triumphs.

The next activities will help your child learn some valuable skills, which is their particular virtue.

By the time Uncle Beazley is an adult, he will be twenty feet long. That's an interesting fact, but only if you can visualize twenty feet. Is that as long as your desk? Your couch? Your rug? Your living room? Your house? Chances are good that your child won't know for sure. You can demonstrate, though, by cutting a twenty-foot length of ribbon.

Gather a roll of ribbon, a 12″ ruler, a black marker, scissors, and masking tape. When all is ready, have your child hold the ruler upright, in a vertical position.

HOW BIG IS UNCLE BEAZLEY?

GRADES

first, second, and third

MATERIALS

roll of colored ribbon that is at least twenty feet long, 12″ ruler, black permanent marker, scissors, masking tape

SKILLS

measuring, counting, estimating

Place the loose end of the ribbon at the top of the ruler and have your child hold it while you run a length of ribbon to the bottom. Then draw a line on the ribbon indicating one foot.

Slide the ribbon up the ruler until the one-foot mark is at the top. Your child will keep the ribbon in place while you pull down the roll until it reaches the bottom of the ruler. Draw another mark. Place this two-foot mark at the top of the ruler before pulling the roll of ribbon downward once again.

Do this twenty times, and then snip the ribbon. By now you probably have a lot of ribbon curled up on the floor.

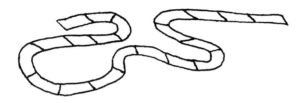

Give your child one end, while you take the other. Then start walking in opposite directions. You might have to untangle some ribbon, but soon you and your child will be standing twenty feet apart, with the ribbon taut between you. Gazing at the ribbon's span, your child will discover that twenty feet is no small matter.

Don't put the ribbon away yet, though. Instead, get ready to measure it in a few new and interesting ways. First lay the ribbon out full-length on the floor and tape it securely in place.

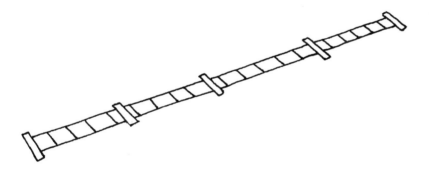

Once you have taped the ribbon, tell your child you want to know how many baby-steps long Uncle Beazley will be when fully grown. To find out, you would like your child to take tiny steps from one end of the ribbon to the other. He will probably be pleased to oblige. But don't start right away. Explain that first you intend to make an estimate, which is a thoughtful guess, of how many steps it will take. How do you make a thoughtful guess? In this case, by looking carefully at both the ribbon and your child's feet. When you have finished looking carefully, you should announce your estimate, and then ask your child for an estimate of his own. If your child does not want to guess a number, don't press. Either way, the child should now start baby-stepping, counting each step.

When he is about halfway down the ribbon, though, ask him to stop. Why? Because you want to reconsider your estimate. Are you still happy with your number? If so, fine. If not, make a change. Your child can change his estimate, too, of course. After you have both reconsidered your numbers, your child should continue walking and counting.

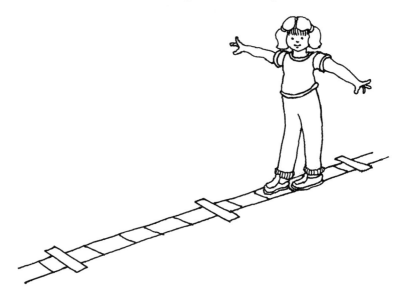

When he reaches the end of the ribbon, evaluate your estimates. Was your number close? Was your child's?

Next measure how many jumps it will take your child to traverse Uncle Beazley's length. How many giant steps? How many shoes will it take to cover the length of the ribbon? How many gloves? Socks? Pieces of notebook paper? No matter which way you measure the ribbon, you and your child (if he is willing) should both make an initial estimate and then, after measuring half the ribbon, reestimate. Before you announce an initial number, though, explain your thinking. "It took fifty-one baby steps for you to get from one end of the ribbon to the other. Giant steps are much longer than baby steps. That means you will need a lot less of them. I estimate you will need twenty." And when you reestimate, explain your thinking again. "It took you six giant steps to get halfway. I know that six and six make twelve. So I'm changing my estimate from twenty to twelve." Will your child understand your logic? Maybe. Maybe not. Even if he doesn't grasp your thinking, he will appreciate that you have reasons when you give a number, which is good in itself.

Don't expect your child to voluntarily explain his own thoughts, however, and don't ask him to. Often children have sound reasons for their estimates but lack the words to express their ideas. Asking for an explanation, then, may merely intimidate your child, which will ruin the fun.

When you finish measuring for the day, roll up the ribbon and put it in a safe place. Then, between reading chapters of the book, you can stretch the ribbon out and remind yourselves of Uncle Beazley's enormous adulthood size.

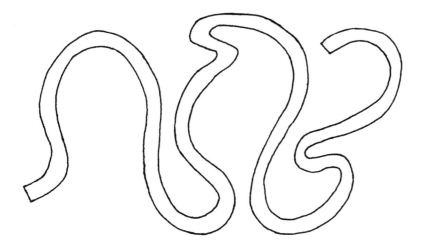

HOW BIG AM I?
HOW BIG WILL
I BE?

GRADES

first, second, and third

MATERIALS

two rolls of colored ribbons in
different colors, black marker,
scissors, 22″ × 28″ sheet of
poster board, glue, an inch
ruler, a centimeter ruler

SKILLS

measuring

You can't avoid talking about
size when you read *The Enormous Egg*. One of the great
pleasures in the book is tracking Uncle Beazley's startling
growth. And not just his length and weight. Shortly after Uncle Beazley hatches, Dr. Ziemer, the kind and amiable paleontologist, measures the baby dinosaur's head, tail, and legs.
Later in the book, Nate takes some measurements of his own.
He discovers that his arm is about the length of Uncle Beazley's upper horns, that Uncle Beazley's lower horn is about
half that long, and that the dinosaur's head stretches about
three feet.

Following Dr. Ziemer's and Nate's leads, consider measuring your child. But don't measure the child's head-to-toe size.
That is too ordinary. Instead, measure his nose, his big toe,
the circumference of his head, and the length of his neck.
Those are interesting things to measure. And you can measure them in an interesting way—with colorful pieces of ribbon, for instance. To begin, pick some part of your child's
body—the thumb of his right hand would be good. Unroll a
piece of ribbon to stretch the length of that thumb and draw a
line to mark the distance.

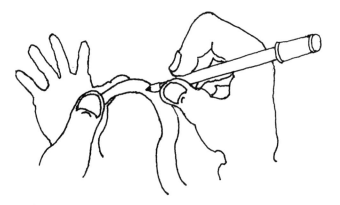

Using the line as a guide, let your child snip the ribbon.

What should you do with this piece of ribbon? You should use it to begin a HOW BIG AM I? HOW BIG WILL I BE? chart. It is simple to do. Take a 22″ × 28″ sheet of poster board and draw a baseline about 5 inches from the bottom.

Glue the ribbon to the chart, making sure that one end is on the baseline. Label the ribbon. Next use a ruler to measure the ribbon's height. I suggest measuring in both inches and centimeters. When you've got the numbers, write them down.

Thumb
5cm
2 in

Dr. Ziemer did not know for sure how big Uncle Beazley would be when fully grown. He could only estimate, using the skeletons of triceratops as reference. There is no way to be certain about the eventual length of your child's thumb, either, but the size of yours is probably a good approximation. This means that if you cut a ribbon the length of your thumb and glue it next to your child's, he can compare how big his thumb is now with how big it will be when he grows up. Since both ribbons start at the baseline, it is easy to see the differences in size. You will, of course, want to measure this second ribbon in both inches and centimeters and record the results. If a girl compares her thumb to her mother's and a boy compares his to his father's, the predictions will probably be more accurate. But it doesn't really matter if you cross sex lines.

Now pick another body part to measure. Then another. And another. The chart is especially effective, by the way, if you always use one color of ribbon to measure your child and a second color to measure yourself. You don't need to complete the chart all at once. You can measure thumbs, front teeth, and ears today. Then measure wrists, smiles, and feet next Tuesday. And so on until the chart is full. That's that, unless you

want to get a second sheet of poster board so that you can
measure some more.

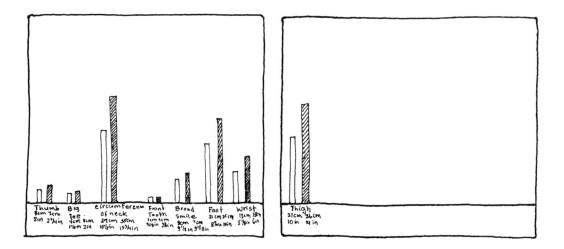

Think of all the measuring your child will do while working
on the chart. He will find the ribbon length of body part after
body part—both his and yours. He will measure those ribbons
in both inches and centimeters, and he will probably do so enthusiastically, since most children love finding out about
themselves. True, it would be even more exciting to measure
Uncle Beazley, but it might be hard to get him in the house.

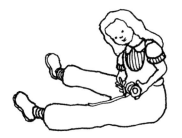

EGG LATIN

GRADES

third

SKILLS

analyzing sounds in words

You have probably heard of Pig Latin. Perhaps, at one point in your life, you were a fluent speaker. If so, you will find it relatively easy to master a variation on the ancient childhood tongue called EGG LATIN, which I have invented in honor of Nate Twitchell's enormous egg. When you speak EGG LATIN, you take a word such as *book* and remove the first sound. Now you have *ook*. Next, take the removed sound, *b*, and combine it with *egg*, giving you *begg*. Move the new syllable, *begg*, to the end of the word. This gives you *ook-begg*, which is *book* in EGG LATIN. Similarly, *hay* would be, in EGG LATIN, *ay-hegg*. To translate words with more than one syllable, you do things a little differently. Here's how it works with the word *triceratops*. First, drop the entire first syllable. This gives you *cer-a-tops*. Now, take that first syllable, *tri*, and move it to the end of the word. This gives you *cer-a-tops-tri*. Next, add a final *egg: cer-a-tops-tri-egg*. To translate *Beazley*, drop the first syllable, *bea*, to get *zley*, move the *bea* to the end of the word and get *zley-bea*. Add an *egg*, and you have *zley-bea-egg*.

It will take time and patience to teach your child EGG LATIN. Teaching it is a good way, though, to spend your time and exercise your patience. When speaking EGG LATIN, your child must concentrate on breaking words into syllables. When he translates Beazley into *zley-bea-egg*, he identifies *bea* as the first syllable of the word, separates that syllable from the rest of the word, and then moves the syllable to the end of the word. The more EGG LATIN your child speaks, the more comfortable he will feel splitting words into syllables. Why is that important? Children who are adept at breaking words into syllables tend to do so automatically when spelling long words. Imagine that your child wants to write *triceratops*. A hard job, if he thinks about the whole word. But it's not such a hard job if he spontaneously divides the word into smaller pieces—*tri-cer-a-tops*. Then again, once you and your child are EGG LATIN speakers, you will share a secret language, which might prove useful on occasion.

If you find, however, that your child cannot figure out how to talk in this new way and has no desire to learn, drop the lessons.

Assuming your child does want to master EGG LATIN, though, what words should you use to teach him? I would start with a selection from *The Enormous Egg: Nate* (*ate-negg*), *Uncle* (*cle-un-egg*), *Beazley* (*zley-bea-egg*), *dinosaur* (*no-saur-di-egg*), *enormous* (*nor-mous-eh-egg*), and *egg* (*guh-eh-egg*).

Ood-gegg uck-legg! Ave-hegg un-fegg!

MRS. PIGGLE-WIGGLE'S MAGIC

WRITTEN BY BETTY MACDONALD
ILLUSTRATED BY HILARY KNIGHT
1949
GOOD READING FOR SECOND AND THIRD GRADERS

*D*oes your child have dreadful table manners? Does he charge around the house breaking everything in sight? Interrupt while you're speaking? Your darling child? Maybe sometimes he does. What should you do about such misbehavior? If you knew Mrs. Piggle-Wiggle, you could call on this remarkable little woman for help. Who is Mrs. Piggle-Wiggle? She is a widow who lives in an upside-down house and always has time for the boys and girls in her neighborhood. The children love visiting Mrs. Piggle-Wiggle. She never gets angry. She understands children's needs and wants. She sees the best in everyone and everything. And she bakes great cookies.

Most important of all, childhood foibles don't upset Mrs. Piggle-Wiggle. She realizes children pretend to be sick in order to avoid school. She expects outbreaks of nasty tattling. Better yet, she cures children of their naughty ways.

In every chapter of *Mrs. Piggle-Wiggle's Magic*, except the first and last, a new family requests Mrs. Piggle-Wiggle's help, and Mrs. Piggle-Wiggle, using her collection of magic formulas, comes to the rescue.

Betty MacDonald, the author, takes common childhood problems and, using exaggeration, makes children laugh rather than cringe at their misdeeds. Then she offers foolproof cures, thus demonstrating that even if a child is rude, careless, or selfish, such bad traits need not last a lifetime.

There are four Mrs. Piggle-Wiggle books: *Mrs. Piggle-*

Wiggle, *Mrs. Piggle-Wiggle's Magic*, *Mrs. Piggle-Wiggle's Farm*, and *Hello, Mrs. Piggle-Wiggle*. The books are not sequential, so you can start with any of them. In my opinion, the funniest and most imaginative is *Mrs. Piggle-Wiggle's Magic*.

The books, written in the 1940s and 1950s, reflect their time. Dads go to work while moms stay home. Girls bake cookies while boys play pirates. There are a couple of racial references that made me uncomfortable, although not in *Mrs. Piggle-Wiggle's Magic*—another reason I prefer this book. It's easy, though, to discuss these issues with your child, if you choose to. And the books are so much fun and so special, a discussion or two won't stop you and your child from enjoying the stories.

The activities below won't cure either you or your child of any bad habits—at least not permanently. But they will give your child amusing ways to practice some important skills.

Mrs. Piggle-Wiggle only cures children, but let's be honest, adults are not without flaws. I'm sure your child can find something in your personality worth altering. Maybe you are too much of a neatness freak. Possibly you have this ridiculous hangup about sweets. Could it be that you're overly particular in regard to bedtime? Wouldn't it be wonderful—from your child's point of view—if a magical drink could cure you of your most irritating trait? Perhaps there can be such a cure—a fantasy remedy, to be sure, and of limited duration. Still, that's better than nothing.

After reading one or two Piggle-Wiggle stories with Jamila, I asked her to name my most annoying imperfection. She looked confused, and so I made a few suggestions. Was it my requirement that she learn to spell five new words a week? Was it my insistence on giving her work to do at home? Did I make her read too much? That was it. I made her read *much* too much. Naturally, I had a different point of view, but for the

MY MOM (OR DAD) NEEDS A CURE

GRADES

second and third

MATERIALS

paper, pencil, a variety of edibles, serving spoon, measuring spoons and cup with metric markings, jar with a secure lid

SKILLS

writing, adding, subtracting, measuring

sake of this particular activity, I accepted her evaluation. I asked if she wanted to cure me of this atrocious habit. She answered with a very loud "Yes!" followed by an inquisitive "How?"

I explained that recently I had learned the way to make a short-term cure, one suitable for any and every problem, from my dear friend Mrs. Piggle-Wiggle. Yes, Mrs. Piggle-Wiggle herself. Naturally, Jamila was skeptical. She knew how to take advantage of make-believe, though, and so she went along with the illusion. The cure, I informed Jamila, required a magic formula. There were any number of ways to make the formula, but certain rules must be followed.

First, the formula must be a drink made up of exactly five ingredients. Second, there had to be at least 100 milliliters of formula but not more than 250 milliliters. Third, the ingredients had to be perfectly measured and then poured into a jar. Fourth, to work, the formula had to be recorded on paper. Fifth, when all the ingredients were in the jar, the formula must be given a thorough shaking. Finally, the cure had to be absolutely delicious.

Not only had Mrs. Piggle-Wiggle taught me how to make the cure, she had also typed up a list of possible ingredients:

yogurt (any flavor)	milk
chocolate syrup	maple syrup
chocolate milk	pineapple juice
orange juice	apricot nectar
apple juice	grape juice
lemonade	ginger ale
raspberry jam	apricot jam
melted ice cream	butterscotch sauce
chocolate pudding	marshmallow fluff
mashed banana	applesauce
mashed strawberries	mashed blueberries
honey	cranberry juice

Jamila's first job was to select five of those ingredients. If she wanted an ingredient that was not on the list, Mrs. Piggle-Wiggle wouldn't mind so long as her selection was liquid or almost liquid, and edible. Jamila gave the matter some thought and chose vanilla yogurt, melted vanilla ice cream, maple syrup, orange juice, and apricot jam. I didn't happen to have the necessary items on hand, so I told Jamila that if she would write a shopping list, I would go food shopping before our next session.

When Jamila showed up for her subsequent appointment, I had everything she needed on my worktable: paper and pencil so that she could record the formula, a carton of yogurt, a cup of melted vanilla ice cream, a bottle of maple syrup, a container of orange juice, a jar of apricot jam, a mason jar with a lid, and a serving spoon. I also had a set of measuring spoons and a measuring cup—both with metric markings. If you don't already own them, you can buy metric measuring supplies at any good housewares store.

"Time to make the cure, Jamila. What ingredient do you want to put in first?" I asked.

"Yogurt," she said.

"Fine. My measuring cup has lines showing 50, 75, 100, 125, 150, 175, 200, 225, 250, 275, and 300 milliliters.

My spoons hold 2.5, 5, 7.5, and 15 milliliters. That gives you a lot of choices. How much yogurt do you want to include?"

Jamila studied my measuring cup for a moment and then said, "One hundred milliliters."

"Sounds good. Go ahead and fill the measuring cup to the 100-milliliter line. Be careful. Don't forget, all of your measurements must be exact," I said.

After she filled the measuring cup to the right spot, I told her to pour the yogurt into the mason jar and record the amount on the paper.

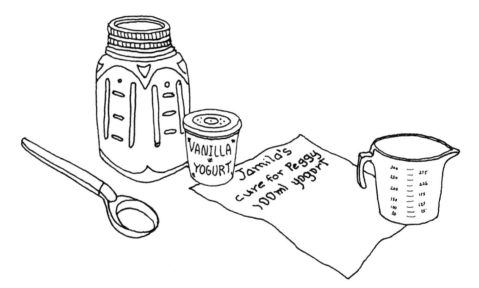

"What goes next?" I asked.

"Orange juice," she said.

"How much?"

Again, she looked at the measuring cup, but this time she frowned. "I want 80, but I don't see a line marked 80," she complained.

"No problem. Fill the measuring cup up to 75 milliliters. Then you can use the 5-milliliter measuring spoon to make up the difference," I said.

Jamila grinned and went to work measuring, pouring, and writing.

"You put in 100 milliliters of yogurt and 80 of juice. Can you figure out how much formula you have so far?" I asked.

"Easy, 180," she said.

I was surprised that Jamila, who had just entered second grade, answered this question so quickly. Lots of second graders, and some third graders, have trouble solving such a problem, even if they use paper and pencil.

After praising her work, I said, "You can only have 250 milliliters in the formula, and you already have 180. I think you're getting pretty close to the maximum."

"How much more can I put in?" she asked.

"We have to subtract 180 from 250 to find that out," I answered, taking a fresh sheet of paper and writing the numbers. Although Jamila could add 100 and 80 in her head, I knew she had not learned to do such a difficult subtraction problem. That being the case, I did the math.

"You can put in another 70 milliliters, but no more," I said when I finished calculating.

"And I still have three ingredients left. I'll only use a tiny bit of maple syrup," she said.

"Okay. How much?"

"Five," she answered after looking over the measuring spoons.

And so 5 milliliters of maple syrup went into the mix, and then Jamila recorded this on her formula sheet.

"You can include 65 more milliliters," I said. "And you have two more ingredients."

"Can I put in 60 of the ice cream?" she asked.

"Sure," I said, "but you'll have to use the cup and the spoon. First fill the measuring cup to the 50-milliliter line."

She did.

"Now you need 10 more milliliters. There isn't a 10-milliliter spoon, though," I said.

"I can use 5 and 5," she suggested.

"Good solution!"

Jamila added the ice cream to the jar and wrote the amount on her sheet.

"How much jam can I add?" she asked.
"You can put in 5 milliliters if you want, or less."
"I want 5," she said.
"Go ahead, then."

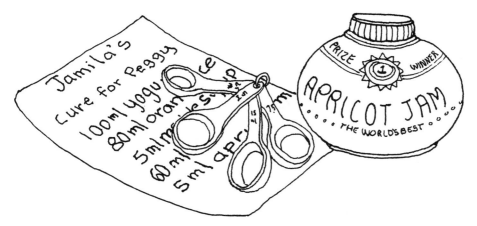

After she had added the jam and recorded it, I said, "Now you have to shake the jar. But first let me screw on the lid."

Jamila blended the cure; then I took the lid off the jar and poured a sip of brew into a glass for Jamila to taste.

"It's delicious," she said.

"In that case, the cure ought to work. You put in the five ingredients, you measured perfectly, you have 250 milliliters and not a drop more, you wrote everything down, and it is delicious," I said, pouring the rest of the formula into another glass. Then I drank Jamila's sweet concoction. I drank it all.

As soon as I emptied the glass, I put my hand to my forehead and said, "Jamila, I feel so strange. I thought we would read two books today, but I don't think we can. I think we have to play games instead." Which is what we did for the remainder of the hour.

If you decide to let your child cure you of some awful trait, you can set your own rules. You can agree to be cured of clean-up-your-room syndrome but refuse a cure for you-can't-eat-sweets disease. You can set your own time limit. The cure could last an hour, two hours, or more or less. You might declare that the formula is the time-release variety. Let's say your child wants to cure you of turn-off-the-televisionitis. For this cure, you swallow the formula at four o'clock Saturday afternoon, the medicine kicks in at eight o'clock Sunday morning—just in time for normally forbidden cartoon shows—and the medicine wears off two hours later.

To get the cure just right, you and your child will surely have to fiddle with your measuring cup and spoons, the way Jamila and I did. All metric spoons I have seen come in gradations of 2.5 milliliters, 5 milliliters, 7.5 milliliters, and 15 milliliters. Measuring cups vary, though. Whatever markings are on your cup and spoons, you can always get the right amounts one way or another.

Making a cure calls for measuring, writing, and calculating. Any time your child has trouble doing the math, or is reluctant to add or subtract, do the work yourself. And if you end up doing all the math, that's okay, too. Your goal isn't to drill your child in arithmetic. Your goal is to have a great time, with a tidbit of measuring, a smidgen of writing, and a little math, possibly very little math, thrown into the mix.

*J*osie did not like to read. She did not like to write. She announced these two facts adamantly and regularly. So far I had done nothing to change her mind or soften her stance. Fortunately, Josie loved listening to stories, which was a promising sign. Fortunately, as well, her parents spent a lot of time reading to her. They read to her every night. They read to her in the afternoon. They read to her on buses and in restaurants. They were wise parents.

One afternoon, Josie entered my office giggling.

"What's so funny?" I asked.

"Mrs. Piggle-Wiggle," she said.

"Tell me about it."

"My mom was reading the best story on the bus. It was about a boy with really bad table manners. He makes all this noise when he eats and he lets everyone see the food in his mouth. My mom and I were laughing so hard," she said.

"I know that story! It's in *Mrs. Piggle-Wiggle's Magic*. Has your mom read the tattletale story to you yet?"

"That was so good!" she exclaimed.

"I have an idea. Let's make a board game all about Mrs. Piggle-Wiggle," I said.

"How can we do that?" she asked.

"I've never made one before, so I'm not really sure. But we can start and see what happens. Do you want to try?"

"Okay," she said.

"We will need a board, of course," I said.

"Of course," she repeated.

"Lucky for us, I have a big sheet of yellow poster board in my closet," I said.

I found the poster board—a 22″ × 28″ sheet—and placed it on the floor, with the rough side up (because ink doesn't smear on the rough side). Then Josie and I sat on the floor, too.

MRS. PIGGLE-WIGGLE'S BOARD GAME

GRADES

second and third

MATERIALS

22″× 28″ sheet of poster board, thin and thick markers, 3″× 5″ index cards, scissors, game tokens, playing die

SKILLS

reading, writing, encouraging an active imagination

Mrs. Piggle-Wiggle's Magic
265

"What now?" she asked.

"I think we should make a long road divided into about thirty sections. Then we can each put a token on the first section of the road and race to the end. Whoever gets to the end first will win," I said.

Although Josie nodded, I wasn't certain she understood my idea. I hoped that if I drew the road, my plan would make sense to her. I took a thick black marker and got to work. Soon the board looked like this:

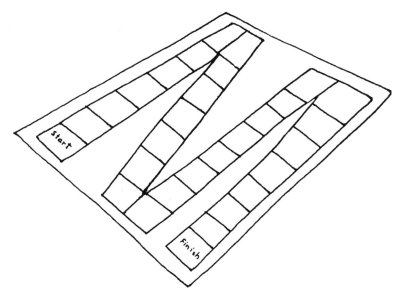

"I get it!" Josie said. "We race to see who can go from start to finish the fastest. Do we use dice?"

"Dice. Hmmm. Yes, we'll use a single die. Every time you throw it, you go that many sections down the road. I think there should be some good-news sections and some bad-news sections," I added.

"What do you mean?" she asked.

"Let's say at the beginning of the game, I roll a three. I go to the third section, right?"

"Right."

"When I get to that section, imagine it says: 'You need a cure for fidgeting. Wait here one turn while Mrs. Piggle-Wiggle cures you.' "

"That would be bad. You would lose a turn," she said.

"On the other hand, it might say 'Mrs. Piggle-Wiggle bakes you cookies. Move ahead two spaces to get them.' "

"That would be good. You'd move up," she said.

"Exactly. So before we play, we need to fill spaces with good news or bad news. I bet you can come up with lots of ideas," I said.

"You need a sneeze cure," she blurted out.

"Perfect! Do you have to wait for the cure, or go back two spaces to find it?" I asked.

"Go back," she said.

"Great. Pick a section of the road and write: 'You need a sneeze cure. Go back two spaces,' " I said.

"I have to write?" she asked.

"Yup. And I'll need to write, as well. Working together, it shouldn't take us too long to finish the board."

This made sense to Josie. I handed her a thin black marker and she began writing in the tenth space. She had an odd way of spelling *sneeze*, but so what?

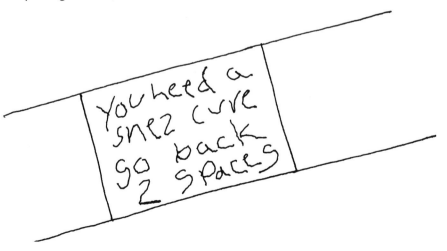

"My turn," I said. Then, in the fifth section of the road, I wrote, "You get a cure card."

"What's that mean?" Josie asked.

"I thought we could make a pile of cure cards. If you have a cure card, you don't lose a turn waiting for Mrs. Piggle-Wiggle's help or go back to find her. You can cure yourself," I said.

"Neat, but where are the cure cards?"

"I guess we have to make them. We can use six index cards and on each one we can write, 'One free cure.' Like this," I said while writing on the card.

"We need five more. Will you write two of them?" I asked.

"I guess," she said.

For the next couple of minutes we made cure cards together. When we finished, I filled five more spaces with the words "You get a cure card." So far we'd filled in nine spaces—Josie's space, six free-cure spaces, start, and finish.

I decided that was enough for today, but during our next session we worked on the board again. I filled more spaces than Josie—often as not writing down ideas she dictated. This was fine with Josie, and fine with me, too. I knew that it was important to finish the board quickly or making it would become tedious. By the time our hour was almost up, we had filled in thirteen new spaces. We now had words in twenty-two of the thirty spaces. Twelve of these were good news spots and ten bad. Not wanting to spend another session making the board, I said, "We have eight spaces left. I think we should make them all free spaces. If you land on a free space you don't move ahead, or lose a turn, or get an extra turn. You just stay in the space until the time comes for you to throw the die again."

Josie agreed with this plan, and after spending a few minutes writing "Free" in the empty sections, we declared the board complete. We didn't have time to start a game that afternoon, but I promised we would begin our next session by playing.

Three days later, Josie bounced through my door and shouted, "Game!"

"Absolutely," I said, "but first you need a game token, and so do I. How about this? We each cut out a square of paper, ones that will fit in the sections of the board. You write *J* for Josie on yours. I'll write *P* for Peggy on mine."

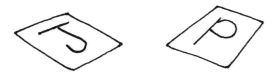

"Do you want to go first?" I asked, holding out a playing die.

"Okay," she said.

She rolled the die, got a four, and landed on a space that said, "Mrs. Piggle-Wiggle cures you of the giggles. Take an extra turn." Josie, the reluctant reader, did not argue about reading the words. She didn't argue about taking her extra turn, either. She landed on "Mrs. Piggle-Wiggle lost her shoe. Go back two spaces and help her find it." Josie read that, too, without complaint or protest. When she finally won the game, she asked if we could play again. And we did. Then I told Josie she could take the game home with her. That way she could play with her mother, another Mrs. Piggle-Wiggle fan.

TREASURE HUNT

GRADES

second and third

MATERIALS

paper, pen, gift

SKILLS

following directions

*I*n the final chapter of *Mrs. Piggle-Wiggle's Magic*, Mrs. Piggle-Wiggle asks the neighborhood children for their help. What can the children do for her? They can find the treasure Mr. Piggle-Wiggle hid in the house before he died. Mr. Piggle-Wiggle, it turns out, was a pirate who had collected a sizable fortune. Instead of leaving his money in a bank or under the mattress, Mr. Piggle-Wiggle filled secret drawers and cupboards with money and gold. Over the years, Mrs. Piggle-Wiggle has discovered almost all the treasure. She is sure, though, that there is one more stockpile of gold, which she must find because she hasn't any money left. And so the children start treasure hunting. Soon Mimi discovers a hoard of concealed gold, silver, jewels, and money. Problem solved, and the book ends.

The day after you finish reading the last chapter, consider planning your own treasure hunt, one that will go on for several days, as a way of saying good-bye, at least for a little while, to Mrs. Piggle-Wiggle. Begin by writing a note that says something like this: "A treasure awaits you. But it will not be easy to find. It will take days and days. If you do exactly as you are told, I know you will succeed. Your first task is to look under the green lamp in the living room. Sincerely yours, Mrs. Piggle-Wiggle."

Place this note under your child's dinner plate, or inside his coloring book, or anywhere else you can be sure he will find it and read it.

When your child makes his way to the green lamp, he should find another message. This one, written by you earlier in the day, should say something like this: "Tomorrow after school, look under your pillow. There you will find a new letter. Do whatever it tells you. Good luck, Mrs. Piggle-Wiggle."

The next day, when your child looks under the pillow, he will find a note from Mrs. Piggle-Wiggle directing him to the cookie jar. And in the cookie jar he will find a note leading him to the bottom drawer of his bureau. And in the drawer he will find a note telling him that tomorrow he must look inside the refrigerator.

You decide how many days you want your child to hunt before leaving him a message like this: "Here is your last letter! Open the kitchen cabinet where you find the cereal. Your treasure is waiting for you next to the oatmeal box. I hope you like it. Love, Mrs. Piggle-Wiggle."

When your child opens the cabinet door, he will see a gift-wrapped package—his treasure. What should be in the package? It might be an outfit for a favorite doll, a miniature car, a set of colored pencils, or a stuffed animal. Anything you choose, so long as it's worthy of the search.

To find the treasure, your child will have to read all of your notes, interpret your instructions, and follow them exactly. Beginning readers often have trouble coping with written directions. Sometimes they ignore them, especially ones on school worksheets. But just as often, they have difficulty turning words into actions. They go to a lamp, but not the green one. They open the top drawer instead of the bottom one. When your child hunts for treasure, though, he is sure to give special care when reading the instructions and try hard to obey them perfectly. The moment he finds the treasure, he will understand the value of his meticulous work. A lesson like that is a treasure in itself.

THE BORROWERS

WRITTEN BY MARY NORTON
ILLUSTRATED BY BETH AND JOE KRUSH
1953
GOOD READING FOR FIRST, SECOND, AND THIRD GRADES

Why is it you can never find a safety pin when you need one? What happens to hairpins the moment you turn your head? Does it seem that your pencils, pens, and rubber bands disappear into thin air? In some houses, Borrowers are to blame. Who are Borrowers? They are little people, very little people—small enough for you to hold in the palm of your hand. They live under the floorboards, and they provide for themselves by borrowing food and household items from the larger residents of the house.

If Borrowers dwell in your house, you will never know it for sure. But if they *do*, they will have created a tiny home of their own where they are probably using your lost thimble for a chair, your old letters as wallpaper, and your missing postage stamps as paintings.

You must not confuse borrowing with stealing. Borrowers never steal. They believe—they know—that anything they borrow from humans is theirs by right.

The Clocks, a family of Borrowers—father Pod, mother Homily, and daughter Arrietty—live in a comfy apartment which can be reached through a hole under the grandfather clock that sits in a quiet old house. Every day, Pod goes about the house collecting necessities and a few luxuries for his family: bits of cheese to eat, fuel for the fireplace, a set of tiny books for Arrietty to read. Life is good, although lonely, since the other Borrower families, the Overmantels, the Harpsichords, the Rain-Pipes, and all the rest, moved away long ago. Humans reside in the house, but they don't present much of a problem, until a boy comes to visit. And the boy catches sight of Pod—a true disaster for any Borrower. The boy sees Arrietty and Homily, too. The youngster doesn't want to hurt the Clocks, though. In fact, he wants to help, and so he starts borrowing. The boy plucks furniture out of an old dollhouse, grabs knickknacks from the drawing room, and transports these wonders to the Clock family home. It's a golden age, but it cannot last. Dresden figurines, unlike safety pins, don't disappear without causing alarm. One awful thing leads to another until the Clocks realize that unless they escape their home, they will be caught and likely killed—by a cat, by a ratcatcher, or by Mrs. Driver, the housekeeper.

Do the Clocks survive their horrifying ordeal? They do, and they go on to have more adventures in four excellent sequels: *The Borrowers Afield*, *The Borrowers Afloat*, *The Borrowers Aloft*, and *The Borrowers Avenged*.

The boy is entranced by the Clocks, and so are almost all children who listen to the story. Mary Norton, the author of *The Borrowers*, creates a make-believe world you can almost believe in.

Don't crayons, paper clips, and buttons disappear in your house? Can you say for sure that Borrowers aren't responsible? Adults are quick to answer, "Borrowers cannot be responsible because there are no Borrowers." But for children, the answer is more likely to be "Maybe there aren't any Borrowers, but maybe there are." By giving children a chance to believe in the unbelievable, by balancing herself on a fence between the impossible and the just barely possible, Mary Norton has written a story that encourages youngsters to fantasize with a vividness that few other children's books do.

The following games offer a way to spend some educationally useful time with Borrowers, even if you don't find them in your closets or behind your bookshelves.

*I*f you are lucky enough to have Borrowers living in your house, is there any way to draw them out of their hiding places? You might try making them a beautiful new home—one they cannot resist inhabiting. How will you create such a home? You could take an empty shoe box, transform it into a Borrowers' apartment, and fill it with your own handmade furniture. Eventually, you and your child might end up with a multiroom dwelling, but I suggest you start off by making a one-room apartment. Begin construction with a single shoe box. Set the box on its side and slide the lid underneath to help balance the box.

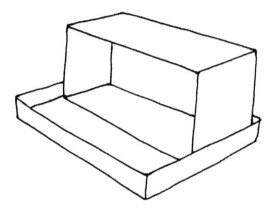

Your child might complain that such a domicile is too little for an entire family of Borrowers. Remind him, though, that generation after generation, Borrowers get smaller and smaller. Many years have passed since the Clocks' era, so that by now Borrowers must be amazingly tiny. A shoe-box-sized room will, therefore, be perfectly commodious.

Once the shoe box is in place, you and your child have to make some crucial decorating decisions. Your first concern should be wallpaper. The Clock family enjoyed putting letters on their walls, but your child might prefer colored construction paper, origami paper, gift-wrap, or a combination of all

A BORROWER'S HOUSE

GRADES

first, second, and third

MATERIALS

shoe boxes, construction or origami or gift-wrapping paper, scissors, glue, tape, poster paint, paintbrushes, a variety of materials (such as index cards, poster board, bottle caps, empty jewelry boxes, empty spools of thread, and so on, depending on how you decorate your house)

SKILLS

learning to think creatively, working on a long-term project

three. Whatever you select, you will have to cut and paste until the paper covers the walls—or at least most of the walls. You can also cover the outside of the box with paper.

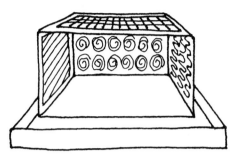

Once the wallpaper is in place, consider the floor. You could decide to paint the floor with poster paint. That would look lovely. But you might want a carpet instead. You can make an excellent carpet out of an old terry-cloth hand towel. Cut it down to size and glue it in place.

Now you need furniture. Your Borrowers must certainly have at least one bed. How will you get one? To answer this question, try thinking like a Borrower. A Borrower would spot a jewelry box, for example, and realize that the bottom, especially if you stuff it with a little cotton, would make an excellent bed. The bed would look even better if you cut a small piece of pretty fabric and place it over the cotton as a bedspread.

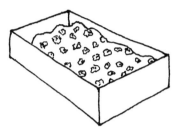

The cap of a spice jar might make a fine nightstand.

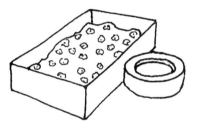

To construct a table, take the cardboard tube from inside a roll of toilet paper and cut about two inches off one end.

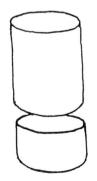

These two inches will be the base of the table. For the table-top, cut an index card into a square, or a rectangle, or any other shape you think will look good.

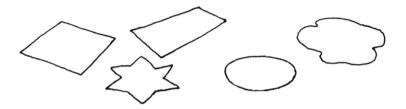

Then tape the index-card top to the toilet-paper-roll base.

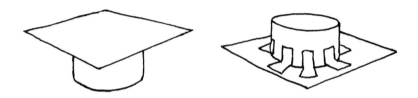

An upside-down eggcup snipped away from an egg carton—either a Styrofoam or a cardboard carton—can make a good chair. You will want to cut the eggcup so that it is in proportion with your table.

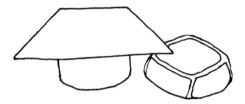

Once you get started, you or your child will surely come up with all sorts of interesting ways to furnish your house. Assuming you used the bottom of a jewelry box to make a bed, what can you do with the top? If you tinker with it, could you turn it into a sofa? A refrigerator? A closet?

When one room is full of furniture, you can build an extension to the house. Just tape a second shoe box on top of, or alongside, the first, and continue decorating.

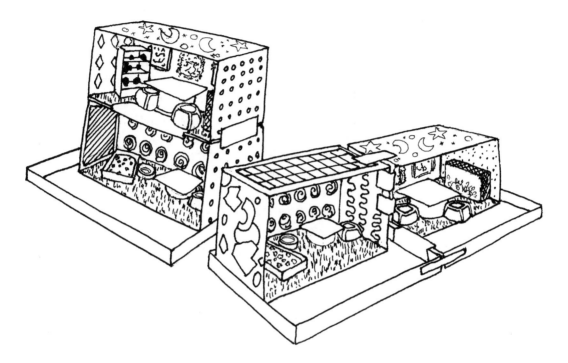

It takes a lot of creative thinking to transform a shoe box into an appealing home for a Borrower. Some people look at a button and see a button. More flexible thinkers look at the button and see a bead for a necklace, a wheel for a tiny model car, or a serving plate for a Borrower's dining room table. Flexible thinking is creative thinking, and creative thinking is intelligence.

It will take time, effort, and patience to finish A BORROWER'S HOUSE. After you start, it might turn out that it is too ambitious a project. If so, don't force your child to finish the house. It's okay to leave the job undone. But keep the box around for a while—just in case inspiration strikes again.

BEAT THE SOUND BORROWER

GRADES

first, second, and third

SKILLS

hearing individual sounds
in words

*B*orrowers take objects—physical objects. But try to imagine a different kind of Borrower, not a being who makes off with postage stamps but someone who specializes in taking sounds away from words. Let's call the new kind of Borrower a Sound Borrower. If you decide to play BEAT THE SOUND BORROWER with your child, you will become a Sound Borrower by snatching sounds away from words. And your child will try to outsmart you by speaking without the borrowed sound. It works like this. You begin by picking a word—*garden*, for instance. Then tell your child that, being a Sound Borrower, you have decided to borrow the *g* sound from the beginning of *garden*. If your child can say *garden* without the borrowed sound—*arden*—he will get a point. If he cannot, you get a point. Then on to the next word. Can your child say the word *trap* after you borrow the *p* sound? If he can, he gets a point. If he cannot, you get the point. After you borrow sounds from five words, the person with the most points wins.

When you first play, I suggest you borrow sounds from important words in *The Borrowers*. Ask your child to say *Pod* without the *p, Arrietty* without the final *ee* sound, *Harpsichords* without the initial *h*, and *Clock* without the first *c*.

It is a lot easier for your child when you borrow the first sound in a word—the *b* in *boy* to get *oy*. It is harder when you borrow the last sound—the *p* in *stamp* to get *stam*. It is hardest when you borrow one of the middle sounds—the *r* in

Driver to get *diver*. It is best to start with the easiest borrowings. Then, if your child is accumulating points without stress or strain, make things a little harder.

Here is a list of words from *The Borrowers* with suggested sound borrowings ranked by level. You might want to use some of them in your first games.

Easy borrowings:

Pod with a borrowed *p* sound

potato with a borrowed *p* sound

Clock with a borrowed *c* sound

letter with a borrowed *l* sound

seen with a borrowed *s* sound

Harpsichords with a borrowed *h* sound

boy with a borrowed *b* sound

Sophy with a borrowed *s* sound

ferret with a borrowed *f* sound

humans with a borrowed *h* sound

giants with a borrowed *g* sound

safety pin with a borrowed *s* sound for *safety* and a
   borrowed *p* sound for *pin*

nursery with a borrowed *n* sound

Rosa with a borrowed *r* sound

Pickhatchet with a borrowed *p* sound

Harder Borrowings:

Pod with a borrowed *d* sound

Arrietty with a borrowed *ee* sound

diary with a borrowed *ee* sound

teacup with a borrowed *p* sound

read with a borrowed *d* sound

Lupy with a borrowed *ee* sound

seen with a borrowed *n* sound

stamp with a borrowed *p* sound

nursery with a borrowed *ee* sound

Hardest Borrowings:

Driver with a borrowed *r* sound
small with a borrowed *m* sound
grating with a borrowed *r* sound
emigrate with a borrowed *i* sound
Crampfurl with a borrowed *r* sound
blotting with a borrowed *l* sound
Clock with a borrowed *l* sound

BEAT THE SOUND BORROWER is a very useful game to play with young readers and writers. What accounts for the fact that some children learn to read and spell more rapidly and skillfully than others? Intelligence is not the answer. Quite a few very bright children with remarkably high I.Q.s find learning to read a difficult task. Effort is not the answer. In the early grades, before children give up hope, struggling readers often put in considerably more time and effort than their friends who learn to read without strain.

What is the answer, then? Children who learn to read easily usually have the ability to remove sounds from words so masterfully that they can instantly say *slip* without the *s* (*lip*) or without the *l* (*sip*) or the *p* (*sli*). Children who do not have this ability often find that reading is a struggle.

For whatever reasons, this skill comes more or less automatically to some children, while others have to work at it. Virtually all children, though, can learn to remove sounds from words—given practice and time. One way to practice is to drill your child. But this is not much fun and your child is bound to resist. Another way is to play games like BEAT THE SOUND BORROWER. Consider, then, playing a round at the end of every chapter or every other chapter as you read the book. It won't take very long, and it can do your child a lot of good.

BEEZUS AND RAMONA

WRITTEN BY BEVERLY CLEARY
ILLUSTRATED BY LOUIS DARLING
1955
GOOD READING FOR FIRST, SECOND, AND THIRD GRADES

No one describes an idealized suburban childhood better than Beverly Cleary. She depicts a friendly world of large houses, stay-at-home moms, good neighbors, and lots of cheer. But even pleasant lives have complications. In each of Cleary's books the characters confront one problem or another, and in *Beezus and Ramona* the problem for nine-year-old Beezus is her little sister, Ramona, age four.

Ramona is a pest. She scribbles on the book Beezus borrowed from the library. She causes a commotion in Beezus's art class. She rams her tricycle directly into the checkerboard while Beezus is in the middle of a game against her best friend, Henry Huggins. Worst of all, Ramona almost ruins Beezus's tenth birthday. It is not easy being Ramona's big sister.

It is easy, however, for adult readers and young listeners to laugh as Ramona causes all sorts of trouble. When you stop laughing, though, you are left with some serious questions—the same questions Beezus confronts. Does a big sister have to love her little sister? All the time? No matter what? And if she doesn't always love her sister, does that make her a bad person? At some point or another, all children ask such questions, if not about a sibling, then about someone else they are expected to love—an aunt, an uncle, even a mother or a father. So when Beezus's mother says, "Why, there's no reason why you *should* love Ramona all the time," it is reassuring, and not just for Beezus.

Here are a few activities based on the book. Although there is no reason you and your child *should* love them, I certainly hope you do.

MU TORERE

GRADES

first, second, and third

MATERIALS

paper, colored markers, four pennies and four dimes (or four red checkers and four black, or four white squares of paper and four black)

SKILLS

learning to think logically and strategically

*B*eezus and her best friend, Henry Huggins, love to play checkers, and it is an excellent game. If your child doesn't know how to play yet, after you have read about Beezus and Henry's ill-fated match you might set aside a few minutes to provide helpful checkers instruction. If your child already knows how to play, you can introduce another excellent board game called MU TORERE.

MU TORERE was invented by the Maoris, the native population of New Zealand. When Maori players want to make a MU TORERE board, they scratch one in the ground or use charcoal to draw one on stone. You will need a board, too, before you can start the game, but you can draw yours on a sheet of white paper. The board should look like this:

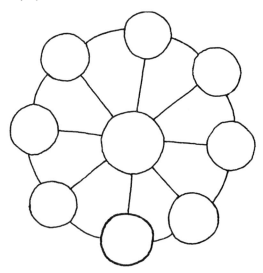

After drawing the board, you must select tokens. Each player gets four. One player can use four pennies and the other player four dimes, or four squares of white paper and four squares of black. It doesn't matter so long as the tokens fit inside the circles.

Place all eight pieces on the board like so:

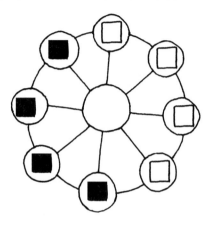

The eight pieces never leave the board. This means that there is always an empty circle. When it is your turn, you want to move one of your four tokens onto that empty circle. Your child wants to do the same on his turn.

There are two rules. One: there must be a line between where you are and where you want to go. This is a legal move:

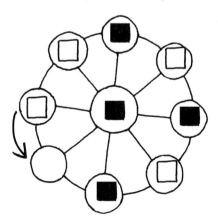

This is not:

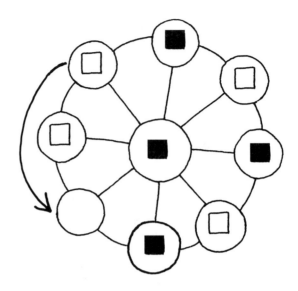

Two: you can move into the center cell only if the piece you want to move is next to at least one of your opponent's pieces. This is a legal move:

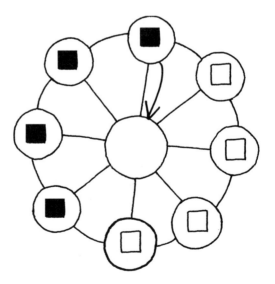

This is not:

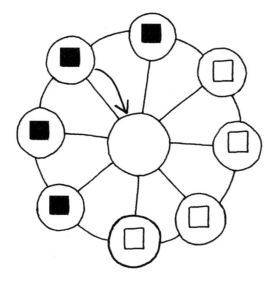

Here is a board set up for a game. I have numbered the
tokens to make it easier to describe the moves.

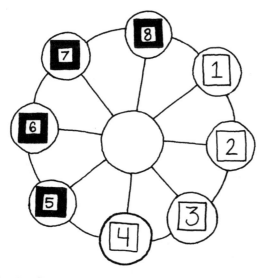

White is the first player. White can move either token number one or number four. That is because the only open circle is

the center circle and, according to the rules, you can move a token there only if it is next to at least one of your opponent's tokens. Let's say white moves token number four.

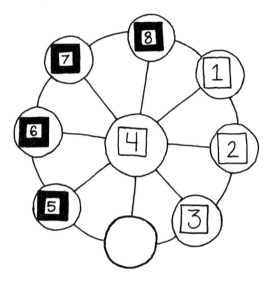

Next it is black's turn. Black must move token number five. It is the only legal move available.

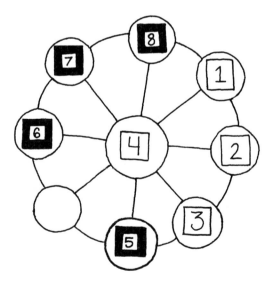

White goes again. White can move only token number four.

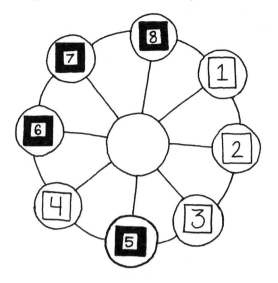

Now black has the choice of moving either number five, number six, or number eight into the center circle. Black must decide which is best. White and black alternate turns until one of them cannot make a legal move. At that moment, the other player wins. Look at this board.

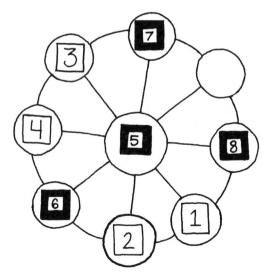

Right now it is white's turn, but since black is blocking white's way to the empty circle, white goes down in defeat.

Sometimes one player sees the winning move within a minute. Other times ten minutes go by, and it seems that both players are going round and round, repeating moves without either making progress. And then, suddenly, a player discovers the winning move and conquers.

During your first matches, being unfamiliar with the game, both you and your child will move your pieces without analyzing your actions. You will see an open circle and place a token on it. After a few games, though, a player, even a young player, begins to consider choices. Which piece is best to move, a child may wonder, the one on the right of the open circle or the one on the left? In time, the child will discover that certain moves lead to victory, while others spell doom. The child will become a strategic player, which means he will plot, plan, and organize his moves. It is exactly because strategy games encourage children to plot, plan, and organize that they are such a valuable way for youngsters to spend time. As a strategy game for young players, MU TORERE has three advantages over Beezus's favorite game, checkers. First, MU TORERE takes only a few minutes to play, so it is possible to arrange a short game after your child finishes homework and before sitting down for dinner. Second, in MU TORERE, unlike checkers, there are only a few options for each move, which makes it easier for a child to evaluate his choices. Third, if a little brother or sister rams into the board with a tricycle, it won't take much effort to get your pieces back into action. I'm sure Beezus would appreciate that.

*O*n her birthday, Beezus receives a book called *202 Things to Do on a Rainy Afternoon*. Reading it, she discovers how to create a Christmas tree ornament out of cellophane straws. It is easy to imagine Beezus making the ornament some rainy day. It might be fun for you and your child to do likewise, and you can, by using the instructions below. If you follow them correctly, you and your child will create a lovely ornament—one that, when you hold it up to the light, will resemble stained glass. It will not be a Christmas tree ornament, though. You can use a Christmas tree ornament only once a year and then only if you celebrate Christmas and celebrate with a tree. Instead, this will be an ornament you can use and enjoy year-round.

To make the ornament, you need a few sheets of newspaper, a roll of waxed paper, a box of crayons, a pencil sharpener, a safety pin, a clothes iron, and scissors.

Lay out the newspaper on a firm flat surface—a surface suitable for ironing. Now place a sheet of waxed paper, about one foot long, on top of the newspaper. Your next task is to sprinkle crayon shavings all over the sheet of waxed paper. For your initial ornament, it is best to use three colors. Your child can select any three he likes, but they should be different hues and not shades of the same color. Also, be sure that at least one crayon is a light color—yellow, pink, or sky blue, for instance. After your child chooses, take one of those crayons and peel off the paper wrapper. Then slide the crayon into a pencil sharpener and start twisting so that bits, pieces, even ribbons of crayon fall on the waxed paper. Sometimes a crayon tip will break in the sharpener. You can clear the crayon away using the pointed end of a safely pin. Move the shavings around a bit so that the color is not all in one place. Follow the same procedure with the second crayon and then the third. You want to cover the waxed paper with color, but don't heap on layers and layers of crayon. If there is too much

A RAINY-DAY PROJECT

GRADES

first, second, and third

MATERIALS

newspaper, waxed paper, crayons, pencil sharpener, clothes iron, safety pin, scissors, hole puncher, yarn or string

SKILLS

following directions, developing an interest in arts and crafts

Beezus and Ramona

crayon on the sheet, you risk losing the transparency you want in the finished ornament. Make sure to leave a crayon-free border of waxed paper.

Now take a second piece of waxed paper, at least as large as the first, and place it on top of the shavings. See to it that all of the shavings are covered. Run a warm iron, *not* a hot iron, over the top sheet of waxed paper. As you glide the iron about, you will see the colors melt, liquefy, slide, and blend. The longer you iron, the more the colors merge. Stop while you can still distinguish individual colors. Now let the crayon cool for a few minutes. While cooling, the crayon will form a gluelike bond between the two sheets of waxed paper.

Once your waxed crayon sheet has cooled, you can cut it into any shape or shapes you want.

You can make a small circle and a small diamond:

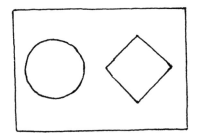

Or a big circle and a big diamond:

Or a star: Or a flower:

Hold your finished shape up to the light and enjoy the stained-glass effect. Try taping the ornament onto a window-pane; when the sun shines through, the colors are spectacular.

If you want to hang your ornament—from a tree or house-plant, or any other inviting place—simply punch a hole in the top of your shape, pull a piece of string, yarn, or ribbon through the hole, and then form a knot. Use the resulting loop to hang your artwork.

That's it—unless you want to make a second ornament. If you have no need for another ornament in your house, you can use the colorful shapes as coasters for cold drinks—hot drinks will cause damage. The ornaments (or coasters) make nice gifts for grandparents, aunts, uncles, and even for pesty little sisters. Would Beezus make an ornament for Ramona? A good question. What does your child think?

APPLESAUCE

GRADES

first, second, and third

MATERIALS

apples, water, cinnamon, maple syrup, metric measuring spoons and cup, pot with a cover

OPTIONAL MATERIALS

raisins

SKILLS

learning to use metric measurements

I love the apple scene in *Beezus and Ramona*. Naughty, naughty Ramona sneaks down to the basement, finds a huge basket of apples, and proceeds to take a single bite out of each one. Oh, Ramona, how could you!

What does Ramona's mother do to salvage all those partially gnawed apples? She prepares a great big pot of homemade applesauce. After reading the apple chapter in *Beezus and Ramona*, you and your child might set aside time to make your own applesauce. Perhaps you have a favorite applesauce recipe, but in case you don't, you can use mine.

I've written the ingredients in metric units with the traditional cups and teaspoons in parentheses. I suggest you use the metric measurements. Making applesauce or any other recipe using metrics is one of the best ways to help your child feel familiar and comfortable with this way of measuring. Given that metrics will play an increasingly prominent role in the coming years, this is a very good idea. You can buy metric measuring cups and spoons at most housewares stores if you don't already own a set.

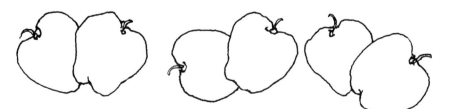

Ramona-Inspired Applesauce

Makes about 875 milliliters (3½ cups)

6 apples (any apples will do, but my favorite is a combination
    of 3 yellow Delicious and 3 McIntosh)
125 milliliters (½ cup) water
2.5 milliliters (½ teaspoon) cinnamon
15 milliliters (1 tablespoon) maple syrup
125 milliliters (½ cup) raisins (optional)

1. Peel the apples and cut them in quarters.
2. Remove the stems, cores, and seeds.
3. Slice the apples into bite-size pieces.
4. Put the apple slices in a pot and add the water, cinnamon, and syrup.
5. Cover the pot and cook over medium heat for 15 minutes.
6. Uncover the pot and cook over very low heat for another 15 minutes. Stir the apples occasionally as they cook.
7. Take the pot off the stove, and let the apples cool.
8. With a fork, mash the softened apple pieces. Your sauce will be chunky or smooth, depending on how long you mash. You can keep the apples in the pot as you mash them, or transfer them to a bowl. If you do use a bowl, you will have to put the sauce back in the pot when you are done mashing.
9. Add the raisins, if you wish.
10. Return the uncovered pot to the stove, and cook over low heat for another 10 minutes. Stir the sauce occasionally as it cooks.
11. Take the pot off the stove, and let the sauce cool.
12. You can serve the applesauce warm or at room temperature.
13. Store any uneaten sauce in the refrigerator.

As you eat, raise a spoonful and toast Ramona. For without her shenanigans, you might not be enjoying your homemade applesauce today.

THE HUNDRED DRESSES

WRITTEN BY ELEANOR ESTES
ILLUSTRATED BY LOUIS SLOBODKIN
1944
NEWBERY HONOR BOOK
GOOD READING FOR SECOND AND THIRD GRADES

Wanda Petronski is poor, so poor that she wears the same shabby blue dress to school day after day. Why, then, does Wanda claim she has one hundred dresses lined up in her closet? And why does she repeat this story in front of all the girls every day?

Wanda even describes her dresses. She says she has a green dress with a red sash and a pale blue dress with red trimmings. Peggy, one of Wanda's classmates, encourages Wanda's talk and pretends to believe her. Then, as Wanda walks away, Peggy and the other girls roar with laughter—laughter they know Wanda hears. Maddie laughs, too, even though she does not like teasing Wanda. But Maddie is afraid to stop and even more afraid to tell Peggy, her best friend, how she feels.

The teasing goes on until the day of the class drawing contest. On that morning, Peggy and Maddie walk into their classroom and see—covering the walls, mounted on the blackboards, tacked to the ledges, posted on the windowsills—one hundred dazzling drawings of dresses. Each dress is unique. Each dress is beautiful. And Wanda drew each dress herself. Wanda Petronski never lied. She had one hundred dresses— one hundred exquisite drawings of dresses.

The Hundred Dresses has interesting ethical implications, which you might discuss with your child. Or you might not. Either way, the book has enough drama and suspense to hold any child's attention.

The following games and activities have no moral implications, but they do present your child with beneficial lessons in organizing information, estimating, counting, and writing. And, like Wanda, I do not lie.

*H*illary adored the book *The Hundred Dresses*. When I asked what made the story so special, she answered, "The drawings. I wish I could draw a hundred dresses like Wanda did."

I decided to give her the chance.

Before our next work session, I drafted a sheet of ten dress outlines exactly like the one on page 302. Then I went to the photocopy store and made ten copies of the page, thus producing a hundred dress outlines ready for Hillary's artistic touch.

When I showed Hillary the sheets, her first reaction was "Did Wanda really color that many dresses?"

Although Hillary had heard the words *one hundred dresses* throughout the book, the reality of the number and the reality of Wanda's accomplishment was not clear to her until she saw all those dresses.

DRESSES, DRESSES, DRESSES

GRADES

second and third

MATERIALS

photocopies of page 302, colored pencils, paper, pencil

SKILLS

organizing information, appreciating the accomplishments of a fictional character, visualizing one hundred

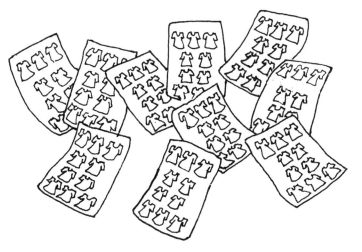

"It is amazing," I said. "If you want, you can use the sheets to see how many different dresses you can design."

Hillary smiled. "I think I can do a lot," she said.

I handed her a box of colored pencils and she went to work. After about twenty minutes, she had finished thirty dresses. She looked at the remaining seventy dresses and wondered if she had enough ideas to color them all.

I offered a suggestion: we would make a chart describing different aspects of dress design. Then she could use the chart to spark ideas. Hillary was not sure what I meant, but since I insisted on it, she allowed me to begin.

"Let's see," I said while pulling out a piece of paper and getting ready to write. "Dresses come in different colors, the fabrics often have patterns, and some dresses have decorations on them. The chart should have a column for each: patterns, decorations, and colors. I think we should begin by listing fabric patterns. There are little polka dots, big polka dots, stripes, checks . . ."

"And flowers," Hillary said, looking down at her own shirt.

"And swirls," I added.

"Little triangles," Hillary contributed.

"Hold on. Give me a chance to write these down," I said.

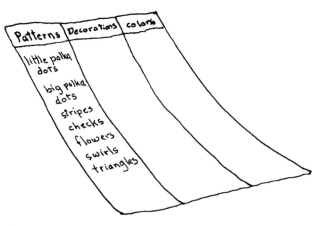

"That's enough patterns. Time to start listing decorations."

"What do you mean by decorations?" she asked.

"I mean things that you put on a dress, like pockets and collars . . ."

"And bows," Hillary added.

"That's it," I said. Soon we had ten decorations on the chart.

Next we listed colors. We did not include every conceivable shade of every hue, only the most obvious ones.

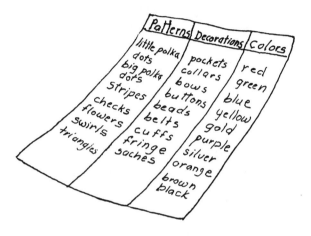

Patterns	Decorations	Colors
little polka dots	pockets	red
big polka dots	collars	green
stripes	bows	blue
checks	buttons	yellow
flowers	beads	gold
swirls	belts	purple
triangles	cuffs	silver
	fringe	orange
	sashes	brown
		black

"Here's how to use the chart," I said. "First, you select a pattern."

"Stripes," Hillary announced.

"Good. You're going to make a dress with stripes. Will the dress have any decorations?" I asked.

"Buttons and pockets," she said after scanning the chart.

"Excellent. Now, what about colors?"

"The stripes will be blue and green. The buttons will be gold. And the pockets will be solid yellow."

"Sounds like a beautiful dress to me. Go ahead and draw."

"That's lovely," I said when she was done. "Maybe now you'll draw a dress with little polka dots and a big collar next. Or a dress with big polka dots, a small collar, and fringe." Hillary liked both ideas.

"The chart helps, doesn't it?" I asked.

"Oh, yeah! I know I can make a hundred dresses now," she crowed.

I was glad Hillary was so enthusiastic. Even so, I only let her color two more dresses during the session. When it was time for her to leave, I gave her the chart and the ten pages of dresses to take home. I told her to design as many dresses as she wanted and, once she'd done all she cared to, bring in her work for me to see.

I assumed Hillary would finish another sheet, or maybe two, before giving up, but I was wrong. She completed all one hundred dresses. Each dress was unique, each was beautiful. I was amazed, and Hillary was very proud of herself.

DRESSES, DRESSES, DRESSES taught Hillary that organizing information can help solve certain problems. Why did I wait until Hillary ran into difficulties before suggesting the chart? As long as she could design dresses on her own, making a chart would not seem especially valuable. Worse, the work would interrupt her drawing, which might irritate her. When she ran out of inspiration, and the chart got her going again, its value was self-evident. Hillary enjoyed making the chart, once we got started. If she had not enjoyed the task, though, I would have pulled back, saying something like, "I don't think this chart is a good idea after all. Let's forget it." Then I would have assured Hillary that her dress collection was wonderful just as it was.

When you finish reading the book, ask your child if designing a hundred dresses sounds appealing. If it does, sometime in the next couple of days make ten photocopies of page 302 and give the sheets to your child. Be sure the child understands that it is not necessary to color all the dresses and certainly not necessary to do so at one time. If your child gets bored after producing five or ten or twenty dresses and has no interest in making a chart or returning to the project, that's okay. No matter how many dresses your child draws, you will have made Wanda's achievement clear, and there is great merit in that alone. What if your child loves dress making and never runs out of ideas? In that case, you might introduce the chart anyway, after the child completes a few sheets. True, organizing information about dresses will not seem as valuable to your child as it did to Hillary, but it should prove useful, nevertheless. If your child does not care to make a chart, though, then forget about it.

Don't assume that this activity is just for girls. Many boys will like the artistic challenge. Some of the world's greatest fashion designers are men, after all.

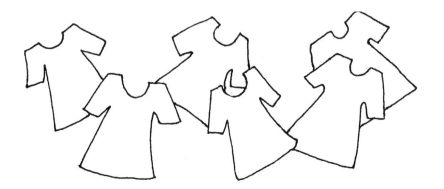

Maria thoroughly enjoyed *The Hundred Dresses*. It was, in her words, "the best book ever written." Given her enthusiasm for Wanda, and especially for Wanda's dress collection, I thought that she might like making a SCRAPBOOK OF DRESSES.

"What's a SCRAPBOOK OF DRESSES?" Maria asked when I introduced the idea.

"It's a book we make ourselves, and it's filled with pictures of dresses."

"I'm bad at drawing," Maria said.

"You don't have to draw the way Wanda did. You can cut out dresses from fashion magazines and paste them on blank sheets of paper. Every time you finish a page, we'll put it in a notebook binder."

"A hundred dresses?" Maria asked.

"Not that many. Maybe fifteen, maybe twenty. We can get started and see what happens."

Maria grinned.

"Your first job is to select a binder."

I pulled four notebook binders off a shelf. The binders were all the plastic type with ½″ rings. Each was a different color: green, yellow, pink, and orange. "Which do you want?"

"I like the pink," she answered.

After handing it to her, I said, "You need to write a title on the cover and your name—since it is your scrapbook. You can use my permanent markers."

SCRAPBOOK OF DRESSES

GRADES

third

MATERIALS

plastic binder with ½″ rings, permanent colored markers, fashion magazines, scissors, hole puncher, blank paper, glue, pencil

SKILLS

developing an appreciation for the value of writing

It took Maria about ten minutes to complete the cover.

"Beautiful job," I said when she was done.

"Thank you," she replied.

"I imagine we can get a couple of pages in the binder today, if we work hard," I said.

"Will you help with the cutting?" Maria asked.

"Sure, I'll do some of the cutting and some of the pasting, but you'll pick out all the dresses."

"Can we leave the ladies in the dresses?" Maria asked.

"I think that's best. If you want to include some of the background, that's okay, too. Then, after you paste the picture, you'll write a sentence telling about the dress," I said.

I handed Maria a copy of *Seventeen* magazine. It did not take her long to find a dress she liked. While she cut out the blue-and-white springtime outfit, I took a hole puncher and punched holes in several sheets of blank paper so that they would fit in the binder.

When Maria finished cutting, I helped her paste the dress on one of the sheets.

That done, I said, "Time to write."

Maria frowned. "I don't have anything to say," she insisted.

"If you owned this dress, where would you wear it?"

"To a party," she answered.

"Then you should write: 'This is a party dress,' " I said.

"Do I really have to?" she groaned.

"Yes, you really have to. I don't think it will take very long, and the sooner you finish writing, the sooner you can pick a new dress."

That got her going.

We agreed it was an excellent first page, and I snapped it in the binder.

"Can we do another page?" Maria asked.

"Sure," I said.

Maria looked through the magazine, stopped at a certain point, and said, "This is the dress I want, but you can't see all of it in the picture."

"No problem, just cut out the part you do see," I said.

"Will you cut this time?" she asked.

"Okay, but then you paste," I said.

When Maria finished pasting, I asked what she liked about the dress.

"It's pink, and pink is my favorite color."

"Excellent reason. You can write 'Pink is my favorite color.' "

And she did, with only a minor complaint.

In the meantime, I cut out a third dress, which Maria had selected. This photograph was small enough to fit on the same sheet as the pink dress.

Next Maria cut out a picture of three girls standing together. She put this group photo on a new sheet of paper and wrote, "These are all pretty dresses."

That was enough work for one day.

Over the next couple of weeks, we spent about fifteen minutes at the beginning of each appointment working on the scrapbook. Soon we had twenty dresses. I asked Maria if she felt like stopping or if she wanted more dresses in her book. She wanted more.

"I wish I could have a hundred," she said.

"That would take too long, but you can go for thirty."

At any given moment, making the scrapbook did not require much writing on Maria's part—a sentence, or sometimes two, for each photograph. That might not seem like much for a third grader, but those sentences began to add up. By the time she'd finished the book, she had actually done a fair amount of writing. As Maria looked through her pages, she enjoyed reading each caption. She was happy I insisted that she write, because, as she said, "It makes the book more interesting." Whenever a child is pleased about writing, that's good. That's very, very good.

If you decide to make a SCRAPBOOK OF DRESSES with your child, be prepared to spend time on the project. It may take several evenings and a rainy Saturday before you see the pages amass in a satisfying way. Leave a good supply of teen fashion magazines lying about the house, and your child might end up cutting, pasting, and writing even when you're not around. On the other hand, your child might lose interest after pasting four or five dresses. If that happens, don't campaign to get the project going again. Making the book serves a purpose, but only if your child truly enjoys the work.

CLOSET ESTIMATION

GRADES

second and third

SKILLS

estimating numbers

*C*LOSET ESTIMATION is a good game to play either in the course of reading *The Hundred Dresses* or after you finish the book. Begin by asking your child to imagine how many dresses are in Wanda's closet—not her drawings of dresses, her real dresses. That is not so hard. One is a reasonable guess. What about Maddie? How many dresses does she own? More than one, certainly. Maybe four or five? Peggy, no doubt, has an even greater number. Eight or nine perhaps? Unfortunately, you cannot visit Peggy's house or Maddie's to check your estimates. You can do the next best thing, though. You can play CLOSET ESTIMATION in your own home. Start by contemplating your dress collection. Does your child have any idea how many dresses hang in your closet? What is his estimate? Do you yourself know how many dresses you own? Take a guess. After both you and your child make and share estimates, open the closet door. Count every dress, and then compare your estimates with the actual amount.

It is unlikely that the number of dresses will match either of your estimates. That's all right. Estimates are intelligent, thoughtful guesses, not precise calculations, and exact numbers are not the point. This is a hard concept for many children to appreciate. Children usually believe that when it comes to numbers, answers should be perfect, and they are not easily convinced that close is sometimes the goal. Since the ability to make sensible estimates is an important skill, it is a good idea to help your child feel comfortable approximating values. Let me suggest, then, that after estimating and counting dresses, you turn your attention to skirts, blouses, and shoes. When you tire of evaluating the clothes in your room, consider your child's wardrobe—and you don't need to stick to the closets. There are good estimating and counting opportunities in dresser drawers, too. Think of socks, jeans, belts, sweaters, and pajamas. It is not necessary to estimate and count all the clothes in your house in a single day. You might count dresses today, skirts tomorrow, belts next week, and so on for as long as the job amuses. And the day it is no longer fun, stop.

THE HALF-A-MOON INN

WRITTEN BY PAUL FLEISCHMAN
ILLUSTRATED BY KATHY JACOBI
1980
GOOD READING FOR SECOND AND THIRD GRADES

*T*he *Half-A-Moon Inn*, a book of mystery and magic, is set in the long-ago world of wooden carts, wandering ragmen, wayside inns, and highway robbers. The author, Paul Fleischman, does a wonderful job of evoking that faraway world, and children listening to his tale quickly find themselves transported to a little seaside cottage, where Aaron, a twelve-year-old boy, lives with his mother. Aaron can hear perfectly but, for unexplained reasons, cannot speak. On the day before his twelfth birthday, Aaron must do something he has never done before, stay home alone. His mother promises to be away for a single night. But the weather does not cooperate, and a blizzard prevents her return. After waiting two days and two nights, Aaron decides to leave the cottage and look for her. Unfortunately, instead of finding his mother, he ends up at the Half-A-Moon Inn, an establishment run by the thoroughly evil Miss Grackle. Miss Grackle, who needs a boy to live at the inn and do her chores, prevents Aaron from running away by stealing his boots and stockings.

Guests stay at the inn, but, being mute, Aaron cannot ask for help. He writes messages, but in those days very few people knew how to read and write, and no one can decipher his words. Consequently, Aaron cannot escape, nor can he warn the illiterate guests that Miss Grackle plans to steal their purses. Instead, each night he joins Miss Grackle, who, by means of a magic recipe, opens the eyelids of her sleeping patrons and watches their dreams dance across their eyeballs.

Eventually, Aaron and Miss Grackle get what each deserves. Aaron is reunited with his mother. Miss Grackle freezes to death—a just reward for a woman with an icy heart and a cold soul. And so all is well by the end of *The Half-A-Moon Inn*.

Children love the book. It has the wonderful effect of provoking them to fantasize about the story even before the book's end. One girl informed me that she spent time thinking about Aaron and Miss Grackle during the day and then dreamed about them at night. This spellbinding power turns out to be a little weaker, though, when children read the book on their own—even when they can manage all the words. *The Half-A-Moon Inn* needs to be read aloud by an adult voice. Since it is such a pleasure to read, why not make the adult voice yours?

Paul Fleischman offers something that is more than a pleasure. For this is an enchanting story in which a central element rests on the importance of reading and writing.

Here are three games you might find worth playing. The first will get you and your child writing poetry. The other two will give your child a tiny idea of what life would be like without the ability to speak.

Mathias was fascinated by Miss Grackle's magical ability to view dreams. Dreams, I discovered, were a major concern of this third-grader, and before the book's end, he was discussing his own dreams. He told me about pleasant dreams, bizarre dreams, and scary nightmares. Given his interest, I wondered if he would care to write a book of poems about dreams.

I suggested the project, and Mathias reacted ambivalently. The thought of writing a POETRY DREAM BOOK appealed to him. But he found writing a difficult task, which was why he was seeing me twice a week. The idea of composing a whole book was, therefore, intimidating. He relaxed a bit when I explained the project in greater detail. First I promised to give him as much help as he wanted. Then I explained that he would write poems in three different styles. If he liked a style, he could write several poems of that type. He would not write all of the poems at one time, and five or six poems, each written on its own sheet of paper, would be plenty for a book. Binding the book would be easy, too. When he had enough poems, we would simply staple the pages together. This plan sounded reasonable, and Mathias announced that we could get to work.

POETRY DREAM BOOK

GRADES

second and third

MATERIALS

paper, pencil, colored markers, stapler

SKILLS

writing different forms of poetry

Acrostic Poems

I started by handing Mathias a sheet of paper that looked like this:

"Here is the beginning of a special kind of poem called an acrostic. In an acrostic poem, you select a word and then write its letters one under another—as I've done with *dreams*."

Mathias nodded.

"The first letter in *dreams* is *d*. That means that, for this poem, the first word of the first line must begin with *d*. The word might be *Doodle,* and the line might be *Doodle a noodle.* Or maybe just *Doodle*, because one-word lines are allowed in an acrostic poem. But I don't think *Doodle* is a very good beginning for a dream poem."

Mathias laughed.

"The second letter in *dreams* is *r*. A word beginning with *r*, therefore, must start the second line," I continued.

"I get it," Mathias said. "The third line starts with *e*, right?"

"Precisely. Can you think of a good first line for this poem? It has to begin with the letter *d*, and it should have something to do with dreams."

Mathias squirmed, and his eyes wandered. He calmed down, though, as soon as I jumped in with two suggestions.

"How about *dark* or *deep*?" I asked.

"I like *deep*," he said.

"Good. What do you want to say about *deep*?" I asked.

"*Deep at sleep*?" he whispered.

"That's great," I said. "Write it down before you forget."

He took a pencil and wrote the words.

"Now for *r*," I said. "You might use *ran* or *race* or *red*. Sometimes my dreams seem red."

Mathias liked the idea of red dreams, and so the words *Red dreams* made up his second line.

Getting the first two lines down on paper made all the difference. With only a few more suggestions from me, Mathias finished the rest of the poem in about ten minutes.

Deep atsleep
Red dreams
Every color
And more dreams
Morning
Sleep is over

"I think that's good," Mathias declared and slapped his hand on the table.

"I do, too," I said. "You have a real talent for poetry."

Mathias grinned.

"How about writing a second acrostic for your book?" I asked.

"Fine by me," he said.

We discussed possible words and phrases, all of which had something to do with dreams. He rejected *snooze* and *take a nap*, was tempted by *bedtime* and *sleep tight*, but settled on *nightmare*. It took him about twenty minutes to complete this acrostic.

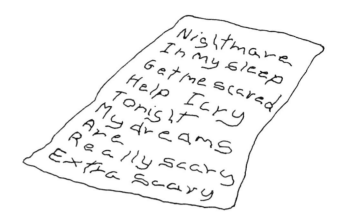

Word Counts

Mathias's next poetic style originated with the great poet W. H. Auden. Auden created a poetic form consisting of exactly six lines. Odd lines (the first, third, and fifth lines, that is) must have seven words each. The even lines must each have five words. The poem does not need to rhyme.

 Before getting to work, it seemed a good idea to give Mathias a visual guide for the words.

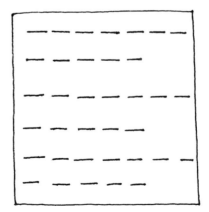

After explaining the idea, and showing Mathias how we would write one word on each dash, I said, "This might be a difficult poem to write. If you want, we can share the work."

"What do you mean?" he asked.

"We could divide the lines. I'll write the first line; you'll write the second; I'll write the third—"

"And I'll write the fourth," he interrupted.

"That's it. Do you want to share that way?"

"Okay. Will you go first?"

"Sure. I need to think about my dreams. What kind of dreams do I have? Some of my dreams are silly. That's a nice line, but it's too short. I know a word I can add, though," I said as I wrote the first line.

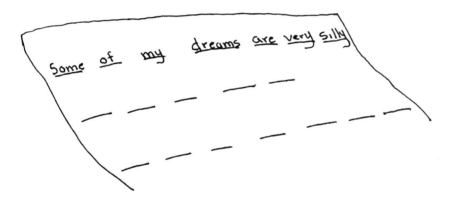

Some of my dreams are very silly

"You have to write the next line. Do you have any thoughts?" I asked.

"Not yet."

"What do you do when you feel silly?" I asked.

"Laugh, I guess," he said.

"You could write something about laughing," I proposed.

Mathias liked this suggestion and tried out different ideas while counting the words on his fingers. Then he announced, "I got it!"

"Excellent. Your line inspired me."

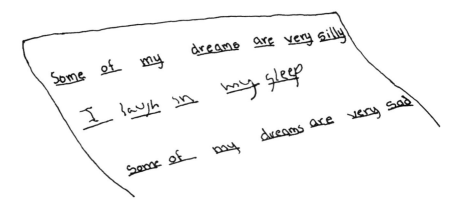

"Sad means crying. I'll write 'I cry and I cry.' "

"Good line. But what should I put next? Any advice?"

"Did you dream last night?" he asked.

"I don't remember. Lots of times I forget my dreams. I could say something about that. But I have to make sure the line is seven words long."

It took writing, erasing, and more writing before I was satisfied. After which, Mathias added the final line.

Some of my dreams are very silly

I laugh in my sleep

Some of my dreams are very sad

I cry and I cry

Sometimes my dreams disappear before I wake

I go look for them

When we finished, I read the whole poem aloud.

"That was fun," Mathias said.

"I agree. How about writing the next poem without me?"

"Okay. How do I begin?"

"You wrote such a good acrostic poem about nightmares. Maybe you would like to write a nightmare poem in this new form."

"That's what I'll do," he said. All on his own, he composed the first two lines.

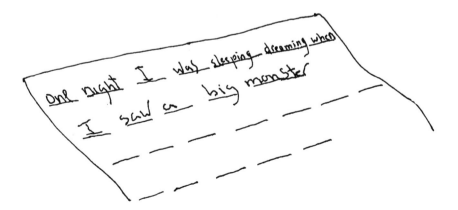

One night I was sleeping dreaming when
I saw a big monster

I was not sure W. H. Auden intended the first and second lines to flow together the way Mathias's did. I figured, though, that a nine-year-old deserves poetic leeway.

Then, with only a little help from me, he finished the poem.

```
One night I was sleeping dreaming when
I saw a big monster
It was red and it was ugly
I was screaming in bed
then I dreamed until I woke up
I went to my school
```

"Wonderful!" I said after reading it aloud.
Mathias beamed.

Word Links

"I have a new way to write poems today," I announced when Mathias arrived for his next appointment.

"What?" he asked.

"It's my own invention, but it's easy to imagine that other people may have thought of it, too. This is how it works. I think of a word—any word—as long as it has to do with dreams. Let's say I pick *sleep*." I wrote *sleep* at the top of a sheet of paper.

"Now you have to think of a word that begins with *p*, because *p* is the last letter in *sleep*," I explained.

"*Pillow*," he said.

"Perfect. I am going to write *pillow* underneath *sleep* so that the *p* in *pillow* is right below the *p* in *sleep*.

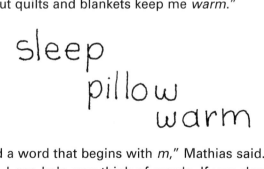

"You see how they link up?" I asked.

"Yeah," he said.

"It's my turn again. I need a word that begins with *w*. Too bad I can't use *quilts*."

"Or *blankets*," Mathias added.

"No, but quilts and blankets keep me *warm*."

sleep
pillow
warm

"I need a word that begins with *m*," Mathias said.

"Right. I can help you think of words. If you don't like my ideas, you don't have to use them. As long as we can think of linking words, we keep writing. When we get stuck and can't think of a good word, the poem ends, and we can begin another," I said.

"What if we never get stuck?" he asked.

"I hadn't considered that. How about we have an eight-word limit? That way we stop after we get stuck or after we write eight words, whichever comes first."

Mathias nodded, and we turned back to the poem.

"We need a sleepy, pillowy, warm kind of word that begins with *m*. *Music*, *magic*, and *Mathias* begin with *m*," I said.

But Mathias didn't think any of them fit, although the notion of using his own name appealed to him.

"Maybe the poem should end here. 'Sleep, pillow, warm.' It's sort of nice just like that," I said.

Mathias agreed. He also agreed that I could begin a second word-links poem.

I wrote *tired*. Mathias followed with *dream*.

"Oh, no, there's that *m*," I said.

"*Monsters!*" Mathias cried out.

"That works. I wouldn't have liked it with our first poem, though. Monsters don't go with *sleep*, *pillow*, and *warm*."

After I wrote *monsters*, Mathias and I continued on until we had eight words.

Tired
Dream
Monsters
scary
Yell
Loud
Disappear
Relax

"What do you think, is this a good way to write poetry?" I asked after reading the entire work aloud.

"It's good," he answered.

On completing this piece, Mathias had six pages of poems—two acrostics, two word counts, and two word links.

"I think we're ready to make the book now," I said.

"I think so, too. What do we do?"

"We need a cover, and a title to write on the cover."

I gave Mathias a sheet of plain white paper and a set of colored markers.

"What do you want to name the book?" I asked.

"*Dream Poems*," he said.

"Excellent title. Write that, then write your name, since you are the author," I said.

"I'm going to put your name, too, because you helped."

"I'm honored," I replied.

When the cover was ready, I placed it on top of the six pages of poetry. Then I held the pages in place while Mathias ran a row of staples along the left-hand side.

The book was done.

Mathias took the completed volume in his hands and read it straight through from beginning to end. When his father arrived, Mathias jumped from his chair holding out his book.

"Look what I did! It's poems. Peggy and I wrote them all!"

Sometime after reading about Miss Grackle's magic dream elixir, ask your child if he would like to write a few dream poems and put them in a book. If your child is interested, you will need to set aside enough time to accomplish the task. If writing a whole book seems like too much work, though, you and your child might write a single poem instead. Select the kind you think your child will enjoy most—acrostic, word count, or word links. Explain the poetic form, and then let the child compose. If help is needed, give it. You can share the writing, if you want, the way Mathias and I did. Post the finished poem someplace special, on your child's bedroom door, perhaps. Then stop for a moment and thank the horrible, dreadful Miss Grackle for inspiring an excellent idea.

ALMOST CHARADES

GRADES

second and third

SKILLS

identifying with a character in a story, expressing yourself without words

*H*ow can you help your child appreciate the frustration Aaron felt when he was trapped by Miss Grackle and unable to ask for help? One way is by playing ALMOST CHARADES, a game where players must communicate without using words.

ALMOST CHARADES is a simplified version of the traditional parlor game. During an ALMOST CHARADES game, you and your child will take turns silently portraying an animal, such as a whale or a turtle; a sporting event, such as baseball or hopscotch; or an activity, such as preparing a bowl of cereal or making the bed. Before you start the game, read through the following list of animals, sports, and activities. If your child wants to read the list for himself, let him. Otherwise, you should read it out loud.

ANIMALS	SPORTS	ACTIVITIES
cat	swimming	shampooing your hair
mouse	baseball	preparing cereal

lion	basketball	making the bed
giraffe	riding a bike	playing checkers
turtle	football	feeding a cat
dinosaur	roller blading	wrapping birthday gifts
butterfly	soccer	making pancakes
bird	tennis	washing dishes
frog	jump rope	buying groceries
spider	hopscotch	playing cards
whale	ice skating	painting a picture

After reviewing the list, tell your child that you are going to select an animal, a sport, or an activity but that you will not say what you picked. Then, without speaking or using any physical object, act out your choice. During your pantomime, your child will try to figure out what you are portraying. If he can, good. If he can't, you will have to tell him with words. Either way, your turn ends and your child's turn begins. The child picks his own animal, sport, or activity and wordlessly tries to communicate his choice to you.

You can play as many rounds as you want—two, three, four, or more. Consider inviting others to join the game. ALMOST CHARADES is a fine way to entertain several children and adults at the same time.

Gaining a better understanding of Aaron's predicament is one good reason to play this game. There is a second equally good reason to play. All children know that they use words to communicate. Many children, though, don't realize how much they communicate with gestures and facial expressions, and this often causes problems. Wave your hands around on the playground, and other children might think you are angry. Smirk, and your mother may get angry with you. Slump in your chair, and your teacher will think you're bored. Playing ALMOST CHARADES is one way, and a humorous way, to show your child that his gestures and the look on his face can be powerful ways of communicating ideas and feelings.

TALKLESS TIME

GRADES

second and third

MATERIALS

a watch

OPTIONAL MATERIALS

pad of paper, pencil

SKILLS

identifying with a character in a
story, expressing yourself
without words

*T*ALKLESS TIME is similar to ALMOST CHARADES in that it helps your child appreciate Aaron's frustrations at the Half-A-Moon Inn. But TALKLESS TIME goes much further than ALMOST CHARADES and will make Aaron's situation much more striking. When you play, you challenge your child to spend half an hour, or as close to it as possible, without talking, whispering, speaking, or vocalizing in any manner whatsoever. For most children, and even for adults, remaining silent for thirty minutes is a nearly impossible challenge. Assuming your child wants to test his ability to stay speechless, you must decide on the best half hour for the experiment. It should be a part of the day when you and your child can stay together, so that you can keep an ear on him. Dinnertime might be a good choice. As the meal begins, check your watch, and then declare the beginning of TALKLESS TIME. During this talkless meal, how will your child ask for more potatoes? How will he complain about the string beans? How will he react when his sister teases him? It probably won't be easy for your child to bite his tongue.

What happens if your child does talk, or, even more likely, has a giggle fit during the half hour? When I challenge a child to a TALKLESS TIME, I always permit some giggling. I even ignore it if a child blurts out a word or two. A gush of words, however, ends the game. After checking my watch, I tell the child how long he maintained silence. For some children, it is just three or four minutes. For others, it is longer. On very rare occasions, a child makes it through the entire half hour.

After your child's silent time, no matter how long it lasts, remind him of Aaron. If staying silent for half an hour is so hard, imagine staying silent for a lifetime!

If your child is willing, tomorrow or the day after, you might try this variation. Give him a pad of paper and a pencil and then begin a second TALKLESS TIME. That way, like Aaron, your child can write messages. After half an hour—or whatever portion of half an hour your child manages to stay silent—ask him to compare the two ways of being talkless. Did writing messages make the job easier or harder? Less frustrating or more frustrating?

Don't be surprised if your child wants you to stop talking for half an hour. Go ahead, give it a try—stipulating that should safety reasons force you to speak, you will do so without hesitation.

Here's one more idea. You and your child can have a TALK-LESS TIME contest. You both stop talking at the same moment, and the person who stays silent longest wins. Imagine how quiet your house will be—for a little while, at least.

THE SEARCH FOR DELICIOUS

WRITTEN AND ILLUSTRATED BY NATALIE BABBITT

1969

GOOD READING FOR SECOND AND THIRD GRADES

*T*he Search for Delicious is thoroughly delectable—an excellent book to read aloud. The tale begins long ago, in an unnamed kingdom, when Prime Minister DeCree decides to write a dictionary. One evening, in the presence of the King, the Queen, and the rest of the royal entourage, the Prime Minister announces his latest definitions, beginning with his definition of *affectionate*. "Affectionate is your dog," he declares, and everyone is pleased. But when DeCree presents his idea for *delicious*, "Delicious is fried fish," he discovers that tastes vary. The King argues that apples must define delicious; the Queen insists on Christmas pudding; the General of the Armies swears by beer. It is soon obvious that the debate over *delicious* will be neither dignified nor well mannered. By the end of the evening, DeCree predicts civil war.

To stop the quarreling, the King announces that Gaylen, a trustworthy lad, will travel throughout the kingdom conducting a poll. The boy will ask every person, in every home, in every village, the meaning of *delicious*. After tallying the results, the food mentioned most often, whatever it may be, will enter the dictionary, and peace will prevail.

But everything goes wrong. The poll causes all sorts of trouble, disaster looms, and it is up to Gaylen to set matters right. The story goes through complex twists and turns before the kingdom is safe and *delicious* is defined. At times, your child may find it hard to keep track of the plot and subplots. Supply a little adult guidance, though, and children can follow Gaylen's travels with a minimum of difficulty and a maximum of pleasure.

The next three activities should also offer a minimum of difficulty and a maximum of pleasure.

DEFINITION POLL

GRADES

second and third

MATERIALS

paper, pencil

SKILLS

organizing information, identifying with a character in a story

*A*fter reading about Gaylen and his adventures polling the citizens of his kingdom, you and your child might be interested in conducting a poll of your own. Your poll will be different from Gaylen's, of course. You won't travel from village to village asking for definitions of *delicious*. Instead, you will conduct a more intimate and limited poll.

Before starting, you and your child must select four foods you believe worthy of defining *delicious*. Let's say you choose pizza, chocolate cupcakes, hamburgers, and pancakes. Your next job is to make a polling sheet for these four finalists. The sheet should look like this:

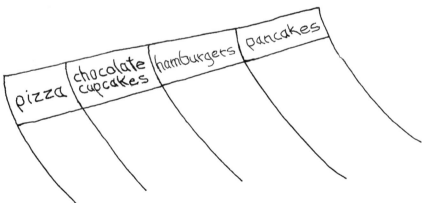

Your child can write the words, or some of them, if he wants to, but if he doesn't want to write, don't make him.

When the sheet is ready, ask your child to select his very favorite of the four foods. After he decides, have him put an X in that column. Next, you make a selection and place an X of your own. You now have two recorded opinions. A good beginning, but to have a legitimate poll, you will need to canvass more people. You might telephone family members, your friends, and your child's friends to ask their views. You can talk to a few people today and a few more tomorrow. You might consider taking the polling sheet with you when you drop your child off at school. That way, you can ask parents and children in the schoolyard to voice their preferences. Make sure to register each vote by putting an X in the appropriate column. How many people should you poll? Aiming for twenty is a good idea. If you ask more, great. If you ask a few less, that's okay, too. When you and your child feel you have enough votes, tally the results and declare a winner.

pizza	chocolate cupcakes	hamburgers	pancakes
X X X X	X X X X X	X X X X	X X X X X X X

Why should you conduct this poll? There are two reasons. First, conducting a poll is a way to make *The Search for Delicious* real for your child. When you read about Gaylen's travels, your child can only imagine what it is like to go from place to place recording opinions about *delicious*. When your child conducts his own poll, though, he will, in a small way, share Gaylen's experiences. Often, when children have trouble understanding stories or books it is because they cannot fully visualize the characters, the settings, or the predicaments presented in the plots. Whenever you can make a story vivid for a child, therefore, it is worth taking time to do so.

Second, the polling sheet can show your child how useful it is to carefully organize information. The sheet, with its individual columns for each food, makes it easy to calculate the number of people you polled and to note which food is in the lead. You do not have to explain the benefits of the chart to your child. He will probably realize the advantages on his own while keeping track of his ever mounting data.

If you enjoyed your *delicious* poll, consider canvassing people about a second word. How, for instance, would you define *happiness*? Is it being with a friend, going to a birthday party, swimming on a hot day, taking a vacation? Perhaps, though, your child would prefer to define *funny* or *scary* or *exciting* or any other word that strikes his fancy.

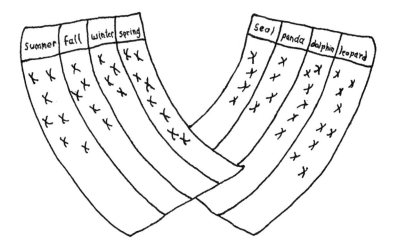

PAPER DOLL

GRADES

second and third

MATERIALS

photocopies on card stock of
pages 338–39, two pair of
scissors, wire ties used for
garbage bags, colored pencils,
removable transparent tape

SKILLS

completing a complex project,
identifying with the character in
a story, encouraging storytelling

How does Gaylen save his kingdom? He gets help from Ardis, a little mermaid who has been weeping for hundreds of years. Why does Ardis weep? She misses her lost doll—a doll made of linked stones. If only she could be with her doll again, Ardis would be happy.

Milly enjoyed everything about *The Search for Delicious*, but she especially loved hearing about Ardis and her doll. When we finished the book, therefore, I thought Milly might like to make her own doll in remembrance of the one that Ardis adored. There was no way for us to fashion a doll out of linked stones. We could, however, construct one out of paper, and we could give it movable joints.

First, though, I needed to do a little preparatory work. I drew two sheets exactly like the doll forms on pages 338 and 339. These sheets contain all the parts you need to make a doll, along with a pattern for a doll's dress. I took the drawings to a photocopy store and asked the clerk to reproduce the pages on card stock. Card stock is thicker than regular paper, and it produces a sturdier doll.

On Thursday, when Milly arrived for her appointment, she looked at my worktable, which was covered with an odd assortment of supplies, and asked, "What's all this for?"

After I explained the project, Milly voiced her approval. I told her that we would begin the doll at the head and work our way down to the feet. Then I cut out the head and neck, and Milly cut out the torso and shoulders.

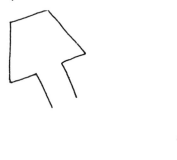

"Next, we attach these two pieces," I said.

"How?" Milly asked.

"We're going to use this," I said, holding up one of the wire ties that come with plastic garbage bags. Using my fingers, I pulled away most of the plastic and paper that covers the wire. Then, taking scissors, I cut a piece about the length of my thumb. I held the doll's neck behind the top of the torso so that the two pieces overlapped, and pierced the wire through from front to back.

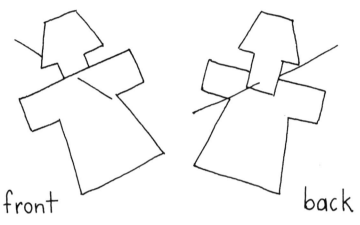

front   back

I twisted the section of wire sticking out the front until I had a small knot, and twisted another knot on the doll's back.

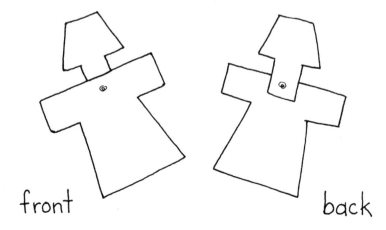

front   back

Next, I drew hair, eyes, a nose, and a mouth on the face.

When I was done, I tilted the doll's head left

and right.

"Neat!" Milly said.

"I think so, too. Now we'll put on the arms. Each arm has two parts—the top part that goes from the shoulder to the elbow, and the bottom part that goes from the elbow to the hand. We'll start with the upper arms. Why don't you cut out one while I cut out the other?"

After that, Milly asked, "Do we put them on the body?"

"You got it—one on each shoulder. I'll hold the arm behind the right shoulder and push the wire through. Then you'll twist the knots," I said.

Milly agreed to this plan.

Next, we cut out the lower arms and attached them. We wanted the thumbs of both hands to face the body. That meant we had to be careful which piece went on the right and which piece on the left.

Using a single wire, we attached the hips to the bottom of the torso, after which we attached the thighs and then the bottoms of both legs. We made sure that the foot on each leg faced outward.

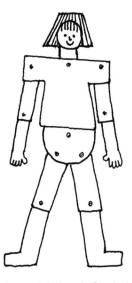

All the pieces in place, Milly shifted the arms, legs, torso, and head around in a dozen different ways, giggling as she observed each new position.

It had taken considerable concentration and patience to make the doll, and I was impressed that Milly never complained or wanted to quit. Quite the opposite, when I asked if she cared to stop maneuvering the doll in order to make the doll's dress, she nodded her head enthusiastically.

We cut out the front and back of the dress.

Holding the pieces on either side of the doll, I used removable transparent tape to connect the left and right straps on the front of the dress to the matching straps on the back. Removable tape, available in most stationery stores, has a very light adhesive, making it easy to remove when you want.

To keep the dress from flapping about, I put more tape near the bottom.

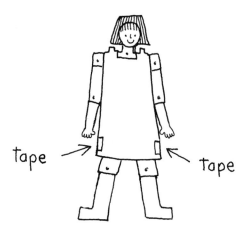

tape → ← tape

"That looks pretty," Milly said.

"Would you like to color the dress?" I asked. "You can use my colored pencils."

"I would," Milly replied.

"Great. I'll remove the tape and take off the dress. When you finish coloring, you can tape the dress on the doll again."

And that's just what she did.

"What do you want to name her?" I asked.

"Ardis!" she said instantly.

"Hello, Ardis," I said to the doll. "Nice to meet you."

Milly laughed, and said, "Nice to meet you, too."

For the next ten minutes, Milly and I played with Ardis the paper doll.

"Ardis, do you want to take a walk with me in the woods?" I asked.

"Yes, can we visit the lake?" Milly asked, speaking for Ardis.

"Sure. Maybe we can find a mermaid. Let's go," I said.

And Milly moved her doll across the table.

After visiting the lake, we walked through the woods collecting apples. Soon we arrived at the castle, just in time to attend a royal ball celebrating Gaylen's success saving the kingdom.

It had taken an entire tutoring session to make the doll and play with it a little. During that hour Milly's love for the book had increased, her appreciation of the imaginative possibilities in reading had deepened, and she had even displayed a good deal of patient effort in helping to construct the doll. All in all, a very successful session.

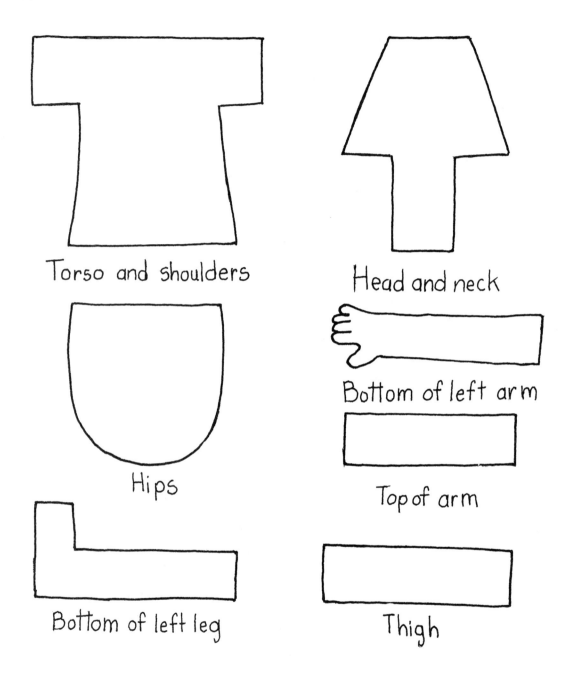

Torso and shoulders

Head and neck

Hips

Bottom of left arm

Top of arm

Bottom of left leg

Thigh

Strap→ ←Strap→ ←Strap

Dress front Dress back

Bottom of right arm Thigh

Top of arm Bottom of right leg

THE DICTIONARY, PLEASE

GRADES

third

MATERIALS

children's dictionary, an
adult dictionary

SKILLS

appreciating the dictionary,
developing vocabulary and an
interest in words

*T*he dictionary figures prominently in *The Search for Delicious*, and dictionaries can be a lot of fun. Sometime when you are not busy reading about Gaylen's search for the definition of *delicious*, you might want to sit with your child, idly turning the pages of a children's dictionary, and discovering interesting words, reading definitions, and looking at illustrations. These investigations can be both pleasurable and instructive, but if you would like a change from idle fun, here is a game that you can play.

Before you begin, make sure your child knows how a dictionary works. He should understand that the entry word appears in **bold** letters and that the definition comes next in regular typeface. Some words have more than one definition. When that's the case, the definitions are numbered. Many children's dictionaries add a sentence or sentences that include the entry word.

When you're sure your child understands these dictionary basics, tell him to look through the dictionary until he finds an interesting entry word (written in **bold** letters). Any word will do. He must not, however, tell you the word he selects. Instead, he should read its definition aloud to you—just the first definition. He must take care *not* to read the sentence that includes the word. Imagine your child says, "The word I picked means, 'To think about something in a careful way.' " Using the definition, you must guess which word your child chose. In this case, several possibilities come to mind: *reflect, contemplate, study, consider, ponder*. To make your job harder, your child can insist that you close your eyes as he hunts for a word. That way you will not know if he picked the word from the front of the dictionary, where you might find *consider* and *contemplate*, or the back, where you might find *reflect* and *study*. You get two chances to name the right word. When I play this game with children, they are usually happy if I figure out the word and even happier if I fail. Either way, they are almost always delighted to continue reading definitions and daring me to name the matching words.

This game is one-sided. Your child always reads the definition, and you always attempt to supply the right word. You are the only one facing a challenge. You can change this situation, if you want. The next time you play, rotate turns with your child. On your own turn, though, you will change the rules, since naming words from definitions is too hard a task for most third graders. You will take an adult dictionary and look through it for a word that your child does not know—*crumpet* is a good choice. Not many third graders know that *crumpet* means, as the dictionary says, a small piece of round bread.

As soon as you're ready, announce your word: *crumpet*. Then you will provide your child with two definitions—one will be the actual definition, the other will be a ridiculous definition of your own creation. Next ask your child to select the true definition. Is *crumpet* a small, round piece of bread? Or is *crumpet* the sound a cat makes when it is angry? The child must choose. Given that he has a fifty-fifty chance of being right, his odds of success are pretty good. And success brings happiness, contentment, delight, and joy.

When you and your child spend time with the dictionary, either browsing or playing THE DICTIONARY, PLEASE, you foster the child's fondness for the dictionary, build his vocabulary, and increase his curiosity about words. And you will help him appreciate the importance of Prime Minister DeCree's project. All of which should bring *you* happiness, contentment, delight, and joy.

APPENDIXES

WHY THE MOON CHANGES SHAPE

Why does the moon go through phases? Here is the explanation. The sun always illuminates one half of the moon—just as it illuminates one half of Earth. If the moon stood still, it would look the same every night of the year. But the moon does not stand still. It travels around the Earth, the same way the Earth travels around the sun. Sometimes the moon is directly between the sun and the Earth. At that moment the sun shines on the half of the moon we cannot see. From Earth, it looks as though the sky is moonless. We call this the new moon. About two weeks later, the Earth is between the sun and the moon. At that moment the sun shines on the entire half of the moon that we see from Earth. We call this the full moon. Between the new and the full moon, the moon seems to get bigger and bigger. It doesn't really vary in size. It's just that we see more and more of it each night as it travels around the Earth. This is called waxing. Between the full moon and the new moon, we see less and less of the moon as it continues to move around the Earth. This is called waning. It takes 29 days, 12 hours, 44 minutes, and 2.8 seconds for the moon to complete one cycle around the Earth. As seen from Earth, the moon changes shape every night, but we have names for just eight points along the cycle. There is the new moon, the waxing crescent, the first quarter, the waxing gibbous, the full moon, the waning gibbous, the last (or third) quarter, and the waning crescent.

Here is a picture showing all eight phases of the moon.

The black sections are the unilluminated portion of the moon.

The striped sections are the illuminated parts of the moon that we do not see on Earth.

The white sections are the illuminated parts of the moon that we do see on Earth.

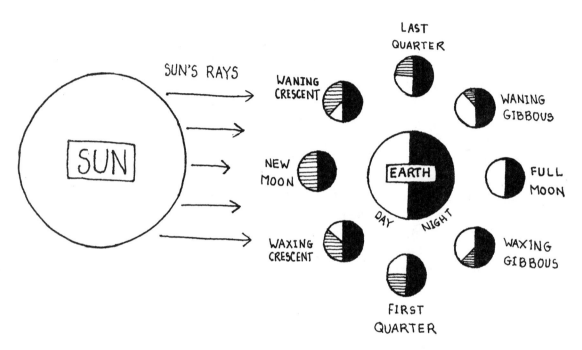

A NOTE TO TEACHERS

Games with Books is a guide for parents, but, with a few minor adaptations, teachers can use almost every activity. You can play some games with an entire classroom of children. After reading *Chrysanthemum* to a class of kindergartners, for instance, you could play THE NAME GAME by making a graph comparing the number of letters in Chrysanthemum's name with the number of letters in each student's name. Some games are appropriate for a smaller number of children. When you finish reading *Charlotte's Web* aloud to first, second, or third graders, you could play a syllabication game called BLEND THE FRIENDS with a group of six, seven, or eight youngsters.

Many of the games work best, though, when played by two people—one grownup and one child. There are several ways you can arrange for such individualization. You might send a letter to your students' parents requesting that mothers and fathers spend a half hour (or more) during the year helping out in class. Explain that a few days before the visit you will send home instructions for a particular game. Then when Dad or Mom comes to class, he or she will play that game one-on-one with a student in a corner of the classroom, in a hallway, or in any other available place. If a game takes only five minutes, it is possible that one parent will have time to play with four or five students. A parent who has a good time might be willing to make a return appearance.

Parents often ask teachers what they can do outside of school to help their children. *Games with Books* offers answers. Select a book for a parent to read aloud at home. It might be one you have already read in class. Then show the parent how to play one of the book's matching games. You might suggest that the parent of a first grader read *Blueberries for Sal* aloud to his child. After the story ends, parent and child can head to the kitchen and prepare Blueberry Honey Sandwiches. Explain to the parent that aside from being a fun thing to do, preparing the sandwiches will also increase the child's intuitive sense of metric measurements. Likewise, if a preschooler or kindergartner is having trouble with hand-eye coordination or small motor control, you might suggest that the parent read *Harold and the Purple Crayon* aloud and then play PURPLE MAZE, a game that directly addresses those issues.

If you want to do something more elaborate (and a little more expensive), you could put either a picture book or a chapter book along with instructions for several games inside a tote bag. Give a child the book bag to take home. Then the child's parents can read the book aloud and play the games before returning the bag to school. If you send home a picture book, the family can keep the book bag for a week. You might have to let families hold on to chapter books for a while longer. To make sure that everyone in your class gets a turn, it is possible you will have to create more than one book bag.

Consider, too, assigning a game for homework. You could ask each child in a kindergarten or first-grade class to learn one or two facts about life in Japan subsequent to reading *Crow Boy* aloud. Or you could start making a FULL MOON BOOK with first or second graders in school after reading *Many Moons*, and have the children finish it at home. Or you could have each child in a first-, second-, or third-grade class make A BORROWER'S HOUSE at home during the course of reading *The Borrowers* in school. When you finish the book, all the children can bring their work to class, and you can have an exhibition of shoe-box households.

The benefits of reading aloud to children are well established. Furious battles rage over reading instruction, but experts on every side of the question agree on one thing: listening to stories is an essential part of the process. Children who listen to a lot of stories read aloud come to understand a great deal about the printed page. They appreciate that there is a difference between the drawings and the squiggles called letters. They know it is possible to figure out the story from the pictures, but they also know that in order to tell the story the same way time after time, you must make sense of the letters. Eventually they realize that letters come in clusters and that each cluster stands for a single word. They know that you read line by line from the top to the bottom of a page and that you read each line from left to right (at least, you do in English). That is a lot of book knowledge for a very young child to possess. Viewing the printed page in these complex ways is not biologically predetermined. It is something that a child learns by sitting alongside an adult and watching as the adult follows the print and turns the pages.

Children acquire crucial concepts about the structure of stories while listening to books read aloud. Young listeners gain a sense of story grammar, an appreciation for literary language, an understanding of characters' personalities, an awareness of plot development. Reading comprehension is dependent on children's secure progress in the conceptualizing of stories. The disturbing middle-grade slump in reading scores results from children's lack of literary awareness as much as from problems deciphering words.

Most important of all, children who listen to a lot of stories read aloud by caring adults come to love books and have, therefore, a firm motivation for learning to read.

Preschool and kindergarten teachers usually read aloud daily, but teachers of older children, especially teachers of second and third graders, don't always keep up the practice, and it is easy to see why. The school day is short, and there are so many things to accomplish in so many subject areas. Even so, it is extremely worthwhile to take fifteen minutes, a half hour, or more each day to read a good book aloud to a classroom of children. Reading aloud will inspire the good readers in your class to read more, and encourage the children who are struggling to keep up the hard work.

By using *Games with Books* you can make reading aloud a practical way to spend classroom time, since the books you read act as motivational springboards for teaching essential academic skills. The books and activities in *Games with Books* are designed for children ranging from preschool to third grade. The games highlight a wide spectrum of skills. You will find that the activities for some books focus on more than one subject area. Read *Katy No-Pocket* with a kindergarten or first-grade class and you can follow up by playing WHO IS HIDING IN KATY'S POCKET?, a game that develops children's phonemic awareness, or by playing BE AN OFFICIAL MASTER POCKET COUNTER, a game that helps children develop numerical skills. Usually, you will select a book you want to read and then choose which activities are best for your class. But you could do things in reverse. Let's say you want to start a poetry unit with a class of second or third graders. Why not read *The Half-A-Moon Inn* as an introduction to the unit? After the class hears about Miss Grackle's amazing magic dream recipe, have each child write a dream poem. You can teach the poetic forms I suggest in POETRY DREAM BOOK or teach any other poetic forms you like. Staple the poems together and you'll have a classroom anthology.

There are four main phases to skills instruction: previewing, introducing, practicing, and reviewing. In *Games with Books*, you will find games well suited for each phase. Reading *The Search for Delicious* aloud to second or third graders and then conducting a classroom, or even a school-wide, DEFINITION

POLL is a wonderful way to preview upcoming lessons in graphing and statistics. Reading *Martha Blah Blah* to kindergartners and then playing either MISSING LETTERS or FEEL THOSE LETTERS is a fine method for having students practice naming the letters of the alphabet. Would you like to review alphabetical order with a class of third graders? Playing MR. ASTOR'S ANTS, a game inspired by *Mr. Popper's Penguins*, can make the lesson fun.

As you use *Games with Books*, you may invent your own activities based on the books you read aloud. Excellent. By linking educational games and books, you will make efficient use of your instructional time, encourage your students to become book lovers, and engage children in enjoyable activities that just happen to help them master vital academic skills. Play games with books, and everybody wins.